BIBLICA ET ORIENTALIA

(SACRA SCRIPTURA ANTIQUITATIBUS ORIENTALIBUS ILLUSTRATA)

47

biblica et orientalia - 47

HOLGER GZELLA

COSMIC BATTLE AND POLITICAL CONFLICT

Studies in Verbal Syntax and Contextual Interpretation of Daniel 8

EDITRICE PONTIFICIO ISTITUTO BIBLICO – ROMA 2003

ISBN 88-7653-350-8
© E.P.I.B. – Roma – 2003
Iura editionis et versionis reservantur

EDITRICE PONTIFICIO ISTITUTO BIBLICO
Piazza della Pilotta, 35 - 00187 Roma, Italia

Dis manibus

James A. Montgomery (1866-1949)

inter viburna cupressus

Acknowledgements

This monograph is the result of my research done on the Book of Daniel at the Pontifical Biblical Institute, Rome, during the academic year 2001-2002. It was Agustinus Gianto, S.J., Professor of Semitic Philology and Linguistics, who, with his keen acumen and liberality, guided the research and later encouraged me to expand the original work into a monograph for inclusion in *Biblica et Orientalia*. I owe him my heartfelt thanks for his constant interest and unfailing support throughout my student days at the Biblicum. I shall remember them with joy when the days of darkness will be many (Eccl 11,8). Although anybody familiar with his works will realize the great extent to which his ideas have inspired me, I take full responsibility for the views expressed in this book.

My interest in the theological significance of linguistic and literary features of Old Testament texts goes back to Erich Zenger, of Munster, who introduced me to Biblical Studies, and to Jan Lambrecht, S.J., of Leuven. Much of my understanding of the intrinsic relationship between Theology and literary scholarship is indebted to Christian Gnilka and Thomas Pröpper, both of Münster.

I am also grateful to Werner Mayer, S.J., for everything I was able to learn from him, even beyond the boundaries of Assyriology proper. Last but not least, I want to express my gratitude to another mentor of mine *in semiticis*, Craig Morrison, O.Carm., who has steadily fostered my love for Aramaic. He has also contributed a number of stylistic improvements to an early draft of the present study.

I should add that my triennial stay at the *Collegium Germanicum et Hungaricum* in Rome would have been much less challenging – and less enjoyable too – without the inspiring company there and elsewhere in the Eternal City. I would like to mention, among others, Christian Wirz, Christof Strüder, Eka Beridze, Georg Müller, Hermann Backhaus, Martin Marahrens, and Stephan Lüttich, from whom I have received much moral support. I shall remember with appreciation and loyalty that I originally came to Rome at the instigation of Franz-Hermann Lürken, although many things have changed since then.

Holger Gzella
March 2003

Contents

Abbreviations

In general, the abbreviations employed here correspond to those in *Biblica*'s "Instructions for Contributors". One may, however, note especially the following sigla:

BHS	Biblia Hebraica Stuttgartensia
GK	W. Gesenius and E. Kautzsch, *Hebräische Grammatik*
HAL	L. Koehler and W. Baumgartner, *Hebräisches und Aramäisches Lexikon zum Alten Testament*
JM	P. Joüon and T. Muraoka, *A Grammar of Biblical Hebrew*
KAI	*Kanaanäische und aramäische Inschriften*, eds. H. Donner and W. Röllig
KTU	*The Cuneiform Alphabetic Texts from Ugarit, Ras Ibn Hani and Other Places*, eds. M. Dietrich, O. Loretz and J. Sanmartín
MT	Masoretic Text
RAC	*Reallexikon für Antike und Christentum*
RIMA	*Royal Inscriptions of Mesopotamia. Assyrian Periods.*
TWAT	*Theologisches Wörterbuch zum Alten Testament*

1
Introduction

Despite its rich linguistic subtleties, symbolism, and apocalyptic theology, the vision of the ram and the he-goat in Daniel 8 has received little attention in modern scholarship. While 18th century scholarship dwelled much on that chapter and applied its imagery to contemporary history,[1] 19th and 20th century Daniel interpretation has shifted its focus to Daniel 7. This shift may be occasioned by the more complex and allegedly more interesting situation there, that is, the succession of the four beasts and the famous "Son of Man".[2]

Such a preference may also be in part occasioned by the growing amount of comparative material from Ancient Near Eastern sources available from the middle of the 19th century onwards.[3] Such material almost automatically attracts many scholars who are more interested in identifying a particular mythological "background" than in understanding the text of Daniel 7 itself. The most obvious examples are the Canaanite myth about the conflict between Baal and Yamm and the final enthronement scene (KTU 1.2:IV:6-28),[4] and its Mesopotamian counterpart, the battle between Marduk and Tiamat, which is described at great length in the *Enuma eliš*.[5] Other suggestions which have been made during the last

---

[1] Cf. Nuñez, *Vision*, 1982.

[2] For a summary of various approaches cf. Eggler, *Influences*, 2000.

[3] The middle of the 19th century is the turning-point which radically changed the material and textual base of Ancient Near Eastern history and literature because of the great archaeological and epigraphic discoveries. Cf. in general Larsen, *Conquest*, 1996.

[4] See Day, *Conflict*, 1985. One of the first scholars to suggest a Canaanite background was Aage Bentzen in his famous book *King and Messiah* (1970).

[5] So Gunkel, *Schöpfung*, 1985, esp. 323-335. A.E. Gardner tries to revive this thesis along the well-known lines of "Ancient Near Eastern mythological background" without any real progress: Gardner, "Daniel 7,2-14," *Bib* 82 (2001): 244-252. Moreover, she appears to be quite mistaken to conclude from the supposed diaspora origin

fifteen years or so include the hybrid beings in the *Vision of the Nether-world* beheld by an Akkadian prince[6] or the freak births in the *Šumma izbu* series of oracles.[7]

This shift of interest in scholarship is understandable. The quest for such a "background" or, more ambitiously, for a specific literary "model", is often a major, if not the only, goal pursued by Old Testament scholars who were also familiar with Ancient Near Eastern Studies. The underlying hypothesis is the assumption that the Old Testament beliefs and thoughts find its matrix in the larger Ancient Near Eastern culture.

One gets the impression that hunting for similarities appears to be an end in itself, even though the principles applied are unhistorical and thus methodically extremely unsound,[8] many commentators are unaware of the fundamental distinction between a myth and a text,[9] the particular climate of a greater intellectual liberty and independence from the "canonical" Mesopotamian culture in the periphery (especially in the west) is not taken into account and, in addition to that, hardly anybody asks how merely tracing down Near Eastern "parallels" without any investigation into the underlying motives could possibly add significantly to one's understanding of either the Old Testament or of Ancient Mesopotamia. Or is it rather a general and slightly irrational fascination caused by the immediate availability of an enormous amount of antiquarian knowledge which has, long before the World Wide Web, turned biblical texts into "hypertexts" that are supposed to contain "links" to the whole of Ancient Near Eastern culture?

---

of the court tales that the visions, too, were written either in Babylonia or by a Babylonian Jew (ibid. 251-252), without paying any attention at all to the enormous problems of dating the Book of Daniel and its various parts.

[6] Kvanvig, *Roots*, 1988, 536-602.

[7] Porter, *Metaphors*, 1985, 15-29; the text has been edited by Leichty.

[8] See the fundamental critique by Parker, *Stories*, 1997, 3-8. He rightly stresses that a comparison of cuneiform mythic-epic tradition of the second millennium with Israelite prose narrative of the first millennium is a multiple category mistake.

[9] A myth is essentially a constellation, it is not identical with any particular text describing mythical scenes etc. Cf. Assmann, "Verborgenheit," *Göttinger Miszellen* 25 (1977): 7-43.

Such an outlook is deeply rooted in the genesis of Ancient Near Eastern Studies as an academic discipline, precisely because the points of contact with the Bible originally attracted the academic and non-academic public to the great cuneiform cultures and provided the necessary financial means. The focus on the "biblical" perspective is thus both the *raison d'être* of the field and its Original Sin (since cuneiform studies would not have been pursued so eagerly without such an interest, one may call this a *felix culpa*).

Along these hermeneutical lines, however, Daniel 8 appears to be much less appealing than many other texts, simply because its frame of reference, including the correspondence between image and meaning, seems to be all too obvious to merit an in-depth study, especially when the narrative as such does not strike the reader as particularly interesting either. It is illuminating that in most discussions the problems of interpretation posed by Daniel 8 are, in accordance with the scholarly tradition, limited to uncovering some hypothetical astral symbolism behind the figures of the ram and the he-goat, as if this were the only question worth asking.

The present study is aimed at a fresh appreciation of the various literary elements which constitute Daniel 8 as a whole, namely the narrative frame, which provides a connection with the rest of the Book of Daniel, the vision report and its application to Jewish history under Antiochus IV. This monograph differs from the few preceding treatments of the subject by trying to consider the clues for interpretation furnished by the narrator himself and hence to avoid an *a priori* understanding of the vision as a historical *allegory* which provides a symbolic representation of the forces of particular history. Instead, the vision narrative itself will be treated as a "mimetic" representation of reality, not as a theoretical construction. A thorough analysis of the verbal syntax will confirm the plausibility of such a view, since the use of a specific narrative pattern and particular verbal forms present the personal experience of the visionary as the report of an eye-witness.

Therefore the application of the vision constitutes a different level on which one can read the text.[10] The double function of the images as

---

[10] Such a distinction is alien to modern scholarship on Daniel 8, but has already been made in the 10th century by the Karaite scholar Jephet Ibn Ali in his Arabic commen-

functional constituents within the narrative textual unit and as references to something else on the level of a particular reading of this unit not necessitated by its initial presentation (both only come close to falling together for an instant at the climax in 8,11-12) will so be kept intact. In addition to that, there will be a full discussion of the ancient versions of Daniel 8, their individual character, and their relationship to the Hebrew. Such a discussion will also shed new light on several problems of textual criticism and indeed on methods of translation and interpretation in antiquity.

1. Apocalypticism and Symbolism: A First Thought

An analysis of both the frame and the literary presentation of the animal fight clearly shows that the vision is considered to be an insight into a transcendent reality by the seer. Hence it reveals a superstructure above the world of his everyday-experience. Moreover, it will be seen that the vision itself and its interpretation in the second half of Daniel 8 are by no means identical, for the interpretation introduces several aspects not present in the vision report, especially those referring to Antiochus himself. At the same time, these new aspects foreshadow basic topics in Daniel 10-12 (such as intrigue and politics).

Thus, the scene is not made up as an encoded and merely theoretical depiction of the sensually perceptible world, to which most modern studies of this subject want to reduce it, but it is a glance into the cosmic universal pattern beyond political history. It presents a fight of supernatural forces, of which the course of history from the Achaemenid Empire to the spread of Hellenism is only a specific manifestation, a mirror-image of the true battle which takes place in the supernatural realm. Such an interpretation, based on a close analysis of the linguistic facts, is, as will be shown in the next section, in any case closer to the central themes lying at the heart of the Book of Daniel, and indeed to the nature of apocalypticism.

---

tary on the Book of Daniel, cf. the Arabic-English edition by Margoliouth, *Commentary*, 1889, 39f (in the translation).

If apocalypticism is taken seriously as what it professes to be,[11] namely the God-given intuition of things inaccessible by means of sensual perception and human intelligence, though nonetheless real, it would be markedly contrary to its self-understanding if it only presented human reality in a merely encrypted fashion.

In the light of its own claims, apocalyptic literature wants to show something which goes beyond. It is the literary expression of a certain historical perspective, namely the reaction to what is, at least subjectively, perceived as a crisis. As a form of literature (oracles and testaments are related genres), it provides at the same time a view of the world as it really is *and* a source of consolation to its readers. Therefore its symbolism cannot be solved like a riddle by transposing it back to the categories of the human realm and by uncovering some kind of one-to-one correspondence.

Nevertheless, the apocalyptic imagery is not completely detached from the human world, but strives to uncover basic structures behind it, just as the "Art of the Fugue" itself is a superstructure which can be applied to different musical "realities" (or "worlds") by being played on the organ, by a string quartet, by a brass quartet etc. So the *application* of an apocalyptic vision to history is an instance of "Reader-Response Criticism"[12] (in Daniel 8 within the text itself), an *example* of how to make sense of a vision, but not the only "solution". Such an understanding of apocalyptic symbolism also comes much closer to modern approaches to cultural anthropology, such as the one of Clifford Geertz, which sees a fund of general meanings stored up in symbols, "in terms of which each individual interprets his experience and organizes his conduct."[13]

---

[11] This is also part of the generally accepted definition by John Collins of an apocalypse as "a genre of revelatory literature with a narrative framework, in which a revelation is mediated by an otherworldly being to a human recipient, disclosing a transcendent reality which is both temporal, insofar as it envisages eschatological salvation, and spatial insofar as it involves another, supernatural world." (Collins, *Apocalypse*, 1979)

[12] For an introduction to the theoretical framework cf. McKnight, *Post-Modern Use*, 1988.

[13] Geertz, *Interpretation*, 1973 (2000), 127.

2. Daniel 8 in the Context of the Book of Daniel

The visionary frame in Dan 8,1-2.27 provides explicitly, as will be seen, a strict connection of the content of ch. 8 with the remaining Book of Daniel, yet at the same time it marks this chapter as an overall unit by providing a new beginning with some historical information at the outset and taking up the court narrative again at the end.

From the unambiguous use of this literary device, the frame, it emerges that Daniel 8 has been consciously inserted into the literary entity of the final version, regardless of the original diversity of the material thus assembled (the markedly different textual tradition of Daniel 4-6 still reflected in the Old Greek allows an insight into the complex history of this text as a whole and has given rise to various hypotheses about its genesis[14]).

So the final redaction of Daniel 8 presupposes the vision in ch. 7 as well as the court narrative, although these stories are not anymore important in Daniel 7-12 (unlike the dreams in chs. 2 and 4). Prior to an analysis of the details, there shall be a brief outline of the general theo-

---

[14] The two most important modern theories have been proposed by Rainer Albertz (*Religionsgeschichte*, 1992, 591-676) and John J. Collins (*Daniel*, 1993, 24-36). The differences between both approaches can at least in part be explained by the different interests of the authors. Albertz tries to explain the growth of the Book of Daniel against the various socio-political backgrounds reflected in it. He distinguishes a *Vorphase* (320-221 BC, collection of the legends in Daniel 4-6 LXX which reflect an optimistic *Oberschichtsperspektive* on the opportunities provided by the Ptolemaic period), a first *Hauptphase* (221-200 BC, composition of Daniel 2-7 which treat the martyrdom of pious Jews who have to suffer under a totalitarian power), and a second *Hauptphase* (176-160 BC, addition of Daniel 1 and 8-12 which propose a pacifistic intellectual opposition to terror and persecution). Collins, however, concentrates on the literary side and sees the origin of the text (1) in separate legends (lying at the heart of Daniel 2-6) which then (2) have been collected (Daniel 4-6, beginning of the two different textual traditions of LXX and Masoretic Text) and supplemented (3) by other narratives originally in Aramaic (including Daniel 1!). After that (4), Daniel 7 has been composed and Daniel 2-3 have been integrated; finally (5), Daniel 8-12 have been compiled and integrated into the text, while Daniel 1 has been translated into Hebrew in order to provide a Hebrew frame. (Phases 1 and 2 in Collins correspond to the *Vorphase* in Albertz, phases 3 and 4a to the first *Hauptphase*, phases 4b and 5 to the second *Hauptphase*.)

logical outlook and the major thematic lines of the Book of Daniel, along which ch. 8 is intended to be read and which it continuously reflects.

a. A Theology of Power

Daniel 8 develops a theme already well known from earlier parts of the Book, namely the connection of supernatural powers with the powers of the world.

The working of the powers of the world, their possibilities and their limits, has been amply demonstrated by the "court tales" in Daniel 1-6. These stories emphasize how the king of an empire can deport foreign peoples and employ them for his own purposes (ch. 1), can decide on life and death of individuals (chs. 1 and 3), order himself to be worshipped by his subjects (ch. 3) and even defile objects designed for religious ceremonies (ch. 5). The working of the divine (with which the king *ex officio* is associated and to which he has a privileged access) is always present, but, at least on the visible level, very much in the background.[15] It is like one central theme which appears in many variations.

In the second part of the court tales, the limitations of worldly powers even at face-value are being pointed out with growing intensity, first in confrontation with other forces of the world, then with the divine itself. The king who wants to be worshipped by his entire realm becomes himself a helpless victim exposed to the manipulating intrigues and slanderous acts of his officials (Dan 3,8ff).[16] He even becomes an outcast afflicted by sickness and can only return to a truly human life by accepting God as the supreme power (Daniel 4; cf. 3,28; 6,27f). If he is unwilling to learn, he will be doomed to destruction (Dan 5).

One may conclude that the growing awareness of the supremacy of God's kingdom against mighty foreign empires becomes a *Leitmotiv*

---

[15] God is continuously the true agent already in Daniel 1, cf. 1,2.9.17 (with נתן).

[16] The presentation of the courtiers' behaviour is marked by a very fine irony indeed, but along the general interest between power and helplessness in the Book of Daniel it acquires a theological function. From a historical point of view, Dan 3,8ff transcends mere literary fiction and furnishes a miniature depiction of how such slandering will have taken place. Several of the texts collected by Parpola, *Letters*, 1993, provide a vivid image of how high-ranking individuals flattered the king, but at the same time denounced each other (cf. no. 72, ll. 6ff; more cautious: no. 290, ll. 13eff).

which ties together the early chapters,[17] creates suspense and keeps the story moving.

The underlying conflict between supernatural and worldly powers is presented in a most explicit fashion in the visions, especially in Daniel 2 and Daniel 7, since a vision grants its beholder an insight into the hidden reality beyond what can be perceived by the senses. In Daniel 2, perhaps the most "symbolic" vision in the whole Book of Daniel, the statue consisting of different materials which symbolizes the totality of worldly power by a synchronic overview of the subsequent major empires is destroyed by the rock, representing the supernatural power. In Daniel 7, the mythical representatives of the forces of chaos are dominated by those of order. Humanity, encapsulated in "the one like a man", is given universal dominion by God.

These visions attempt to explain the struggle of forces whose *effects* can be seen in the world. The instances of conflict between good and evil there constitute the momentarily visible side of a larger framework, a cosmic battle. They do not exhibit "allegories" or transpositions of structural patterns which occur in the human world on a fictional level in order to illustrate them, but universal structures which are being realized in the course of history, even if their totality is invisible.

The opposition between worldly and supernatural powers is thus essential to the visions. It expresses a theodicy problem for the Jews of ca. 165 BC,[18] who acknowledged the God of Israel as the real ruler over creation and history, yet had to suffer under foreign dominion and a lack of respect for their religious traditions. This is also the thematic frame which is constitutive for Daniel 8. In Daniel 8, the author illuminates as the central element of his account the profanation of the sacred (8,11-12),[19] but then takes up the historical dimension again by indicating that the end of this profanation has already been determined for a specific

---

[17] Albertz, "Social Setting," in *Book of Daniel*, eds. Collins and Flint, 2001: 175; see also Gane, "Genre Awareness," in *To Understand*, ed. Merling, 1997: 141, on the dominant role of transcendent kingship in Daniel 1-6.

[18] See Harrington, "Ideology," *SBL Seminar Papers* (1999): 540-551.

[19] These verses are depicted as the climax of the whole narrative by various literary and rhetorical means, as will be pointed out in the detailed analysis.

time (8,13-14).[20] This means that transcendent planning reaches into strictly historical categories. The need for self-reflection, intellectual maturity and repentance, which was so prominent in Daniel 2 and 4, has in Daniel 8 given way to a sinister presentation of the imminent forces of evil. But their limitations are reinforced, for the restoration of the cult reestablishes the sacred aspect of humanity and expresses the victory of order over chaos. There is no moral message anymore, but a demonstration of how things are and how they will invariably be.

b. The Framework of Apocalypticism

From the preceding observations it emerges that apocalypticism, that is, the insight into things still hidden, does not only deal with another world, but that it is contextualized in various ways. There is, first of all, an explicit setting in the exilic situation of Israel, with continuous references to the, from the point of view of the narrator, relative past (the growth of the Persian Empire) and future (the spread of Hellenism and the *Religionsnot* under Antiochus IV) political history.

In Daniel 8 the historical dimension of the Babylonian exile as the literary setting – and so the relative "present" of the text – is provided by chronological and geographical information given in the frame. The historical background of the final redaction of the Book of Daniel, by contrast, is reflected in the visionary parts. It takes up some ideas from the setting, such as the conflict between Jewish and pagan culture or the vulnerability of worldly power, but presents a much more sinister overall view by putting a far greater emphasis on the theme of war or the demoniac nature of foreign rule. Thus, the historical dimension is universal and embraces past, present and future, almost typologically elaborating on the contrast between setting (as a foil for the reader) and background.

Since the visions do not merely illuminate the inner nature of things, but can, when interpreted correctly, also predict the future, there

---

[20] This does not mean that the Book of Daniel is totally deterministic in its outlook. On the contrary, God's action is often displayed as motivated by human prayer. However, the major course of history seems to be fixed in favour of the salvation of the Jewish people. Cf. Baldwin, "Free Will," in *To Understand*, ed. Merling, 1997: 163-172.

is no exact borderline between history and apocalypticism. On the contrary, historical events can only be understood in the light of a wider cosmic framework. Since all power-struggles in the world reflect the combat between supernatural forces in the invisible realm, a revelation (ἀποκάλυψις)[21] of the working of these forces is at the same time a revelation of the way things really are (8,3-12). A visionary insight is not the appearance of a symbolic and theoretical construction, but the possibility, momentarily granted by God, to see and hear things with the eyes and ears of the angels, as is made clear above all by Daniel 8.

This insight, contrary to all sensual experience, is so bewildering that it is in need of explanation, while explanation is not conceived as a decipherment of encrypted information, but as the establishment of a link between the cosmic superstructure and its individual realization in political history (8,13-26).

In fact, Daniel 8 goes further than the bulk of visionary literature in that it gives the application of the vision, too, in a visionary framework and so stresses most vividly that even the ability to interpret the things revealed results from a divine favour (this is already emphasized in Dan 1,17). It is the right interpretation which provides the link between the strange images seen by the visionary and the course of things which will come to pass.

3. The Language of Daniel 8

The Book of Daniel belongs to the texts commonly said to be written in "Late Biblical Hebrew". This linguistic stage allegedly exhibits various peculiarities in spelling, grammar, and vocabulary, duly pointed out by the standard histories of the Hebrew language.[22] "Late Biblical Hebrew" is thus a theoretical construction based on a catalogue of individual non-Classical features atomistically drawn from all of these texts together as if they were unified in any way.

---

[21] See Gane, "Genre Awareness," in *To Understand*, ed. Merling, 1997, for reflections on the idea that "apocalypticism" is not restricted to Daniel 7-12, but permeates the whole Book of Daniel.

[22] They generally follow Polzin, *Late Biblical Hebrew*, 1976, and repeat his criteria.

It is, however, clear that the generic concept "Late Biblical Hebrew" engulfs only a small number of linguistically rather diverse writings. Although there are some non-Classical features shared by several of them, many differences may be due to the literary genre, such as narrative (Ezra-Nehemiah, Daniel), re-working of history (Chronicles) and argumentation (Qohelet).

For this reason it is by no means easy to postulate different variations of "Late Biblical Hebrew" among the late texts, such as more (Daniel, Ezra-Nehemiah) and less (Chronicles)[23] classicizing works or compositions which are "on the way" to Mishnaic Hebrew (Qohelet). The so-called characteristic features of "Late Biblical Hebrew" on the whole simply do not reflect any unified linguistic stage.

Moreover, it has been suggested that Qohelet is an early text rather than a late one.[24] One may also bear in mind that Qohelet has, even though it is not a narrative text, at least two certain instances of *wayyiqtol* and can hardly function as secure evidence for the gradual decline of this form. So even the material basis for a classification of that kind is still uncertain.

Since there is very little evidence for grammatical features known from Mishnaic Hebrew in Ezra-Nehemiah, Daniel and Chronicles,[25] it seems doubtful whether one may really postulate a gradually growing assimilation of the Hebrew of the later biblical compositions towards Mishnaic Hebrew. In the light of this evidence the Hebrew of the Book of Daniel shall not be compared to such a catalogue of individual features and assigned a place within the allegedly linear development of the language towards Mishnaic Hebrew in the following observations. This would presumably be another instance of the "teleological fallacy" to

---

[23] The linguistic similarities and differences between Ezra-Nehemiah and Chronicles are still subject to discussion. Most previous scholarship on this subject has attempted to use linguistic evidence in order to defend or to criticize the view that both texts have been written by the same author, but it seems hard to arrive at either the one or the other conclusion on such grounds alone. Cf. Talshir, "Reinvestigation," *VT* 38 (1988): 165-193.

[24] Cf. Fredericks, *Language*, 1988, who wants to date Qohelet in the 8th or 7th century BC. Fredericks's views remain controversial, however; the traditional opinion prefers a date somewhen between 250 and 190 BC.

[25] See Kropat, *Syntax*, 1909, 73-74.

which all historical sciences are prone, including the history of languages. Instead of that, there shall be a brief discussion of the most striking linguistic peculiarities on their own. Such a less theoretically-biased interpretation of the facts may in the end contribute more to the linguistic character of the Book of Daniel than a mere label.

An obviously late orthographical feature is the *plene* spelling וָאָקוּם in Dan 8,27, even though the last syllable was originally short (*wā'āqŏm*).[26] Orthography on its own is no secure criterion, as it may result from a later scribal variation, but it is noteworthy that וָאָקוּם recurs in other late post-exilic texts,[27] while earlier compositions have the consonantal text ואקם.[28]

Apart from that, the Hebrew of Daniel, especially in ch. 8, is full of peculiar lexical features, but is not at all clear whether they are, as often stated, "colloquialisms" or "colloquial Aramaisms". In fact, it may often be impossible to attain certainty as to the stylistic status of these peculiarities. Some of them are classic examples arguing for a later date, such as the form of the first person singular pronoun אני instead of אנכי,[29] מַלְכוּת instead of מַמְלָכָה[30] or the verb עמד which takes up meanings of קום (Dan 8,23; 11,2.3), maybe an "inverted calque" from Aramaic, where קום has the meanings of both Hebrew verbs.[31]

More important, however, are the numerous idiosyncracies which cannot be found elsewhere in Biblical Hebrew. It is therefore less probable that they are distinctive features of "Late Biblical Hebrew", they are rather peculiar to the language of Daniel as such and carry little weight for dating the text. One of them, תָּמִיד (normally an adverb: "continuously") meaning "daily offering", can be found in the Mishna,[32] but this does not necessarily imply that Daniel reflects a common late usage, it

---

[26] See below on the narrative frame for a slightly more extensive discussion of this verse.

[27] Such as Neh 2,12; 2 Chr 6,10.

[28] Cf. 1 Kgs 3,21.

[29] Kutscher, *History*, 1982, §§46.119.

[30] Ibid., §§121.123. In Chronicles, the latter is replaced three times by the former.

[31] Kutscher, *History*, 1982, §123; Rooker, *Transition*, 1990, 149.

[32] See below on Dan 8,11-12 for a more extensive discussion.

may well have been coined by the author of ch. 8 and made its way into Mishnaic Hebrew only afterwards. A clearer case is פלמוני in 8,13, a syncope of פלני and אלמוני ("whoever") which is unattested elsewhere. It is unlikely that this is an ordinary feature of later Hebrew, since the Old Greek and Theodotion did not understand it and translated it as if it were a proper name (τῷ φελμουνι), although the Vulgate (thanks to Rabbinic learning?) has understood it correctly, translating *alteri nescio cui*.[33]

Several other lexical idiosyncracies most probably highlight important keywords, even though it is not clear whether they are "late". Apart from תָּמִיד with the unusual meaning "daily offering", one may note the double designation צְפִיר־הָעִזִּים (literally "the he-goat of goats") for the he-goat or the dual קְרָנַיִם which adds the dual ending to the plural stem. Since Daniel 8 is the only text where this form occurs with קרן, it may reflect an ancient vocalization and not a scribal modification.

It will become clear from the subsequent narrative analysis that all of these even morphologically remarkable words and forms denote crucial concepts within the theological framework of Daniel 8 and occur in grammatically anomalous or at least noteworthy constructions. One may point above all to the numerous instances of a lack of agreement in gender between subject and verb in the climactic section 8,8-12.

Therefore it would be a strange coincidence if these features were not consciously applied, especially since the language of the Hebrew Book of Daniel makes ample use of keywords for sign-posting in order to guide the reader. It is evident that terms denoting power, such as יד (literally: "hand"), נתן ("to give") or מלך ("king"), which recur in Daniel 8, have been very prominent in the court-narrative, particularly in Daniel 1, where the many cases of a combination of יד and נתן are noteworthy. In Daniel 7-8, the most important keyword is קרן ("horn"). Its metaphorical use ("power") is widespread in the Old Testament; within the visions in Daniel 7 and 8, it may forecast the theme of war which becomes dominant in the more historically-oriented chapters Daniel 11 and 12, that is, the military campaigns and the persecution of the Jewish sages.

These phenomena hint at the subtle stylistic differences between the court tales which prefer a third-person narrative (except the dream

---

[33] See the commentary section below on this verse.

report in ch. 4, but there the vision is part of a larger story praising Daniel's mantic skills) and the visions in chs. 7-12 which are first-person accounts whose focus is solely on the revelation. The court tales thus present a rather "factual" idea of history. This concept is mirrored by means of a plot which keeps going on chiefly due to the mutual interaction of cause and event. Correspondingly, the literary expression of this idea of history in the Book of Daniel appears to be a detached, "objective" presentation of the working of worldly powers and politics which is nonetheless at crucial points replaced by divine interaction. So its depiction penetrates, above all by means of dreams, beyond the historical horizons of the Babylonian exile, preparing the reader for the culmination of God's kingdom in the latter half.

Contrary to the style of the court tales, the visions have a more personal dimension, even though they, too, make a claim to historical objectivity by trying to uncover the forces at work behind everyday reality. Hence the first-person narrative and the prominence of "metaphorical" keywords such as קֶרֶן. Both approaches are of course strictly complementary, as the numerous instances of linguistic and thematic correspondence between the two halves of the Book of Daniel indicate. The literary style is thus a most important carrier of the respective message, since it guides the reader effectively, although often invisibly.

Moreover, it is precisely this sophisticated use of keywords which makes the difference between the vision and its application (one of the central topics of this study) in Daniel 8 itself apparent. While the three stages of the vision (the ram, the goat, the horns) use identical phrases in order to describe the rise, challenge and defeat of the respective protagonist, the commentary section in Dan 8,13ff employs *different* words, even when it explicitly refers to the vision. One may note the different verbs in vv. 8 and 22 (עלה and עמד, both "to come up") or the various terms for the he-goat in vv. 5.8.21 (צְפִיר הָעִזִּים and הַצָּפִיר הַשָּׂעִיר; the latter could be a *double entendre*, because הַשָּׂעִיר can also mean "the demon").

An analysis of the commentary section (see below) will also show that this part introduces a new semantic field, namely the wisdom terms used for Antiochus ("a king of bold countenance and understanding riddles") – these did not feature at all in the vision report.

The preference for technical language which is so clear in Daniel 1 (Persian loan-words denoting concepts associated with the royal court) or, in the Aramaic section, Daniel 3 (the list of officials in 3,2 and the one of musical instruments in 3,5) can still be seen in the introduction to Daniel 8. The use of precise geographical terms and the correct administrative designations הַבִּירָה ("the fortress") for Susa or הַמְּדִינָה for the "satrapy" of Elam fits well into the author's ambition to employ at times rare, but appropriate words for the sake of precision. One may add the strange אוּבַל in 8,2, but its meaning is not entirely clear: see below for a more extensive discussion of the frame. All this creates a strong impression of a very conscious use of language, above all the lexicon, at various stylistic levels.

The verbal morphosyntax of the Hebrew of Daniel, however, appears to be quite close to pre-exilic Hebrew narrative. Very characteristic for such a "classicizing" tendency is the use of "lengthened imperfects" for the first person ("cohortatives"), such as in Dan 8,13.[34] These are also very frequent in the Qumran documents and biblical texts from Qumran (even when they are absent in the Masoretic Text, cf. Isa 42,1 in 1QIsaᵃ).[35] The meaning of such "cohortative" forms can hardly be distinguished from the simple imperfect (at least not on contextual grounds). Thus they are presumably employed for stylistic reasons.[36] Perhaps their sound was appreciated as particularly solemn, but no convincing explanation of their prominence in later writings has yet been found.

Apart from that, Daniel 8 makes full use of the many possibilities of the Classical Hebrew verbal system as they are known from pre-exilic prose whose style was apparently considered no less authoritative than

---

[34] See Driver, *Use of the Tenses*, 1892, §69, for references. The use of the "lengthened imperfects" is not evenly spread in the later biblical texts: Chronicles, for example, have almost exclusively the short imperfect, see Japhet, "Common authorship," *VT* 18 (1968): 337.

[35] Cf. Schniedewind, "Antilanguage," *JBL* 118 (1999): 245-246, who rightly calls this phenomenon a "pseudo-classicism".

[36] Cf. Kutscher, *Isaiah Scroll*, 1974, 40.326-328; Abegg, "Hebrew of the Dead Sea Scrolls," in *Dead Sea Scrolls after Fifty Years*, Vol. 1, eds. Flints and VanderKam, 1998: 336-337, who detects a lengthening in 35% of the singular and 65% of the plural forms.

its content.[37] Daniel 8 continuously uses *wayyiqtol* as the standard verbal form for successive past events taking place against a background described by *qatal* forms and thus keeps *wayyiqtol* and other forms strictly apart. One can even find instances of the infinitive construct with preposition following ויהי with the meaning of a temporal clause (cf. Dan 8,1, right at the beginning: וַיְהִי בִּרְאֹתִי). This is a very classical construction which shows no traces of the later tendency to leave out ויהי.[38]

Nonetheless, these serious attempts at writing largely in pre-exilic prose style are complemented by some individual features commonly associated with the style of later Hebrew. Former generations of scholars were perhaps too rash to call the latter features "colloquialisms" or indeed "Aramaisms" and to draw unverified conclusions concerning the origin of the Book of Daniel from them.

But in very many cases it is simply not possibly to identify a particular "colloquial" nuance. An interesting example is the use of אֵין without expressing the agent in 8,5 (וְאֵין נוֹגֵעַ בָּאָרֶץ, cf. 8,27). It occurs only here in the Hebrew Bible, but can occasionally be found in Mishnaic Hebrew.[39] Moreover, the rare use of the article as a relative particle in 8,1 seems to belong to post-classical usage.[40]

In general, the linguistic profile of the Hebrew Book of Daniel is even more complex. Together with the standard *qatal-wayyiqtol* pattern, it also uses periphrastic constructions (such as in Dan 8,5) and *w^eqatal* for the end of a narrative sequence. *W^eqatal* and *waw* plus *qatal* (as in Dan 8,7) are strictly kept apart. From v. 13 onwards, the linguistic code changes from narrative to dialogue and then to prophecy.

Consequently, the author adapts his use of verbal forms to the underlying linguistic conventions of the literary genre. The most striking

---

[37] Joosten, "Pseudo-Classicisms," in *Sirach, Scrolls, and Sages*, eds. Muraoka and Elwolde, 1997: 147-148. Cf. Rabin, *History*, 1973, 37, for a similar explanation of the classicizing tendency of Qumran Hebrew.

[38] As in Chronicles, cf. Kutscher, *History*, 1982, §67; Kropat, *Syntax*, 1909, 22-23.74-75. ויהי is avoided in Qumran Hebrew as well: Qimron, *Hebrew*, 1986, 72-73.

[39] Cf. mAvot 3,17 and van der Peursen, "Negation," in *Sirach, Scrolls, and Sages*, eds. Muraoka and Elwolde, 1997: 224.

[40] Most of the examples available are to be found in Chronicles and Ezra, see JM §145d-e.

instance is his shift to *yiqtol* with future rather than modal meaning in the prophetic section. He makes use of a maximum of syntactical and stylistic possibilities available to him.

2
The Text of Daniel 8

For the present inquiry, the basic point of reference will be the Hebrew text of the Masoretes (MT), although a few corrections have been incorporated. These corrections have been indicated according to the conventions of Classical Philology, the mother of textual criticism. In effect, the following signs will be used:

< ... >	A word which is not in the Masoretic Text has been added.
[MT: ...]	The reading of the Masoretic Text has not been accepted, but is given nonetheless for consultation purposes.
[K: ...]	Indicates the Ketib, although the Qere has been accepted as the superior reading.
† ... †	The text between the daggers is taken to be corrupt.

The Hebrew text and its translation have been put on facing pages. This will hopefully make the work easier for consultation, although it should be borne in mind that the discussion of linguistic points generally presupposes a study of the original text, since all those stylistic subtleties of Daniel 8 can hardly be reflected in another language. It is obvious that the translation has no artistic ambitions whatsoever; it is only meant to reflect the Hebrew text as the present author understands it. The presentation of the subject-matter in the rest of this monograph will mostly follow the segmentation as it is proposed here.

Since external textual evidence will be taken into account for some major points which bear on the interpretation of the text, the text-critical situation of the Daniel 8 shall be briefly summarized in order to make the material foundation of subsequent decisions accessible. For this reason, the textual notes are not presented with the exclusive aim of establishing a reading text, but are also geared to make understand better tablishing a reading text, but are also geared to make understand better the discussion in the more interpretative parts of this study, as the textual facts themselves often provide a starting-point for wider-ranging literary scholarship.

Lastly, the individual translation technique and style of the ancient versions has not yet been taken into consideration by scholars who worked on Daniel 8. Therefore textual critics often too readily change the MT on the basis of the versions without being aware of the fact that these translations may in certain cases not be faithful representations of their respective *Vorlage*. It will be evident that, in the light of these precautions, which try to clarify the nature of the relationship between the different text forms, several textual problems can be solved in a different and, perhaps, sometimes more satisfactory way. Proposals for changes in the MT based on external evidence will carry greater conviction when "interpretational" renderings in the versions can be ruled out.

1. A Reading Text and Translation of Daniel 8

Opening part of the frame: time, place, circumstances (vv. 1-2)

1 בִּשְׁנַת שָׁלוֹשׁ לְמַלְכוּת בֵּלְאשַׁצַּר הַמֶּלֶךְ^a
חָזוֹן נִרְאָה אֵלַי אֲנִי^b דָּנִיֵּאל אַחֲרֵי הַנִּרְאָה אֵלַי בַּתְּחִלָּה:
2 ^aוָאֶרְאֶה בֶּחָזוֹן וַיְהִי בִּרְאֹתִי
וַאֲנִי בְּשׁוּשַׁן הַבִּירָה אֲשֶׁר בְּעֵילָם הַמְּדִינָה
וָאֶרְאֶה בֶּחָזוֹן וַאֲנִי הָיִיתִי עַל־אוּבַל אוּלָי:

Battle narrative (vv. 3-12)

3 וָאֶשָּׂא עֵינַי וָאֶרְאֶה וְהִנֵּה אַיִל אֶחָד <גָּדוֹל>^a עֹמֵד לִפְנֵי הָאֻבָל
וְלוֹ קְרָנָיִם וְהַקְּרָנַיִם^b גְּבֹהֹת וְהָאַחַת גְּבֹהָה מִן־הַשֵּׁנִית
וְהַגְּבֹהָה עֹלָה בָּאַחֲרֹנָה^c:
4 רָאִיתִי אֶת־הָאַיִל מְנַגֵּחַ <מִזְרָחָה>^a יָמָּה וְצָפוֹנָה וָנֶגְבָּה
וְכָל־חַיּוֹת לֹא־יַעַמְדוּ לְפָנָיו וְאֵין מַצִּיל מִיָּדוֹ^b וְעָשָׂה כִרְצֹנוֹ וְהִגְדִּיל:
5 וַאֲנִי הָיִיתִי מֵבִין
וְהִנֵּה צְפִיר־הָעִזִּים^a בָּא מִן־הַמַּעֲרָב עַל^b־פְּנֵי כָל^c־הָאָרֶץ
^dוְאֵין נוֹגֵעַ בָּאָרֶץ^d וְהַצָּפִיר קֶרֶן חָזוּת^e בֵּין עֵינָיו:
6 וַיָּבֹא עַד־הָאַיִל בַּעַל הַקְּרָנַיִם אֲשֶׁר רָאִיתִי עֹמֵד לִפְנֵי הָאֻבָל
וַיָּרָץ אֵלָיו בַּחֲמַת כֹּחוֹ^a:
7 וּרְאִיתִיו^a מַגִּיעַ אֵצֶל הָאַיִל
וַיִּתְמַרְמַר אֵלָיו וַיַּךְ אֶת־הָאַיִל וַיְשַׁבֵּר אֶת־שְׁתֵּי קְרָנָיו
וְלֹא־הָיָה כֹחַ בָּאַיִל לַעֲמֹד לְפָנָיו
וַיַּשְׁלִיכֵהוּ אַרְצָה וַיִּרְמְסֵהוּ
וְלֹא־הָיָה מַצִּיל לָאַיִל מִיָּדוֹ:
8 וּצְפִיר הָעִזִּים הִגְדִּיל עַד־מְאֹד
וּכְעָצְמוֹ^a נִשְׁבְּרָה הַקֶּרֶן הַגְּדוֹלָה
וַתַּעֲלֶנָה^b †אַחֵרוֹת† [MT: חָזוּת]^b אַרְבַּע תַּחְתֶּיהָ
לְאַרְבַּע רוּחוֹת הַשָּׁמָיִם:

Opening part of the frame: time, place, circumstances (vv. 1-2)

1 In the third year of the reign of King Belshazzar a vision appeared to me, yes, to me, Daniel, after the one which had appeared to me before.
2 Then I concentrated on the vision and saw, while I was looking, that I was in Susa the fortress, which is in the satrapy of Elam. I concentrated on the vision and was by the river Ulai.

Battle narrative (vv. 3-12)

3 Then I looked up and saw a <great> ram standing in front of the river. It had two Horns.[41] Both Horns were high, but one was higher than the other, and the high one came up last.
4 I was seeing the ram charging <eastward,> westward, northward and southward. No beast could withstand it, and there was no one to rescue from its power. Thus, it did as it pleased and became great.
5 And I was reflecting – yes, it is the he-goat! It came from the west upon the face of all the earth without touching the ground. As for the he-goat, there was a conspicuous horn between its eyes.
6 Then it came toward the ram, the one with the two Horns that I had seen standing in front of the river, and ran at it with burning anger.
7 And I was seeing it approaching the ram: it was enraged against it, hit the ram and broke its two Horns, so that there was no strength in the ram to withstand it. Then it threw it down to the ground and trampled upon it. There was no one to rescue the ram from its power.
8 Then the he-goat became very great indeed, but when it had reached the peak of its might, the great horn was broken, and in its place four other ones[42] came up, corresponding to the four winds of heaven.

---

[41] I have capitalized "Horns" in the translation in order to point out that this important keyword is visually highlighted in various ways in the Hebrew text as well.

[42] MT: "a conspicuousness of four".

9 וּמִן־הָאַחַת [a]מֵהֶם יָצָא קֶרֶן־אַחַת[b] צְעִירָה [מִצְּעִירָה :MT][b]
וַתִּגְדַּל־יֶתֶר אֶל־הַנֶּגֶב וְאֶל־הַמִּזְרָח וְאֶל[c]־הַצֶּבִי:
10 וַתִּגְדַּל עַד־צְבָא הַשָּׁמָיִם
וַתַּפֵּל אַרְצָה מִן־הַצָּבָא וּמִן־הַכּוֹכָבִים וַתִּרְמְסֵם:
11 וְעַד שַׂר־הַצָּבָא הִגְדִּיל
וּמִמֶּנּוּ [a]הוּרַם [הֵרִים :K][a] הַתָּמִיד וְהֻשְׁלַךְ מְכוֹן מִקְדָּשׁוֹ:
12 וְצָבָא תִּנָּתֵן עַל־הַתָּמִיד בְּפָשַׁע
וְתַשְׁלֵךְ אֱמֶת אַרְצָה וְעָשְׂתָה וְהִצְלִיחָה:

Angelic dialogue (vv. 13-14)

13 וָאֶשְׁמְעָה אֶחָד־[a]קָדוֹשׁ מְדַבֵּר
וַיֹּאמֶר אֶחָד[a] קָדוֹשׁ [b]לַפַּלְמוֹנִי הַמְדַבֵּר[b]
עַד־מָתַי הֶחָזוֹן[c] הַתָּמִיד[d] וְהַפֶּשַׁע שֹׁמֵם
[e]תֵּת וְקֹדֶשׁ†[e] וְצָבָא[f] מִרְמָס:
14 וַיֹּאמֶר [a]אֵלָיו [אֵלַי :MT][a]
עַד עֶרֶב בֹּקֶר[b] אַלְפַּיִם וּשְׁלֹשׁ מֵאוֹת וְנִצְדַּק קֹדֶשׁ:

Epiphany of the interpreter (vv. 15-18)

15 וַיְהִי בִּרְאֹתִי אֲנִי דָנִיֵּאל אֶת־הֶחָזוֹן וָאֲבַקְשָׁה בִינָה[a]
וְהִנֵּה עֹמֵד לְנֶגְדִּי כְּמַרְאֵה־גָבֶר:
16 וָאֶשְׁמַע קוֹל־אָדָם בֵּין אוּלָי
[a]וַיִּקְרָא וַיֹּאמַר גַּבְרִיאֵל הָבֵן לְהַלָּז אֶת־הַמַּרְאֶה:
17 וַיָּבֹא [a]אֵצֶל עָמְדִי[a] וּבְבֹאוֹ נִבְעַתִּי וָאֶפְּלָה עַל־פָּנָי
וַיֹּאמֶר אֵלַי הָבֵן בֶּן־אָדָם כִּי לְעֶת־קֵץ הֶחָזוֹן[b]:
18 וּבְדַבְּרוֹ עִמִּי נִרְדַּמְתִּי עַל־פָּנַי אָרְצָה
וַיִּגַּע־בִּי וַיַּעֲמִידֵנִי עַל־עָמְדִי:

9 And out of one of Them had come one single, little horn and grew exceedingly great toward the south, toward the east, and toward the glorious (land).

10 It grew up to the host of heaven and cast down to the ground some of the host and some of the stars and trampled upon them.

11 Even up to the prince of the host it grew, and from him the offering was taken away.[43] Thus it overthrew the place of his sanctuary.

12 So a host had to be given over, in addition to the offering, in the course of transgression. It threw truth down to the ground and had success in what it was doing.

Angelic dialogue (vv. 13-14)

13 Then I heard a holy one speaking and another holy one said to whoever it was who was speaking: "For how long is the vision, the regular offering, the transgression that makes desolate and his making sanctuary and host a trampling?"

14 And he answered him:[44] "For two thousand three hundred evenings and mornings. Then it will be the case that the sanctuary will be set right."

Epiphany of the interpreter (vv. 15-18)

15 And while I (yes, I, Daniel) was seeing the vision, I sought understanding: There was someone standing before me, looking like a man!

16 Then I heard the voice of a man by the Ulai. He called out: "Gabriel, make yonder man understand the vision!"

17 So he approached the place where I was standing, and while he was approaching I was terrified and fell prostrate. But he said to me: "Understand, O mortal, that it is the end of time to which the vision refers."

18 And while he was speaking with me, I was in a trance, on the ground. Then he touched me and made me stand on the place where I stood.

---

[43] Or: "and he took the offering away" (according to the Ketib).

[44] MT: "And he answered me".

Application of the vision to contemporary history (vv. 19-25)

19 וַיֹּאמֶר^a הִנְנִי מוֹדִיעֲךָ אֵת אֲשֶׁר־יִהְיֶה בְּאַחֲרִית הַזָּעַם^b
כִּי לְמוֹעֵד קֵץ:

20 הָאַיִל אֲשֶׁר־רָאִיתָ בַּעַל הַקְּרָנָיִם מַלְכֵי^a מָדַי וּפָרָס:

21 ^aוְהַצָּפִיר הַשָּׂעִיר^a מֶלֶךְ יָוָן
וְהַקֶּרֶן הַגְּדוֹלָה אֲשֶׁר בֵּין־עֵינָיו הוּא הַמֶּלֶךְ הָרִאשׁוֹן:

22 וְהַנִּשְׁבֶּרֶת וַתַּעֲמֹדְנָה אַרְבַּע תַּחְתֶּיהָ
אַרְבַּע מַלְכֻיּוֹת מִגּוֹי^a<וֹ> יַעֲמֹדְנָה וְלֹא בְכֹחוֹ:

23 וּבְאַחֲרִית מַלְכוּתָם כְּהָתֵם^a הַפֹּשְׁעִים^b
יַעֲמֹד מֶלֶךְ עַז־פָּנִים וּמֵבִין חִידוֹת:

24 וְעָצַם כֹּחוֹ ^aוְלֹא בְכֹחוֹ^a וְנִפְלָאוֹת יַשְׁחִית^b
וְהִצְלִיחַ וְעָשָׂה וְהִשְׁחִית עֲצוּמִים ^cוְעַם־קְדֹשִׁים^c:

25 ^aוְעַל־שִׂכְלוֹ^a וְהִצְלִיחַ מִרְמָה בְּיָדוֹ
וּבִלְבָבוֹ יַגְדִּיל וּבְשַׁלְוָה יַשְׁחִית רַבִּים
וְעַל־שַׂר־שָׂרִים יַעֲמֹד וּבְאֶפֶס יָד יִשָּׁבֵר:

Final order to the visionary (v. 26)

26 וּמַרְאֵה הָעֶרֶב וְהַבֹּקֶר ^aאֲשֶׁר נֶאֱמַר^a אֱמֶת הוּא
^bוְאַתָּה סְתֹם^b הֶחָזוֹן כִּי לְיָמִים רַבִּים:

Closing part of the frame: the effects of the vision (v. 27)

27 וַאֲנִי דָנִיֵּאל ^aנִהְיֵיתִי וְנֶחֱלֵיתִי^a יָמִים^b
וָאָקוּם וָאֶעֱשֶׂה אֶת־מְלֶאכֶת הַמֶּלֶךְ
וָאֶשְׁתּוֹמֵם עַל־הַמַּרְאֶה וְאֵין מֵבִין:

Application of the vision to contemporary history (vv. 19-25)

19 Then he said: "Behold, I will inform you of what will be at the end of the wrath, since it is for the appointed time of the end.
20 The ram which you saw, the one with the two Horns: the kings of Media and Persia;
21 and the he-goat: the king of Greece; and the great horn between its eyes: this is the first king.
22 But as for the one that was broken and four came up in its place: four kingdoms shall arise from <his>[45] nation, but not with his strength.
23 And after their rule, when the sinners have come to an end, a king shall arise, of bold countenance and understanding riddles.
24 So his strength will be great [but not by his own strength], and an incredible destruction he will cause, having success in what he will be doing and destroying the mighty ones and the people of the holy ones.
25 And after his cunning he shall make deceit prosper by means of his control and shall be arrogant in his innermost self. Without warning he shall destroy many, and will stand up even against the prince of princes. But without anybody's hand he will be broken.

Final order to the visionary (v. 26)

26 But the appearance of the evening and the morning that has been told is true. As for you, however, seal up the vision, for it refers to many days.

Closing part of the frame: the effects of the vision (v. 27)

27 But I, Daniel, was undone and sick for a number of days. Then I arose and did the king's business. But I was dismayed by the vision, and there was nobody who could gain insight.

---

[45] MT: "from a nation".

2. Textual Commentary

V. 1:   a) The title "king" is not explicitly mentioned in the Old Greek, while Theodotion and the Vulgate agree with the MT. There is no need to consider this an explicating plus and thus to delete it from the Hebrew (so Collins, *Daniel*, 1993, 325), because the reading of the Old Greek is not necessarily a true variant. Additionally, there is no other external evidence. Instead, the translator may have thought that the idea of kingship was already implied in βασιλεύοντος ("while he was king"). Accordingly, he did not follow the Hebrew text word by word; he tends to do that in other places as well. In 8,3, for example, he leaves out וְהִנֵּה, which is revealing for his understanding of the Hebrew syntax, see below. In 8,27, too, the Old Greek seems to merge two Hebrew words into the single ἀσθενήσας, "having been sick". For a not totally dissimilar case one may compare the Hebrew and the Greek text of Jer 2,6, a series of adjectives which is not strictly parallel to the Hebrew.[46]

However, the most significant reason why the omission of the title "king" in the Old Greek does presumably not point to a different original text is the fact that the translator – apparently on purpose – creates an exact harmonization with the Old Greek translation of Dan 7,1. There the text has ἔτους πρώτου βασιλεύοντος Βαλτασαρ χώρας Βαβυλωνίας for the Aramaic original בִּשְׁנַת חֲדָה לְבֵלְאשַׁצַּר מֶלֶךְ בָּבֶל ("In the first year in which Belshazzar was king of Babylon"). Here, too, the participle βασιλεύοντος renders the Hebrew noun מֶלֶךְ, while there is no לְמַלְכוּת ("during the kingship", as in 8,1). Other observations can corroborate the suggestion that the translator wanted to join Dan 8,1 explicitly with Dan 7,1. Exactly the same Hebrew pattern of dating individual episodes ([name of the king] לְמַלְכוּת [year] בִּשְׁנַת) which recurs in 1,1, 2,1 and 8,1 is translated in three different ways by the Old Greek (cf. ἐπὶ βασιλέως Ιωακιμ in 1,1 and καὶ ἐν τῷ ἔτει τῷ δευτέρῳ τῆς βασιλείας Ναβουχοδονοσορ συνέβη in 2,1). Hence it seems that the translator of the Old Greek wanted to make the connection between the two chapters

---

[46] Cf. Muraoka, "Literary Device," *Textus* 8 (1973): 24-25.

Daniel 7 and Daniel 8 (which is very important for the interpretation of the vision, see below on the narrative frame) especially evident by means of harmonization. However, in doing so he lost the initial connection which the Hebrew of 8,1 makes with 1,1 and 2,1, that is, with the court tales.

The translator could have had this idea by observing that the pattern of dating changes again with 9,1, for in 9,1, 10,1 and 11,1 it is consistently [name of the king]לְ [year] בִּשְׁנַת.[47] Moreover, with Dan 7,2 begins a first-person narrative (while the introductory remark in Dan 7,1 is still in the third person) which continues throughout the whole of Daniel 8 and 9. It may also be the case that the translator has seen that the title מֶלֶךְ is given in 1,1, but, as the king is already known, has been omitted in 2,1. These suggestions are not mutually exclusive, but may well go together. Particularly the latter observation may theoretically be an internal argument for the view that 8,1 originally had *not* read מֶלֶךְ, but omitting the title in the Hebrew is, in the light of this evidence, certainly the *lectio facilior* and so in itself less probable, especially since the weight of the evidence exhibited by the versions speaks against it. In any case, the Old Greek emphasizes the intrinsic connection between Daniel 7 and Daniel 8 even more strongly than the Hebrew. Such a point of view can be further supported in the light of variant b) and the rendering of v. 2, see the next two notes. The Old Greek has thus seen that such a connection is crucial for an understanding of the function of Daniel 8 in its context. While the visions in Daniel 2 and 4 had served a particular purpose within the narrative plot of the court tales, the visions in Daniel 7-12 are much more independent and "universal". Hence Daniel 8 has to be read in the light of Daniel 7 rather than Daniel 1-6. The translator's handling of Dan 8,1 strongly indicates that he has been aware of this. The whole question is thus much more complex than previous commentators had been willing to admit.

b) Contrary to the MT, the Old Greek has a nominal sentence and places the finite verb into a relative clause. It thus seems to understand v. 1 as a kind of title: ὅρασιν ἣν εἶδον ("the vision which I saw", so Pap.

---

[47] Other books of the Septuagint, too, tend to make connections between individual texts (which may already be present in the Hebrew) much more evident, cf. Gzella, *Lebenszeit*, 2002, 243 and esp. 350-359 (with respect to the Psalter).

967 with *attractio inversa* of the case of the subordinate noun to the case of the relative pronoun;[48] MS 88 and SyH have the nominative ὅρασις, which is certainly a *lectio facilior*). Theodotion and the Vulgate reflect the MT. The corrected version of 4QDan^a agrees with the MT, too, although originally it had read נגלה דבר, "a word was revealed", presumably under the influence of Dan 10,1. The reading of the Old Greek may insofar be significant as it appears to go together with the as-similation of the first half of v. 1 to Dan 7,1. There is it stated explicitly in the third person singular that Daniel wrote down his dream (τότε ἔγραψε τὸ ἐνύπνιον), introducing the subsequent text as the content of the book he wrote (καὶ διηγήθη τὸ κεφάλαιον τῶν λόγων). Conse-quently, the first person singular is employed throughout, including the whole of Daniel 8 and 9.[49] Now the translation of Dan 8,1 as a nominal sentence would give the impression that here *another chapter* of the *same* book as in Dan 7,1 begins ("The vision which [...]:"). Hence Dan 7,2-28 would be the first chapter (κεφάλαιον), Dan 8,1-26 the second. With Dan 8,27, there is a caesura, and Daniel returns to the king's busi-ness. This marks the end of the second "apocalyptic" chapter.

V. 2: a) These words are lacking in Theodotion, but the MT is supported by 4QDan^a and the Peshitta. The Old Greek has the rather free translation καὶ εἶδον ἐν τῷ ὁράματι τοῦ ἐνυπνίου μου, "and I saw in

---

[48] This phenomenon is quite frequent in classical as well as post-classical Greek (es-pecially in non-literary texts), see Kühner and Gerth, *Grammatik* II,2, 1898 (1992), §555,4. For Biblical Greek (that is, Septuagint and New Testament) cf. Gen 31,16; Num 19,22; Ps 118,22 (a fairly close parallel to what can be found in Daniel: λίθον ὃν ἀπεδοκίμασαν οἱ οἰκοδομοῦντες οὗτος ἐγενήθη εἰς κεφαλὴν γωνίας); 1 Cor 10,16 and Blass and Debrunner, *Grammatik*, 1990, §295.

[49] From this point of view it is perhaps not irrelevant that the remark in 7,28 MT that the message ends there (עַד־כָּה סוֹפָא דִי־מִלְּתָא) is not translated literally (that is, as a marker indicating the end of a reported text, just as in Theodotion), but "apocalypti-cally" as the end of time (ἕως καταστροφῆς τοῦ λόγου). The precise meaning, how-ever, is unclear. Certainly it cannot be part of 7,27 (as Ziegler suggests), because there it is said that the kingdom to come will be an eternal one, not one only lasting up to a καταστροφή. It may be the easiest solution to understand it – tentatively – as some-thing like "up to the point when the message spoke about the catastrophe I was..." (cf. Bauer, *Wörterbuch*, 1988, s.v. II,4).

the vision of my dream". This is either a conflation of two variant translations (so Collins, *Daniel*, 1993, 325; conflations in the Old Greek recur
in vv. 16 and 25), or τοῦ ἐνυπνίου μου is an idiomatic attempt to render
וַיְהִי בִּרְאֹתִי.[50] But since Hebrew infinitive constructions with a preposition
and a preceding form of היה are generally translated literally in the Old
Greek of Daniel (cf. 8,15), and in addition to that the Vulgate seems to
point to a *Vorlage* without the וַיְהִי בִּרְאֹתִי (*vidi in visione mea cum essem
in Susis*), it may be more plausible to postulate the existence of two
more Hebrew textual variants conflated in the Old Greek. These can be
reconstructed as follows: וָאֶרְאֶה בְחָזוֹן וַאֲנִי בְּשׁוּשַׁן (Vulgate) and perhaps
something like וָאֶרְאֶה בִּרְאֹתִי וַאֲנִי בְּשׁוּשַׁן. The two words וַיְהִי בִּרְאֹתִי could
have easily dropped out of a supposedly original text (still represented by
the MT) וָאֶרְאֶה בְחָזוֹן וַיְהִי בִּרְאֹתִי וַאֲנִי בְּשׁוּשַׁן in an attempt to simplify the
style. The possessive pronoun in the Vulgate may translate the definite
article in בְּחָזוֹן, if indeed the Masoretic pointing here is ancient. The consonantal text on its own does not indicate the presence of absence of the
article. Anyhow, it is certain that καὶ εἶδον ἐν τῷ ὁράματι, together with
the other support from the versions, clearly militates against the shorter
text in Theodotion. The external evidence is therefore strongly in favour
of one of the various longer readings, be it the MT, the Old Greek or the
Vulgate. On the basis of 4QDan[a], the MT is left intact here. As to the
bearing on the interpretation, the longer reading may imply that Daniel
was in Susa only in his vision and not physically (see below).

Apart from that, the Old Greek introduces its own interpretation
of the rest of the chapter, for by using the term ἐνύπνιον it classifies the
whole vision explicitly as a *dream*. The Peshitta corresponds to that interpretation. There is nothing of that kind in the Hebrew, which only
speaks of a *vision* (חָזוֹן). But the rendering in the Old Greek can be understood as yet another interpretative attempt to assimilate Daniel 8 to
Daniel 7, which is very clearly marked as a dream Daniel had while being
in bed (7,1). Such an explanation fits in neatly with the Old Greek's rendering of Dan 8,1 (see the textual note above), so the idea of an intrinsic
connection between the two visions is well and consistently represented
there. Again, an only seemingly minute difference between the Hebrew

---

[50] So Jeansonne, *Old Greek*, 1988, 49.

and the Greek points to a more comprehensive interpretation in the
background.

V. 3:   a) 4QDan[a] and 4QDan[b] add גדול ("great") here. They receive support from Pap. 967 against the MT and the other versions. This
excellent external evidence indicates that the Qumran texts reflect a textual type different from the MT and that this was also the type of Pap.
967's *Vorlage*. It is by no means clear whether this plus is in fact a secondary anticipation of the verbal form הִגְדִּיל ("it became great") at the
end of v. 4 (so Collins, *Daniel*, 1993, 325). Instead, the quality of the at-
testation suggests that the plus גדול may well have been original and has
dropped out only secondarily. In any case the depiction of the ram as
"great" right from the outset fits in well with the description of its dominating presence in vv. 3-4, even though such an indication is missing in
the other references to the ram and its horns (vv. 3.4.6.7.20). The ram is
thus not just a random animal, but the dominating power, and no other
being can stand up against it. In the light of such considerations, גדול
covers a nuance quite crucial to the meaning of the vision.

b) וְהַקְּרָנַיִם ("and the two horns") is omitted by the Old Greek,
Theodotion and the Vulgate, but the omission of this word is easier to
explain than its addition (which creates an additional clause), so it may
be preferable to leave it in the text as the *lectio difficilior*. Moreover, the
rather complex phrase וְלוֹ קְרָנַיִם וְהַקְּרָנַיִם גְּבֹהֹת ("and it had two horns,
and the two horns were high") highlights the keyword "horns" (see the
narrative analysis for the importance of this concept) more effectively
than the weaker וְלוֹ קְרָנַיִם גְּבֹהֹת ("and it had two high horns"). The two
Qumran texts from 4Q, however, repeat קרנים, that is, they lack the definite article. In this case, קְרָנַיִם גְּבֹהֹת would be an apposition ("and it had
two horns, two high horns") instead of an independent clause. The definite article could at first look like an attempt to harmonize this part with
the rest of the sentence which has two more instances of *waw* plus a sub-
stantive with the definite article.

Yet the omission of the article could well be the result of a dittography, so it does not necessarily reflect the original text, but an early
variant in the textual type represented by the two Qumran fragments.
Maybe this dittography was identified and consequently simplified by the

Vorlage of the Old Greek, Theodotion and the Vulgate. This would mean that the versions point to a text originally identical with the Qumran fragments. It can thus not be decided with certainty whether the slightly more striking expression in the MT, which also corresponds better to the rest of the sentence, outweights such excellent external evidence. Perhaps it can be said that, in the light of the importance of קרנים as a most important key-word in this text, both the MT and the Qumran fragments are in any case superior to the simple and weak expression "and it had two high horns" in the versions. So the option in favour of the MT's וְהַקְּרָנַיִם taken here is tentative, but maybe not totally unfounded.

  c) The Old Greek (μετὰ δὲ ταῦτα) takes this word with the next sentence, as the particle δέ clearly indicates, while Theodotion joins it to v. 3. This is a very interesting problem. Perhaps the translator of the Old Greek opted for this solution because he wanted to avoid an asyndetic beginning of v. 4. By doing so he made a narrative sequence out of v. 3 and v. 4 (with v. 4 following chronologically on v. 3), against the Hebrew, which has a so-called background depiction without progress in the mainline story. The Vulgate, however, is ambiguous, since *postea* can refer to the end of v. 3 or to the beginning of v. 4. The far-reaching implications of these renderings, apparently unnoticed so far by commentators, will be discussed below in the narrative analysis.

  V. 4: a) The MT, together with Theodotion, the Peshitta and the Vulgate, is lacking the "east" which is preserved in Pap. 967, MS 88 and the Syro-Hexaplaric version. The Qumran fragment 4QDan[a], which has ומזרחה after "west", now indicates that there was once also a Hebrew text giving a complete list of directions, *pace* Munnich,[51] who thinks that the different order of the points of the compass in the Qumran tradition indicates that the tripartite list in the MT is original; according to him, Pap. 967 has been secondarily corrupted. Presumably מזרחה originally followed מנגה immediately and was omitted by haplography,[52] at least in the textual tradition reflected by the MT and the other ancient versions mentioned. מזרחה as the first direction is in any case still docu-

---

[51] Munnich, *Daniel*, 1999, 61f.

[52] So Collins, *Daniel*, 1993, 325.

mented by MS 88 and the Syro-Hexaplaric text, which have the order "east – north – west – south" (a westward rotation beginning with the east), and Pap. 967, which has the order "east – west – north – south". Furthermore, such a mechanical error is a convenient explanation. This latter sequence may be the original one, and it is, without the "east", preserved in the MT.[53] The slightly different word order in 4QDan[a] can be plausibly explained by the hypothesis that מזרחה had already disappeared by the time this text or its archetype was written. It has only been reinserted, together with the conjunction ו, by a scribe, but after ימה and not after מנגח, where it used to stand initially. 4QDan[b], too, probably read מזרחה, because otherwise the line would be too short (48 letters) in comparison with the rest.[54] So both texts of Dan 8,4 from Qumran concord against the MT, which they otherwise largely support.

  Such a reading would in fact correspond well to the historical facts behind the application later made for this scene, since the Persian empire under Darius I did expand to the east by adding north-west India,[55] and this was known to biblical authors (cf. Est 1,1). The "north" would then mean Asia Minor, the "west" Greece and the "south" Egypt, if one accepts that the identification of the ram with Persia in 8,20 allows to understand the "charging" as the expansion of the empire – even if this is not beyond doubt, see below. If one does not, it is at least apparent that mentioning all four points of the compass gives a stronger impression of universal expansion. So it may be more appropriate in the given context.

  b) The Old Greek has the plural ἐκ τῶν χειρῶν αὐτοῦ.

V. 5: a) Some commentators propose to delete the word הָעִזִּים, see the apparatus of the BHS. But this is purely conjectural and receives no support from the textual tradition. Neither the Old Greek nor Theodotion have the definite article, so the editor of the BHS, too, wants to

---

[53] At least this solution appears more plausible than the one given by Montgomery, *Daniel*, 1927, 329, according to whom (obviously he did not know the Qumran fragment!) ימה (= יָמָּה) has been understood as יֹמָה, "the rising of the sun".

[54] Ulrich, "Orthography," *Of Scribes and Scrolls*, ed. Attridge, 1990: 39.

[55] Herodotus III,94 lists Indians among the Achaemenids' subjects, but the precise date of the conquest is not known. Cf. Kuhrt, *Ancient Near East II*, 1995, 667.

to delete it,[56] although not even the best textual witnesses must be blindly followed when they present only a *possible* reading.[57] However, both the double designation of the he-goat and the definite article have a crucial function in the narrative presentation (see below for an extensive discussion), and for this reason the MT's reading צְפִיר־הָעִזִּים is better left unchanged.

b) The reading אֶל for עַל attested by 4QDanᵃ can easily be attributed to an audial error and does not seem to carry any weight, especially since עַל in later Hebrew has taken over many functions formerly exclusive to אֶל.[58]

c) The Old Greek leaves out the specification כָּל, which is still present in the MT, Theodotion and the Vulgate, but the expression "*every* land" certainly emphasizes the universal dimensions of the he-goat's conquests and makes quite good sense in that context. Although the vision depicts an animal fight, it is clear from the outset that this animal fight is somehow "larger than life".

d) This phrase is missing in Pap. 967 and MS 88, presumably because of haplography, as the preceding clause, too, ends with τῆς γῆς. Thus the reading presented by Pap. 967 and MS 88 is not a major textual variant.

e) The Old Greek seems to have read (or corrected the text to) אֶחָד, as the translation κέρας ἓν indicates. Theodotion does not translate חָזוּת at all, the Vulgate is close to the MT (*cornu insigne*). But given the fact that horns play an important role in this vision and are thus frequently emphasized as crucial key-words (see the narrative analysis below: the horns of the protagonists are always singled out as something special), חָזוּת is exactly what one would expect, unlike a rather weak and straightforward אֶחָד.

V. 6: a) The Old Greek has dropped the personal suffix and translates the whole expression rather freely with ἐν θυμῷ ὀργῆς. This rendering expresses the idea of irrational aggression which is at the heart

---

[56] Cf. also Montgomery, *Daniel*, 1927, 331.

[57] Cf. West, *Textual Criticism*, 1973, 50.

[58] See Kropat, *Syntax*, 1909, 41-42.

of the animal fight quite well. One may also note that θυμός is the uncontrollable motivating element in one's soul in Greek philosophical anthropology, although this fact does of course not prove that certain parts of the Septuagint have been influenced by Greek philosophy, as some scholars in the past have thought.

V. 7:   a) This verb is left out by the Vulgate, which thus totally concentrates on the battle description without mentioning the visionary any more. The tendency of the visionary to disappear to the background is already present in the Hebrew text, although the Vulgate makes it more explicit.

b) The variant reading ב instead of כ, which some Hebrew manuscripts have (cf. the apparatus of the BHS), is of no great importance, since the temporal meaning is expressed by the one as well as by the other preposition. The preposition ב may be a harmonization with Dan 8,3.15-18, however.

b) The word חָזוּת makes little sense here. Either it is a misplaced gloss which should connect v. 8 with v. 5[59] and there was nothing between אַרְבַּע and וַתַּעֲלֶנָה in the original text (this concords with the testimony of Theodotion and the Vulgate; the word has therefore been deleted by Bentzen and Collins ad loc.), or the reading καὶ ἀνέβη ἕτερα τέσσαρα κέρατα in the Old Greek has, with Marti[60] and others, to be taken as reflecting an original אחרות, which has been corrupted (in this case presumably under the influence of v. 5) into חָזוּת. Although the Old Greek's ἕτερα may well be a stylistic improvement without any basis in the Hebrew text, such a corruption, from a palaeographic point of view, is not difficult to explain: the א could have dropped out, perhaps under the influence of the preceding ה, and the ר would then have been misread as a ז.

Hartman and Di Lella[61] correct the text to חֲזִיוֹת ("four conspicuous ones"). This explains a possible corruption into חָזוּת significantly bet-

---

[59] Bevan, *Daniel*, 1892, 131; Montgomery, *Daniel*, 1927, 338.

[60] Marti, *Daniel*, 1901, 57.

[61] Hartman and Di Lella, *Daniel*, 1978, 221 and 225.

ter, but their proposal is not supported by any external evidence. The similar phrase in the corresponding verse in the interpretation, v. 22, has nothing between the *wayyiqtol* verb and אַרְבַּע, but both clauses are *not* exactly parallel (v. 22 has a different verb), so this is no conclusive evidence in favour of a correction of v. 8 in the light of v. 22. Hence, the best solution seems to be a correction to אֲחֵרוֹת, but the passage remains difficult.

V. 9:   a) In order to establish full gender agreement, some commentators have proposed feminine forms instead of the masculine ones in the MT, but this is unnecessary, since the incomplete agreement may serve an important literary function here and highlight the keyword "horn". See below for a more detailed discussion within the narrative analysis.

b) The MT is likely to be corrupt; at least the vocalization, taking the מ as an assimilated form of a מִן (of comparison?), is awkward, although it has been accepted by an authority like König who thinks it means *minus quam parva*.[62] The difficulty has already been perceived by the ancient scribes. A Babylonian-Yemenite manuscript of the Book of Daniel with Babylonian vocalization, dating probably from the 14th century but reflecting at times features of an older Masoretic school,[63] reads מצעירה as a Hiphil participle of צער, "to be small, young", that is, "a small (or: young) horn". But the Hiphil stem of צער is unattested so far, so the reading looks like an artificial attempt to save the consonantal text. Interestingly, it corresponds exactly to Ewald's repointing of the text,[64] even though he could not know the 14th century manuscript.

Perhaps the easiest solution is to omit the מ in מִצְּעִירָה, which leads to the feminine singular of the adjective צָעִיר.[65] The traditional emendation, which goes back to Bevan[66] and is taken up by most of the

---

[62] König, *Syntax*, 1897, §352z.

[63] The manuscript has been edited by Morag, *Manuscript*, 1973.

[64] Ewald, *Lehrbuch*, 1870, 664, n. 1. Morag, *Manuscript*, 1973, xii, accepts this reading as an improvement of the MT.

[65] Cf. Hartman and Di Lella, *Daniel*, 1978, 221; Collins, *Daniel*, 1993, 325.

[66] Bevan, *Daniel*, 1892, 131; see Montgomery, *Daniel*, 1927, 338-339, for an elenchus of other proposals.

older commentaries, is quite similar. However, they take the מ as a corruption of an original ת belonging to a preceding אחרת and thus correct
the text to אחרת צעירה. This does not encounter problems from a paleographical point of view and would indeed resemble the formulation in
7,8 (קֶרֶן אָחֳרִי זְעֵירָה, "another little horn") closely. The apparatus of the
BHS suggests a solution along the same lines.

But several different observations strongly militate against this
proposal and may add some fresh impetus to the discussion. First of all,
קרן אחר צעירה, "a little horn", may again take up the play between defi-
niteness and indefiniteness which is characteristic for the opposition between the ram and the he-goat (see below). Furthermore, it is quite feasible that an original אחר צעירה has, on the basis of Dan 7,8, been corrupted into אחרת צעירה, which, in a second step, was presumably misread as אחר מצעירה. The reading אחר is in any case supported by the Old
Greek, Theodotion (both: ἕν) and the Vulgate (*unum*). In addition to
that, the translation ἰσχυρός, which is again common to the Old Greek
and Theodotion, also suggests that their *Vorlage* had nothing else but
מצעירה,[67] since צעיר on its own is *always* translated correctly with "little,
small" etc. in various books of the Septuagint.[68] If the *Vorlage* of either
had read צעירה, the respective translation would with all probability have
rendered this word with one of the Greek terms for "little, small". Instead, both Greek translators apparently considered מצעירה a substan-
tive, unattested elsewhere, and made a guess which translation would be
appropriate here. Since the final horn is the main aggressor in these
verses, they opted for ἰσχυρός, ironically choosing exactly the opposite
of the original meaning. Interestingly, they achieved a greater consistency
with the general character of the fight among unusually "big" or "strong"
opponents.

This indicates that the translators correctly understood the "cosmic" dimensions of the animal fight. So it is fairly certain that the *Vorlage* of both the Old Greek and Theodotion read אחר מצעירה, exactly as

---

[67] *Pace* Jeansonne, *Old Greek*, 1988, 55, and McLay, *Versions*, 1996, 171, who assume that the Greek versions "appear to be translating a form of עצום" (McLay, ibid.).

[68] Cf. Gen 25,23; 1 Kgs 16,34; Jer 49,20 (= 30,14 LXX); 50,45 (= 27,45 LXX); Job
30,1; 32,6; Ps 68,28; 119,141; Mi 5,1.

the MT, since ἰσχυρός can best be explained on grounds of contextual interpretation and does not point to an otherwise unattested *Vorlage* which had עצום. Perhaps the similarity in writing of מצעירה (the initial מ being analyzed as the widespread preformative creating abstract nouns)[69] and עצום made this rendering especially appealing.[70]

It is rather strange that both Greek translations agree here, since Theodotion often does *not* follow the Old Greek when the MT is hardly intelligible – either Theodotion knew the Old Greek (for which, according to McLay, no definite proof exists),[71] or he reached the same conclusion, because he thought ἰσχυρός would obviously be, especially in the given context, the word required, or the Theodotion text has been corrected toward the Old Greek. Any of these solutions seems theoretically possible. However, if the MT is indeed corrupt (and its reading is not acceptable as a possible Hebrew way to say *minus quam parva*), the corruption must have taken place quite early in the textual transmission.

c) Most modern commentators supply אֶרֶץ before הַצְּבִי and refer to Dan 11,16.41. Montgomery,[72] however, understands צְבִי as a gloss on צבא in the following verse which has at a later stage been assimilated to the geographical term צבי in Daniel 11. For this reason he deletes it completely. He is, in any case, right in stressing that the formulation "toward the south, toward the east and to the glorious land (sc. Palestine)" is strange. So it is understandable that the Old Greek, too, was puzzled and translated βορρᾶν, which would be צפונה in Hebrew – did the translator assume a scribal error in the MT? But such a form of harmonization with the rest of the verse is a clear instance of *lectio facilior* and therefore quite unlikely to be original.

V. 11: a) It is hard to determine whether the Qere (passive form: "it was taken away") or the Ketib (active form: "he took away") is to be

---

[69] See JM §88Ld.

[70] Derivations from roots etymologically not related occur frequently in later Hebrew scholarship and have even been systematically investigated, cf. Eldar, "Genizah Treatise," *Tarbiz* 57 (1988): 483-510.

[71] Cf. McLay, *Versions*, 1996.

[72] Montgomery, *Daniel*, 1927, 339.

preferred. Many manuscripts have the Qere in the text (see the apparatus of the BHS). The Hophal (passive) of this verb is rare in the Hebrew Bible (cf. Ex 29,27; Lev 4,10)[73] and in any case the more difficult reading in the given context, because it implies a change of subject. In the preceding and in the subsequent clause the subject is the horn, while the beginning of the subsequent verse, at least according to the reading and interpretation proposed here (see the narrative analysis below), has a passive expression: the host and the sanctuary were given over. Hence the Qere may theoretically be a harmonization with v. 12. The versions seem to be of little use here, as they apparently have problems with understanding and translating the entire verse, although the Old Greek as well as Theodotion still seem to reflect a passive reading (if one supposes that ἐρράχθη corresponds to הוּרַם), the Vulgate and the Peshitta an active one. The preference for the Qere in this study (following Montgomery),[74] is therefore only very tentative.

V. 12: This difficult verse and its interpretation are discussed at greater length in the course of the narrative analysis, for only the wider context of the passage supplies arguments why it might be sensible to leave the MT intact as much as possible.

V. 13: a) The Old Greek, contrary to Theodotion and the Vulgate (which both support the MT), reads both times אחר and translates ἕτερος, "another one". But this is certainly the result of a confusion between ד and ר (which was perhaps already in the *Vorlage*),[75] since the being in v. 13 is the first to be mentioned, so "another one" does not make much sense. Instead, the transcendent angelic figures seem to appear from nowhere only to add an objective notion to the vision by stressing that there were other beholders as well. So the vision is no allegory, but an insight into the world as it appears to transcendent beings. Therefore it is of no interest *who* they actually were, it is enough to know *that* they were there; consequently, the depiction as indeterminate (אחד) is very

---

[73] In both places the meaning is "to be raised", presumably in the sense of "to be separated".

[74] Montgomery, *Daniel*, 1927, 340.

[75] Both letters can at times hardly be distinguished at all in the manuscripts.

apt.

b) Pap. 967 leaves out the whole expression לַפַּלְמוֹנִי הַמְדַבֵּר, but this is presumably a scribal error (or maybe even a deliberate attempt to leave out an unintelligible text?),[76] since לַפַּלְמוֹנִי הַמְדַבֵּר, being the required indirect object (subject and indirect object change in vv. 13 and 14), performs an important syntactical function. Furthermore, this expression is taken up again by the resumptive personal pronoun in v. 14 (see the textual note on that verse).[77]

c) The Old Greek as well as Theodotion add στήσεται after "vision", without there being any support from other witnesses or indeed the Hebrew text. Perhaps the Greek translators only wanted to clarify the elliptic phrase.

d) Here the Old Greek and Theodotion agree in reading ἡ θυσία ἡ ἀρθεῖσα instead of simply ἡ θυσία, while the Old Greek has an additional καί before the expression. The plus ἡ ἀρθεῖσα receives no support from other witnesses and may be an explanatory gloss from v. 11. So there appears to be little justification for an attempt to correct the MT accordingly by inserting מוּרָם (see the proposal in the apparatus of the BHS, accepted by HAL, s.v.). The reading of the Greek versions reflects a correct understanding of the passage, however, since it points out that it is precisely the *abolition* of the sacrifice which bothers the speaker.

e) This is a *crux*. The text is most certainly corrupt, and the least difficult emendation, which does not alter the consonantal text at all, is to take the *waw* with the preceding word and to read קדש חתו, "his making sanctuary and host a trampling".[78] The 14th century Babylonian-Yemenite manuscript of Daniel[79] has the same consonantal text, but vocalizes instead קָדוֹשׁ of קְדֶשׁ. However, this does not improve the text at all. In addition to that, קָדוֹשׁ occurs at two other places in the same verse and may be an inference from there. The personal suffix would then indicate that the speaker presupposes that the agent is known already, although he has not been mentioned before. This *can* refer to Antiochus

---

[76] See below on the treatment of this expression in the ancient versions.

[77] Correctly seen by Munnich, *Daniel*, 1999, 67f.

[78] See Montgomery, *Daniel*, 1927, 341, accepted by Collins, *Daniel*, 1993, 336.

[79] Morag, *Manuscript*, 1973, xii.

Epiphanes, but does not have to. In fact, omitting a clear specification of the respective agent contributes to the mysterious atmosphere as well as to the dramatic vividness. For the interpretation of the vision is not yet given, so there may still be some ambiguity present, although the imagery allows for some first conclusions and inspired guesses on the reader's side. It will emerge from the subsequent discussion of the text that the tension between the vision itself and its application is crucial to the understanding of Daniel 8. The translation of the Old Greek and Theodotion (both have καὶ ἡ ἁμαρτία ἐρημώσεως ἡ δοθεῖσα) seems to be a tentative suggestion to make sense of an already corrupt text, presumably emending an infinitive תח in the *Vorlage* to a participial form. This idea was taken up by the Vulgate (*quae facta est*) and perhaps also by the Peshitta ("will be completed").

f) The MT's reading is confirmed by Theodotion (δύναμις) and the Vulgate (*fortitudo*), but the Old Greek has ἐρημωθήσεται, hence reading a form of the verb צדה in the Niphal, "to lay waste". This was not necessarily the text of the *Vorlage*, since the translator could have been inspired by the phrase ἡ ἁμαρτία ἐρημώσεως earlier on in the verse, where it corresponds to the rather straightforward וְהַפֶּשַׁע שֹׁמֵם. The latter expression is easier and could have served as a clue for interpreting the more obscure one, especially since both are closely situated to each other in the immediate context, so that is is feasible to assume a case of *qal wachomer* exegesis here.[80] As the "host" makes perfectly good sense in this context, emendations, such as the ones proposed in the apparatus of the BHS, are unnecessary.

V. 14: a) With the principal versions (Pap. 967 and other witnesses of the Old Greek, Theodotion, the Vulgate and the Peshitta) and most commentators, the MT's אלי ("to me") will surely have to be corrected to אֵלָיו ("to him"). There is also good internal evidence, since v. 14 is a direct reply to the question in v. 13; the visionary himself does not participate in this conversation, but follows it from a distance. He is therefore not the centre of attention in the vision. A corruption would

---

[80] Other books of the Septuagint, too, follow this interpretative technique in order to translate obscure Hebrew passages, cf. Gzella, *Lebenszeit*, 2002, 355, for examples.

have been particularly easy with the early orthography אלו, for the *waw* would only have to be confused with a *yod*, often very similar in manuscripts, so the MT has a simple scribal error. This is much easier than explaining אלי as a result of erroneously taking לְפַּלְמוֹנִי as a reference to Daniel himself.

b) The Old Greek and Theodotion add ἡμέραι, "days" before the actual number.

V. 15: a) Pap. 967 has τὸ ὅραμα after διανοηθῆναι, surely an explanatory gloss which receives no support from MS 88 and SyH, nonetheless inserted into the text by Ziegler and kept by Munnich. The insertion of τὸ ὅραμα could have been inspired by Dan 9,24.[81]

V. 16: a) The Old Greek textual tradition has a double translation of this stichos; it may be a conflation of two originally alternative variants (see below on v. 25). The situation in v. 2 is not entirely clear, see above.

V. 17: a) The Old Greek and Theodotion expand this expression to καὶ ἔστη ἐχόμενός μου τῆς στάσεως, the Vulgate has something similar (*et stetit iuxta ubi ego stabam*).

b) The Old Greek expands the text, perhaps for clarity's sake, to "*this* vision" (τοῦτο τὸ ὅραμα).

V. 19: a) The Old Greek, some witnesses of Theodotion's text and the Vulgate add "to me", perhaps a harmonization with v. 17b.

b) The Old Greek adds τοῖς υἱοῖς τοῦ λαοῦ σου, apparently an exegetical plus on the basis of Dan 12,1.

V. 20: a) Both Greek versions, the Peshitta and the Vulgate have the singular, perhaps because they think in terms of a precise identification and thus a state of history in which the Medes had already been absorbed by the Persians: Since there is only one ram in the vision, it can

---

[81] According to Montgomery, *Daniel*, 1927, 377.401, the phrase διανοηθῆναι τὸ ὅραμα in Dan 9,24 is a gloss, but this view has already been refuted by Ziegler (cf. Munnich, *Daniel*, 1999, 63).

only represent one king. The Hebrew text, however, makes it quite clear that there is no complete agreement between the vision and its interpretation (see below), and the plurality of kings to which the single ram is applied may be another (deliberate?) instance of this tension.

V. 21: a) The Greek versions as well as the Vulgate translate הַצָּפִיר הַשָּׂעִיר with ὁ τράγος τῶν αἰγῶν and *hircus caprarum* respectively, that is, just in the same way as they translated the slightly different term צְפִיר־הָעִזִּים in vv. 5 and 8. So they harmonize vision and interpretation by removing a terminological difference, although such a difference may be important to the meaning of the chapter (see below on the interpretation of the vision).

V. 22: a) The expected pronominal suffix (Alexander's successors divide his own empire among themselves) is supported by the Old Greek, Theodotion and the Vulgate. The *waw* could have easily been lost due to haplography, especially since it is followed by a *yod* and preceded by a *yod* and another *waw*. The whole sequence of very similar letters may just have looked like a series of four *waw*s (or *yod*s) in the manuscript, so that it is quite feasible that one of them has dropped out by error.

V. 23: a) The passive rendering (the Old Greek as well as Theodotion: πληρουμένων) or intransitive translation (Peshitta, Vulgate) of this verb does not necessitate repointing it into כְּתֹם, as indeed suggested by the apparatus of the BHS. This has been accepted by Collins.[82] תמם in the Hiphil, too, can be used with the same intransitive meaning as the Qal, cf. Isa 33,1 (כַּהֲתִמְךָ שׁוֹדֵד תּוּשַּׁד),[83] as correctly pointed out by Montgomery.[84] The similarity of wording and pattern in Isa 33,1 (כ with the infinitive construct of תמם Hiphil with a following Qal participle,[85] al-

---

[82] Collins, *Daniel*, 1993, 327.

[83] There is absolutely no need to postulate an implicit direct object, as suggested by HAL s.v., 2: "(ein Mass) vollmachen".

[84] Montgomery, *Daniel*, 1927, 353.

[85] Cf. the following textual note.

though it is the complement of the verb here, and then a *yiqtol* form) and the unusual character of this expression may in fact indicate an intertextual reference. Such a view is even more plausible since the passage in Isaiah, too, is a prophecy announcing the end of an apparently invincible destroyer. A less close parallel is the Qere in Dan 9,24, again a prophecy. This fits in well with the "emotional" use of intransitive Hiphil forms with the same basic meaning as in the Qal, the most noteworthy case in Daniel 8 being the use of גדל in the Hiphil for depicting a nuance of arrogance (see the narrative analysis below). Since תמם in the Hiphil with an intransitive meaning occurs in all three passages within a context which implies a strong pejorative value judgment, it may indicate something more than just an objective temporal constatation. Perhaps it expresses an end strongly desired, a form of longing.

b) Both Greek versions, the Peshitta and the Vulgate vocalize the text הַפְּשָׁעִים and translate correspondingly "sins", which has been accepted by Collins in his translation;[86] the Old Greek and Theodotion also add αὐτῶν, presumably an exegetical plus.[87] Yet in the light of Isa 33,1 (see note a) above) the Qal participle ("when the sinners have finished") may well be possible, even though in Isa 33,1 it goes together with the verb ("when you have ceased to destroy"). One may also note that words for "sin" / "transgression" are generally used in the singular in Daniel 8. This is further support for leaving the MT intact.

V. 24: a) The phrase וְלֹא בְכֹחוֹ in the MT is supported by MS 88 and SyH of the Old Greek, the Hexaplaric texts of Theodotion, the Peshitta and the Vulgate. Since the best textual witness for the Old Greek, Pap. 967, lacks these two words, the view that they have been copied from v. 22 gains plausibility.[88] Perhaps they were added by Origen himself.[89]

b) The MT's reading יַשְׁחִית (with the feminine plural נִפְלָאוֹת per-

---

[86] Collins, *Daniel*, 1993, 327.

[87] So Montgomery, *Daniel*, 1927, 353.

[88] Cf. Collins, *Daniel*, 1993, 327.

[89] At least according to Montgomery, *Daniel*, 1927, 354.

haps being an adverbial complement,[90] "he will cause an incredible destruction"; this interpretation is made explicit by the Old Greek's idiomatic θαυμαστῶς φθερεῖ) is supported by all the versions and does not pose grammatical problems. However, it has been suspected by several modern commentators and the editor of the BHS, while, among others, Montgomery and Plöger retain it. Bevan[91] suggests to emend the text into יָשִׂיחַ and to take נִפְלָאוֹת as the direct object, hence "and wondrous things he will utter". But while a corruption from יָשִׂיחַ into יַשְׁחִית is easy from a paleographical point of view and seems like an assimilation to וְהִשְׁחִית later in the same verse, Bevan's proposal encounters several difficulties, apart from the lack of any support from the ancient versions. This word is in fact not attested elsewhere in Daniel, and the verses to which Bevan refers for the general sense "to speak wondrous things" (Dan 11,36 in the Hebrew and 7,8.20 in the Aramaic) use markedly different expressions: the verb is דבר and מלל respectively, the object in the Aramaic is רַבְרְבָן. Moreover, the entire verse Dan 8,24 is *not* about *boasting*, as 7,8.20 and especially 11,36 (where this idea is repeated several times), but about *destructive action*. Hence, Bevan's emendation must be dismissed.

Another suggestion, which goes back to Charles,[92] consists in correcting the text to a third person singular *yiqtol* form of חשב, that is, "and wondrous things he will devise". Both a Qal and a Piel form are theoretically possible. However, this proposal, too, lacks the strong support a purely conjectural solution would require. It is true that יחשב is used with reference to Antiochus elsewhere, but there the direct object is not נִפְלָאוֹת or something similar, but a *figura etymologica*, a typically Semitic contruction (וְעַל מִבְצָרִים יְחַשֵּׁב מַחְשְׁבֹתָיו, "and he will devise plans against strongholds"), with the object following the verb (unlike 8,24). This is clearly no parallel at all, and it is in any case arguable whether חשב נִפְלָאוֹת would not be a rather positive expression, if it indeed existed, since only God can do wondrous things (Ps 72,18; 86,10; Job 5,9

---

[90] See GK §100d.

[91] Bevan, *Daniel*, 1892, 139, followed by Marti.

[92] Charles, *Daniel* 1929, 218; cf. Collins, *Daniel*, 1993, 340, who accepts Charles' proposal.

etc.). This may actually be the particular force of the peculiar expression נַשְׁחִית נִפְלָאוֹת: Antiochus, who has defiled the Temple, thereby destroying God's wondrous works, behaves himself like a kind of anti-God. The author of Daniel 8 describes Antiochus' destructive action by using נִפְלָאוֹת, a term which elsewhere always refers to God's creative design which man seeks to understand. So there is absolutely no good reason for emending the MT – on the contrary, the Hebrew text as it stands fits the argument of the passage very well indeed.

c) See the following textual note.

V. 25: a) The first two words of v. 25, together with the last two of v. 24, are a *crux*. The MT has been defended by Montgomery,[93] who takes v. 25 as the beginning of a new clause with fronting of the prepositional phrase: "And after his cunning..." Accordingly, he interprets the *waw* in the following וְהִצְלִיחַ as resumptive. This would render the content of the *casus pendens* even more emphatic,[94] which, in turn, aptly corresponds to the idea of "cunning" (not present in the vision itself) as *the* characteristic trait *par excellence* of Antiochus in this passage (see below on the commentary section). Since the *waw* is supported by the versions, the tempting solution to delete it as a dittography due to שִׂכְלוֹ appears not very plausible. Theodotion may at a first glance point into this direction, but he has apparently misunderstood the whole clause, since his translation reflects the misreading of על as ζυγός, "yoke", and an erroneous derivation of שכלו from the verb שכל, "to lay crosswise".[95] His attempt to take these two words as a noun in the construct state necessitates his understanding of הִצְלִיחַ as the verb whose subject this construct state is. Consequently, Theodotion deletes the *waw* and interprets מִרְמָה בְּיָדוֹ as the asyndetical beginning of a new clause. Thus, his translation cannot be taken as first-hand evidence for an original reading הִצְלִיחַ.

On the basis of the Old Greek (καὶ ἐπὶ τοὺς ἁγίους τὸ διανόημα αὐτοῦ), Charles[96] and after him Collins[97] have opted for emending the

[93] Montgomery, *Daniel*, 1927, 350-354.

[94] Cf. GK §143d (with examples).

[95] See Montgomery, Daniel, 1927, 354.

[96] Charles, *Daniel*, 1929, 219.

text. This external evidence can in fact be taken as pointing to a *Vorlage* which once had וְעַל קָדָשִׁים שְׂכְלוֹ. Afterwards, וְעַל קָדָשִׁים has, according to this theory, been corrupted into וְעַם־קָדָשִׁים and placed at the end of v. 24 as another direct object of וְהִשְׁחִית and in parallelism with עֲצוּמִים.[98] The Old Greek may thus either witness to a text which had once read וְעַל קָדָשִׁים at the end of v. 24 and at the beginning of v. 25 once again וְעַל קָדָשִׁים שְׂכְלוֹ, or it may indeed be a conflation of the MT and the – supposedly – original וְעַל קָדָשִׁים שְׂכְלוֹ.

This is, on the whole, fair reasoning, but since the MT is intelligible, presents the *lectio difficilior* and, in addition to that, is supported by the Vulgate (which has the rather free rendering *secundum voluntatem suam*, but it is obvious that this reading reflects the MT), there is no need to insist on an emendation. The Old Greek may therefore just have added an old, but still secondary variant reading וְעַל קָדָשִׁים שְׂכְלוֹ, which had itself originated from an attempt to render the more difficult wording in the MT easier. Such a simplification of unusual constructions in the course of textual transmission is fairly normal.[99] The merging of two originally different textual variants, however, does happen at times in the Old Greek, see above on v. 2 (if this is indeed a conflation) and v. 16 for two more presumable instances. So the MT shall be left intact for the time being, because the reading of the Old Greek does not carry enough weight to be considered genuine, but is likely to be another conflation.

V. 26: a) Theodotion refers this expression to the specification of the date, translating "the vision of the said (τῆς ῥηθείσης) evening and morning"; the Old Greek and the Vulgate take it with "the vision".

b) The Old Greek has καὶ νῦν ("and now"), thus reading the well-known transition marker וְעַתָּה instead of the personal pronoun. This may have something to do with the fact that it also has an indicative

---

[97] Collins, *Daniel*, 1993, 340-341.

[98] Hartman and Di Lella, *Daniel*, 1978, p. 223, think that וְעַל עַם־קָדָשִׁים שְׂכְלוֹ was the original reading, but such a reading is purely hypothetical and has left absolutely no traces in the history of the text.

[99] West, *Textual Criticism*, 1973, 51.

statement (πεφραγμένον τὸ ὅραμα) for the imperative סתם, which the
translator had perhaps mistaken for a passive participle, maybe because
his *Vorlage* had a *plene* spelling סתום. Hence it is feasible that he corrected the א into an ע, as the personal pronoun would not have made
much sense in such a context. Thus, v. 26 in the Old Greek is a stronger
caesura and marks the end of the vision more clearly, above all due to
reading וְעַתָּה.

V. 27: a) Ehrlich[100] and several other older commentators, including Marti[101] and Charles,[102] take נִהְיֵיתִי as a dittography. But this is
too simple, since the presence of the word in their *Vorlage* is unambiguously confirmed by the tentative translations of Theodotion ("I fell
asleep", ἐκοιμήθην) and the Peshitta ("I trembled and was afraid"),
whereas the rendering of the Old Greek (ἀσθενήσας) could be an attempt
to merge both Hebrew terms and does not necessarily betray a Hebrew
variant (see also the note on v. 1 above).

b) The Old Greek has ἡμέρας πολλάς, which could in theory point
to an original Hebrew ימים רבים. In this case the last word could have
dropped out because of haplography. But the fact that יָמִים on its own
meaning "a number of days" is well attested (Gen 40,4; also in later Hebrew: Neh 1,4) and the testimony of the Vulgate as well as the Peshitta,
which both agree with the MT, cumulatively suggest that an emendation
of the text is not necessary.

Instead, the translator of the Old Greek has apparently understood the nuance of יָמִים meaning "several days" in idiomatic Hebrew
and has expressed it in perfectly good Greek, while a slavishly literal
rendering ἡμέρας would have been rather clumsy. He may have chosen
the particular expression ἡμέρας πολλάς because of 8,26 (לְיָמִים רַבִּים,
again ἡμέρας πολλάς in the Old Greek translation).

---

[100] Ehrlich, *Randglossen*, 1908-1914, ad loc.

[101] Marti, *Daniel*, 1901, 63.

[102] Charles, *Daniel*, 1929, 221.

3. The Textual History

The antiquity and reliability of the textual tradition represented by the MT is strongly supported, at times against the Greek versions (cf. vv. 1.2, see above), by two Qumran fragments which contain more than tiny parts of the text, namely 8,1-5 (4QDan^a)[103] and 8,1-8.13-16 (4QDan^b), dating at the earliest from ca. 125 BC (4QDan^a).[104] These fragments deserve particular consideration, since they are fairly close to the time of the final redaction of the Book of Daniel itself. In some cases the Qumran texts may be superior to the MT. The plus גדול in v. 3, for example, fits the sense very well and is also supported by Pap. 967. Therefore it could be the original reading, just like the plus "west" in v. 4, which has very strong versional support and may indeed witness to an original Hebrew text mentioning all four points of the compass, one of which was later omitted (one should note, however, that the latter view has not found universal acceptance, see the textual note on v. 4 above). The double קרנים in v. 3, by contrast, may be a dittography and is in any case less striking than the MT's reading. The reading אל for על is likely to result from another scribal error.

There is also a 14th century Babylonian-Yemenite manuscript which preserves large parts of the Book of Daniel.[105] The consonantal text corresponds to the MT. Its Babylonian vowel signs may reflect at times the work of an earlier Masoretic school which is in some cases at variance with the MT (although in the Hebrew part these variations are very few), but it does not really provide better readings (cf. the textual notes on 8,9 and 8,13 above).

In the Greek textual tradition, church usage has replaced the Old Greek (that is, the original Septuagint version) of Daniel, presumably written during the late second or early first century BC, by Theodotion's

---

[103] Preliminary publication: Ulrich, "Daniel Manuscripts 1," *BASOR* 268 (1987): 17-37, official publication now in: DJD XVI (2000).

[104] Ulrich, "Daniel Manuscripts 2," *BASOR* 274 (1989): 3-26, now in: DJD XVI (2000).

[105] A facsimile edition with a brief introduction has been published by Morag, *Manuscript*, 1973.

version. The Septuagint textual tradition in its Hexaplaric recension is represented by MS 88 (*Codex Chisianus*, 9th-11th c.) and the Syro-Hexapla (616-617 AD), which corresponds closely to MS 88, while the original, pre-Hexaplaric Old Greek is represented by Pap. 967.[106] Joseph Ziegler's edition[107] is based on this textual evidence;[108] the new edition prepared by Olivier Munnich presents a text which has been freshly constituted in the light of all the available evidence, especially recent editorial work on Pap. 967, while Ziegler's Theodotion text has been reprinted which a few slight corrections.[109]

The Old Greek of Daniel 8-12, contrary to Daniel 4-6, adheres very closely to the Hebrew text, and its *Vorlage* is presumably the textual type represented by the MT, although in 8,3 it confirms the Qumran text against the MT, see above.[110] Several striking differences go back to the translator himself and his own interpretation of the text, for example the rendering of the introductory verse. Thus, they cannot be attributed to a different *Vorlage*. There are some minor explanatory additions, such as the addition of πολλάς in v. 27, the plus in v. 19, derived from 12,1, or the addition of a stichos at the beginning of v. 16. Omissions are rare, cf. the title of the king in v. 1 and כל in v. 5; for v. 27 see below. Sometimes, the Old Greek presents a better text. This is the case in 8,14, where the Old Greek has the correct third person pronominal suffix, corrupted into a first person in the MT due to a scribal error. Sometimes, however, it conflates variant readings (cf. vv. 16.25).

The version of Theodotion, also part of Ziegler's edition and reprinted with Munnich's new edition of the Old Greek in 1999, is the one presented by the mainstream of the manuscript tradition and citations. Apart from Daniel 4-6, it appears to follow the Old Greek – and so also the MT – closely and sometimes even confirms it against the MT (as in

---

[106] Some verses from Daniel 7-8 and a part of Daniel 11 are also contained in the Barcelona fragment: Roca-Puig, "Daniele," *Aegyptus* 56 (1976): 3-18. Pap. 967 places cc. 7 and 8 before cc. 5 and 6 in order to establish a better chronological order, but this is most certainly a secondary alteration of the original sequence.

[107] Ziegler, *Daniel*, 1954.

[108] Except for the Barcelona and the Cologne fragments.

[109] Munnich, *Daniel*, 1999.

[110] Cf. Jeansonne, *Old Greek*, 1988, *passim*.

Dan 8,11.13), which has given rise to the opinion that is it really a revision of an older translation.[111] One of its distinctive features is its tendency to simplifiy repetitions, which is in part also true for the Old Greek (see the textual notes on vv. 1 and 27). It is much less idiomatic than the Old Greek and tries to reproduce the Hebrew word by word if this is indeed possible.

The other ancient Greek versions, namely Aquila and Symmachus, together with citations in the Fathers (especially Jerome's commentary), generally reflect the MT, as does the Vulgate, though the latter also betrays some noteworthy influence of Theodotion. Most daughter versions of the Greek have only very limited value for a reconstruction of the original text, so the Armenian,[112] Coptic[113] and Ethiopic[114] versions, while the Arabic translations[115] represent various textual traditions. Some of them mirror the MT. Among the several different Arabic traditions those based on the Greek text, namely the Arabic text printed 1645 in the Paris Polyglot and 1657 in the London Polyglot, are the most important witnesses to the original.[116] The Peshitta[117] follows the MT closely in the translation of the text and thus seems to have used it as its *Vorlage*. Although it has certain additions, these are merely explanatory glosses and have no independent textual value whatsoever.

In the light of this evidence, there can be no doubt that the Masoretic Text, improved by the Qumran fragments and Pap. 967, is the best possible base for an investigation into Daniel 8. Whether this text represents the original or is in itself a translation from an Aramaic original – a thesis nowadays generally associated with the work of H.L. Ginsberg, although it is significantly older than him –, does not affect this

---

[111] For a recent challenge of this opinion cf. McLay, *Versions*, 1996.

[112] Crowe, *Armenian Version*, Atlanta 1992.

[113] Gehman, "Sahidic and Bohairic Versions," *JBL* 46 (1927): 279-330. The additional chapter of the Coptic versions is late (composed ca. 1000 AD).

[114] Critical edition by Löfgren, *Äthiopische Übersetzung*, 1927.

[115] Löfgren, *Studien*, 1936.

[116] Gehman, "Arabic Text," *JBL* 44 (1925): 333.

[117] Critical edition by the Peshitta-Institute: *The Old Testament in Syriac According to the Peshitta Version* III/4, 1980. A detailed comparison of the Peshitta of Daniel with the other witnesses has been undertaken by Taylor, *Peshitta*, 1994.

point very much. The various reconstructions of an allegedly original Aramaic text proposed by scholars of past generations are based on a number of only hypothetical Aramaisms in Hebrew text which are far too arbitrary to be seriously taken into consideration.

4. The Principal Ancient Versions of Daniel 8

The following observations try to assess the individual "profile" of the major ancient versions of the text, i.e. the Septuagint (or Old Greek), Theodotion, the Vulgate and the Peshitta. Therefore a major question will always consist in trying to understand the *interpretation* of the text by the translators and the translation technique, including stylistic unification, they applied as well as the exegetical methods to which they had access. The translation into well-known non-Semitic languages with a highly developed morphological system, such as Greek and Latin, can be, above all, a very valuable source of information concerning the interpretation of the Hebrew verbal system in antiquity – especially when more than one version in the target language exists!

For this reason, Daniel 8 will be treated as a whole in the individual versions rather than verse by verse, which is the customary practice in scholarly literature on the textual criticism of the ancient versions up to now. The aim of this analysis is not to isolate differences relevant for an approximation to the respective hypothetical Hebrew original of the translators (their so-called *Vorlage*) and its change in textual history, but to consider the respective textual units in the versions compared to precisely *one* final form of the text[118] (that is, the MT) as an end in itself. Certainly the textual history of the versions will have to be taken into account as well.

Such a comparative study does not only seem useful for uncovering a minute piece of the history of exegesis and philology, but it can also yield important results for the principal goal of textual criticism, that is, a reconstruction of the original text. It can obviously sharpen the critic's eye for a clearer distinction between faithful translation of the Hebrew

---

[118] For a justification of this approach cf. Lust, "Exegesis," in *VI Congress*, ed. Cox, 1987: 201-202.

text and consciously applied interpretation. This is especially the case since various ancient versions show convergence in method of rendering, even if their actual interpretation often differs widely. Once these techniques as well as stylistic preferences of individual translators are known by means of abstraction, a presumable *Vorlage* may thus be individuated with a much greater objectivity.

a. The Greek Versions: The Old Greek and Theodotion

A direct comparison between the Old Greek and the rendering of Theodotion is revealing not only for the textual history of the Hebrew, but also for the hermeneutics of translation among different Greek translators. This is especially the case since both Greek texts exhibit different interpretations, translation techniques and stylistic ambitions.[119] The Old Greek sees many subtleties of the Hebrew and apparently aims at reproducing them in an idiomatic Greek prose style.[120] Furthermore, the Old Greek tends to simplify redundant expressions (see the textual notes on vv. 1 and 27).

This attempt at an idiomatic Greek style seems to be the translator's usual way of dealing with Hebrew prose narrative; similar techniques are applied in Daniel 1. Other parts of the text, such as the prayer in Daniel 9, which consists of many well-known phrases and formulae from other parts of the Old Testament, give considerably less opportunity for well-constructed Greek clauses. The Greek of Daniel 9, for example, seems to be a verbatim translation of the traditional language of personal prayer by which the translator himself must have been deeply influenced.

It is therefore precisely the linguistically more original prose part of Daniel in which the Old Greek makes a fuller use of linguistic features inherent to the target language, such as the genitive absolute (see below) or the aspectual distinction between aorist, reflecting the "punctual"

---

[119] For a survey of different hermeneutical approaches to the Old Testament in Greek and the ambiguity of the concept of a "literal" translation cf. Gzella, *Lebenszeit*, 2002, 23-79.

[120] Cf. Jeansonne, *Old Greek*, 1988, 131, who asserts that the Old Greek "tries to render faithfully the Vorlage into well-constructed Greek prose".

wayyiqtol forms in the Hebrew, and imperfect which is used, e.g., for the durative participle וְאֵין נוֹגֵעַ בָּאָרֶץ, "without touching the ground", in v. 5.

Contrary to that, the stylistic ambition of the Theodotion version seems to have consisted in a verbatim representation of the Hebrew, if this is morphologically possible. The sentence patterns and idioms, however, still witness to a Semitic source text and are not adapted to the linguistic possibilities of Greek, even though Semitic and non-literary or vernacular Greek syntax show certain similarities which makes it often problematic to trace down "Semitisms" with certainty.[121]

Thus, the participle וְאֵין נוֹגֵעַ in v. 5 is rendered by means of the literal periphrastic construction καὶ οὐκ ἦν ἁπτόμενος, which is as close to the Hebrew original as it is to non-literary and vernacular Greek,[122] although this rendering, too, makes use of the aspectual division of the verbal stems in Greek (which has no real parallel in the Semitic verbal system) and captures the durative *Aktionsart* by using the present-tense stem. The date in v. 1, too, is translated literally with a prepositional phrase (cf. v. 8), while a main clause specifies the geographical circumstances at the end of v. 2.

These observations cannot prove that Theodotion did not see certain subtleties in the Hebrew text. The rare use of the article as a relative particle in הַנִּרְאָה, "the one which had appeared", in v. 1, for example, has been understood correctly by him, as is the case in the Vulgate.[123] Evidence of this kind just indicates that idiomatic Hebrew expressions have not been reproduced by means of adequate Greek renderings. Instead, Theodotion prefers to reproduce the Hebrew word by word, which is often apparent in the case of prepositions, especially in his treatment of עַד.

---

[121] For a sophisticated criteriology with which one can determine whether a Greek text has been translated from a Hebrew or Aramaic original cf. Beyer, "Griechischer Text," in *Studia Semitica*, eds. Macuch, Müller-Kessler and Fragner, 1989: 21-31.

[122] It is clear that participles with εἶναι are well-attested already in Classical Greek (see Kühner and Gerth, *Grammatik* II,1, 1898 [1992], 38ff; here they seem to be emphatic, cf. Thucydides IV,54: ἦσαν δέ τινες καὶ γενόμενοι τῷ Νικίᾳ λόγοι, "even to Nicias himself suggestions have been made"), but they are exceedingly popular in documentary texts (such as papyri) and later vernacular literature, cf. Moulton, *Einleitung*, 1911, 357-360.

[123] See the textual note above for the Old Greek.

While the aspect and *Aktionsart*[124] of verbal forms are generally reproduced well both by the Old Greek and by Theodotion, there are some variations in the treatment of tense and modality.[125] A striking example consists in the rendering of the modal *yiqtol* form לֹא־יַעֲמֹדוּ ("they could not stand") in 8,4 (see the narrative analysis below for the interpretative implications of this verbal form). The modal meaning is reproduced most clearly by the Vulgate (*non poterant resistere*).

Theodotion is straightforward and has a future tense ("they will not stand"); this does not only correspond to the usual way of rendering Hebrew *yiqtol* forms in the Greek Old Testament throughout, but it also harmonizes 8,4 (*yiqtol* with modal meaning in a narrative context) with the verbal syntax in 8,22ff (*yiqtol* with future tense meaning in a prophetic context). Thus, Theodotion is fairly consistent in translating Hebrew verbal forms, even if this is not always totally adequate.

Contrary to all expectations, the Old Greek has an aorist (οὐκ ἔστησαν, "they did not stand") for the modal *yiqtol* in 8,4, although it correctly translates the prophetic *yiqtol* forms in 8,19.22ff with a Greek future and has therefore done justice to the change of literary genre and linguistic coding there. This is extraordinary, since an aorist for a *yiqtol* form is extremely rare in narrative prose texts, although in can occur in archaic passages, where *yiqtol* often functions as a narrative past, just like the Canaanite *yaqtul*, but this is a different linguistic register.[126] However, such a rendering corresponds well to the tendency of the Old Greek to simplify the narrative by translating almost all Hebrew verbal forms as if they indicated successive events. This is especially evident in v. 4, where the Old Greek clearly introduces a subsequent action (μετὰ

---

[124] Not all linguists distinguish between aspect and *Aktionsart* (or, as some would prefer nowadays, "situation type"). Those who do normally limit aspect to the functional opposition between perfective and imperfective use *Aktionsart* for semantic categories, such as durativity or punctuality. However, these terminological issues do not bear on the present discussion and can be easily followed up by consulting the standard handbooks, such as Comrie, *Aspect*, 1976.

[125] The rendering of Hebrew verbs with modal meaning in the ancient versions is still a new topic, for a first systematic treatment cf. Gzella, "Verbformen," in *Beiträge*, ed. Lehmann, 2003 (forthcoming).

[126] Cf. μετεπέμψατό με in the Septuagint for יַנְחֵנִי in Num 23,7.

δὲ ταῦτα, "but after that") at the expense of the distinction between background and foreground (see the narrative analysis below for a more extensive discussion of this phenomenon). As a result, the Old Greek consistently eliminates elements which seem to interrupt the straightforward sequence of these successive events.

On the syntactical level, the Old Greek succeeds more than once in establishing unambiguous logical or temporal subordination through grammatical hypotaxis,[127] mostly by means of participle constructions, while Theodotion's style is generally paratactic: he lines up main clauses with καί. This is especially apparent at the beginning of v. 3, where the Old Greek subordinates the lifting of the eyes (aorist participle ἀναβλέψας) to the main verb εἶδον and introduces the object of the perception as a direct object in the accusative (κριὸν ἕνα μέγαν ἑστῶτα).

In addition to that, the Old Greek may be aware of the polysemy of וְהִנֵּה, which it leaves out in v. 3, because this particle introduces the content of the sensual perception there, but which it translates literally in v. 5 and elsewhere (see the narrative analysis below for a further discussion). Theodotion, however, has two paratactic main clauses (καὶ ἦρα ... καὶ εἶδον); also the content of the vision is an independent clause in his text (καὶ ἰδοὺ κριός εἷς ...). One may compare various rather similar phenomena in v. 16 (OG: ἀναβοήσας εἶπεν, Thd: ἐκάλεσεν καὶ εἶπεν), v. 18 (OG: ἁψάμενός μου ἤγειρέ με, Thd: καὶ ἥψατό μου καὶ ἔστησέν με), or v. 27 (OG: ἀσθενήσας [...] ἀναστὰς ἐπραγματευόμην, Thd: ἐκοιμήθην καὶ ἐμαλακίσθην [...] ἀνέστην καὶ ἐποίουν).

Moreover, the Old Greek adds particles in order to make the logical connection between clauses more evident, such as ἔτι in vv. 2.7[128] or πάλιν in v. 27, even if its use of particles is rather limited and does by

---

[127] This distinction is important, since grammatically paratactic clauses can nonetheless express logical hypotaxis in Hebrew and Aramaic (such as in Deut 22,1), see Beyer, "Griechischer Text," in *Studia Semitica*, eds. Macuch, Müller-Kessler and Fragner, 1989: 28 (cf. also 29, no. 11).

[128] The expression ἔτι γάρ in vv. 17.19.26, however, is a fairly normal translation of the Hebrew כִּי in many books of the Septuagint (cf. Gen 7,4; Isa 10,25), although it is especially prominent in the Old Greek of Daniel (see 10,14; 11,27.35; 12,13). In vv. 17.19 and 12,13 it is also used by Theodotion.

no means exploit the possibilities of the Greek language.[129] The Old Greek also supplies the copula in the nominal clauses in vv. 20-21 in order to make them slightly more elegant ("the ram [...] *is*"), while it translates the one at the end of v. 21 literally – this is the only clause which has a הוּא.

Lastly, the Old Greek resolves at times Hebrew temporal clauses with prepositions into genitive absolute constructions (vv. 1.18) or avoids them althogether, as in v. 2, where it just has the plain genitive τοῦ ἐνυπνίου μου without a verbal constituent. Elsewhere it translates them literally (vv. 15.17), as Theodotion generally does (contrast his ἐν τῷ λαλεῖν αὐτόν in v. 18 with the Old Greek's λαλοῦντος αὐτοῦ),[130] although both have a genitive absolute (πληρουμένων τῶν ἁμαρτιῶν αὐτῶν) for the infinitive plus preposition (כְּהָתֵם הַפֹּשְׁעִים)[131] in v. 23. So neither the Old Greek nor Theodotion is absolutely consistent, but the Old Greek has a slightly stronger tendency to use idiomatic Greek constructions, although Theodotion can evidently handle them as well if he wants to.

From a lexical point of view, Theodotion is again very literal, especially in his treatment of prepositions. However, he can be idiomatic in translating prepositions as well – at times even more so than the Old Greek. This becomes clear from v. 13, where he has ἕως πότε, while the Old Greek has ἕως τίνος. One may also note his verbatim translation of the Hebrew יָצָא in v. 9 with ἐξῆλθεν (cf. the Vulgate: *egressum est*), nicely rendered with the "biologically correct" ἀνεφύη by the Old Greek. Theodotion is also more prone to a word-by-word rendering of Hebrew metaphors, such as מִיָּדוֹ ("from its power") in v. 7, for which the Old Greek has the weaker paraphrase ἀπὸ τοῦ τράγου, even though it translates the same expression in v. 4 almost literally (ἐκ τῶν χειρῶν αὐτοῦ).

---

[129] The use of particles is very untypical for texts which have been translated from Hebrew or Aramaic, cf. Beyer, "Griechischer Text," in *Studia Semitica*, eds. Macuch, Müller-Kessler and Fragner, 1989: 26.

[130] An idiomatic translation of a Hebrew inf. cstr. plus preposition with a conjunction, a genitive absolute etc. is the normal rendering, while a literal translation, as in Theodotion, is less widespread, but occurs in all books of the Septuagint. Cf. Soisalon-Soininen, *Infinitive*, 1965, 80-93.188ff.

[131] See the corresponding textual note for the vocalization.

The use of the plural instead of the Hebrew singular may be an attempt at good Greek, however).

It is also a characteristic feature of the Old Greek that it introduces various, although generally short expansions or brief explanatory glosses into the text. Interestingly, some of them shared by Theodotion as well, even if this observation on its own cannot prove a straightforward dependence. Moreover, the Septuagint also has a number of presumably conflated readings (cf. the textual notes above).

These substantial differences in translation technique and the ambiguity of renderings common to both Greek versions[132] make it very hard to determine whether Theodotion's text of Daniel is actually a revision (or recension) of the Old Greek in the light of a proto-Masoretic Hebrew *Vorlage*, as Jeansonne and most modern scholars suppose, or whether it is indeed a translation of its own (McLay).[133]

For the purpose of this study, the preceding brief analysis of the respective individual character of both Greek texts shall suffice, without there being further investigations into a possible genetic relationship between them. However, it should have become clear by now that the Old Greek as well as Theodotion provide valuable evidence of comparable importance for the textual history and the interpretation of the underlying proto-Masoretic Hebrew *Vorlage*.

b. The Vulgate

The Vulgate is, on the whole, a fairly faithful translation of the Hebrew text. It reproduces many stylistic subtleties, especially in the verbal syntax, without sacrificing too much in favour of an idiomatic Latin prose style. More than once it takes the middle way between an idiomatic rendering and a word-by-word translation of the Hebrew. In addition to that, the Vulgate correctly translates some difficult words or phrases which have been misunderstood by both Greek versions, such as the syncope פלמוני (otherwise unattested in the Hebrew Bible and left

---

[132] Common renderings between two translations do not prove dependence, unless they are highly idiosyncratic (cf. McLay, *Versions*, 1996, 13).

[133] Interestingly, Jeansonne as well as McLay arrive at their respective conclusions also by way of a study of Dan 8,1-10.

out by Pap. 967, see the textual note above) for which it has *alteri ne-scio cui*. In such cases Jerome may well have profitted from his knowl-edge of contemporary Jewish exegesis which could have preserved the right interpretation of several difficult expressions, even if they are *hapax legomena*.[134]

The translation reproduces the distinction between durative and punctual *Aktionsart* in the appropriate use of the Latin imperfect and the perfect. In doing so it also mirrors the careful distinction between back-ground and mainline story in the Hebrew text. In this case, the Vulgate is much closer to the Hebrew than even the Old Greek, for the latter tries to simplify the narrative flow at the expense of such a distinction (see above). The reproduction of the Hebrew grounding in the Vulgate clearly emerges from the use of imperfect forms for the background description in v. 5 (*intellegebam, veniebat, non tangebat, habebat*) and the perfect forms for the description of the sudden attack in vv. 6-7 (*venit, cucurrit, efferatus est, percussit, conculcavit*). This is almost an exact mirror-image of the distinction between *qatal* (or participle) forms and *wayy-iqtol* forms in the Hebrew. The Vulgate also applies the Latin *plusquam-perfectum* appropriately (*id quod videram*, v. 1; *quem videram*, v. 6; see also *cum adpropinquasset* and *cumque eum misisset* in v. 7 as well as *cumque crevisset* in v. 8, an "anterior construction" in the Hebrew, see below).

Even more interesting is the treatment of verbs with modal mean-ing in the Vulgate. The modal nuance of the *yiqtol* form in v. 4 is made clear by adding a modal verb[135] (*non <u>poterant</u> resistere*; cf. *non <u>poterat</u> aries resistere* for the clause וְלֹא־הָיָה כֹחַ בָּאַיִל in v. 7), while the *yiqtol* forms in the "prophetic" section around vv. 20ff are correctly translated with Latin future tenses. But the Vulgate even resolves Hebrew *partici-ple* forms, and not just modal *yiqtols*, into constructions with a subjunc-tive, such as *non erat qui interpretaretur* in v. 27, or indeed a clause with

---

[134] See Kamesar, *Jerome*, 1993, and Rahmer, *Traditionen*, 1861 (a still useful collec-tion of individual examples, although without any systematic treatment), for Jerome's familiarity with interpretative traditions also known from Rabbinic sources.

[135] Adding a modal verb in order to emphasize a modal nuance is common practice in ancient translation technique and also occurs in the Septuagint and the Targum, cf. Gzella, "Verbformen," in *Beiträge*, ed. Lehmann, 2003 (forthcoming).

an additional modal verb (*nemo quibat liberare arietem de manu eius*, v. 7, with the correct durative *Aktionsart*).

Apart from that, the Vulgate also employs various conjunctions and particles in order to connect individual clauses and to establish a logical relationship between them, even more than the Old Greek (see above), although the respective linguistic possibilities in Latin are much more restricted than in Greek. *Et* and *–que* are the most frequent ones, but *autem* and, to a lesser extent, *porro* occur as well, all of them generally corresponding to a Hebrew *waw*. While *et* and *–que* are used in order to provide "conjunctive" connections, *autem* often introduces a new literary unit or sub-unit (vv. 5; 15) or a change of subject (vv. 8; 9; 12; 22), therefore performing certain pragmatic functions. In v. 5, *porro* introduces what in the Hebrew is a *casus pendens*. Thus, the Vulgate resolves the polysemy of the Hebrew *waw* and reproduces to a certain extent the internal structure of the text by formal means, such as *autem*, in order to mark a caesura.

The difficult construction in v. 22 ("But as for the one that was broken...") is neatly rendered by an ablative absolute (*quod autem fracto illo...*); infinitive constructions with prepositions are consistently resolved into temporal clauses with *cum* (vv. 2.15.17.18). Although participles in the Latin often correspond to participles in the Hebrew (cf. vv. 4.13), the Vulgate once replaces two finite verbs with a participle and a finite verb, thus somehow enhancing the stylistic quality in that place (v. 17: *pavens corrui in faciem meam* for נִבְעַתִּי וָאֶפְּלָה עַל־פָּנַי).

Perhaps it was precisely the desire for such a smooth flow of the narrative which has also caused the noteworthy omission of וּרְאִיתִיו at the beginning of v. 7, if it does not result from a different Hebrew *Vorlage*. In any case, there is no other external evidence for a Hebrew text without וּרְאִיתִיו. Thus, the Vulgate has no interruption of this part of the vision report by the narrator. The effect is that the Latin text appears to be more dramatic and vivid. This omission therefore reproduces and even emphasizes the tendency of the Hebrew text to fade out the narrator step by step as the storytelling goes on (see below on the narrative analysis). Furthermore, the use of the article as a relative particle in הַנִּרְאָה, "the one which had appeared" (v. 1), is correctly reproduced in the Latin (*id quod videram*, cf. Theodotion).

Against the background of such stylistic niceties, it is rather astonishing how literal the Vulgate renders some Hebrew expressions. Perhaps the most striking examples are *subter illud* in v. 8 instead of the expected *pro illo* ("in its place", for the Hebrew תַּחְתֶּיהָ, which can of course also mean "beneath it"), or *iuge sacrificium* for הַתָּמִיד, almost a calque which reproduces the originally adverbial nature of תָמִיד. Strikingly unidiomatic is also the juncture *et faciet et prosperabitur* in v. 12, a word-by-word translation of the Hebrew expression וְעָשְׂתָה וְהִצְלִיחָה, which is only grammatically paratactic, since the second finite verb adverbially modifies the first one; the whole expression means nothing else than "to act successfully".

Sometimes the Vulgate has a more general word than its *Vorlage*, see, e.g., *propositiones* in v. 23 for חִידוֹת ("riddles", just as in Ps 78 [77],2),[136] maybe because the translator was unaware of the exact meaning. He nevertheless gets an extraordinarily rare and grammatically difficult expression like לַפַּלְמוֹנִי הַמְדַבֵּר (v. 13), missed by both Greek versions, absolutely right (*nescio cui loquenti*, see above). It is of course no surprise that the most original renderings in the Latin text are to be found where the Hebrew is most difficult, such as *secundum voluntatem suam* for וְעַל־שִׂכְלוֹ in v. 25 (see the textual note above) or *langui et aegrotavi* for the likewise obscure נִהְיֵיתִי וְנֶחֱלֵיתִי in v. 27. But there are only few examples of this kind, since, on the whole, the idiomatic character of the Vulgate of Daniel 8 consists more in its rendering of the syntax than the lexicon.

c. The Peshitta

The Peshitta[137] follows the MT so closely that it is fair to conclude that the Hebrew text which is reflected in the Syriac is practically

---

[136] The rather general meaning of *propositio* in the Vulgate becomes clear from the fact that it is also used for דָּבָר ("thing", "matter", 1 Kgs 18,24).

[137] Critical edition: *The Old Testament in Syriac According to the Peshitta Version* III/4, 1980. A detailed comparison of the Peshitta of Daniel with the other witnesses has been undertaken by Taylor, *Peshitta*, 1994. The correct spelling would of course be *Pšitta*, but I shall stick to the conventional (at least in the English-speaking world) term here.

identical with the MT, or at least very close to it. Many additions in the Syriac consist in possessive suffixes added to substantives which are without these suffixes in the Hebrew. Such an ample (and, strictly speaking, even redundant) use of pronominal suffixes corresponds to normal Syriac prose style and says nothing about the underlying Hebrew text. About the same is true for tendency of the Syriac version to avoid asyndetic constructions by supplying a *waw* at the beginning of a clause. Furthermore, the Peshitta resolves Hebrew infinitive constructions with preposition into temporal clauses.

The most characteristic feature of the Peshitta, however, is the existence of explanatory glosses in the vision report itself. These are generally added to the end of a clause or even of a verse and are meant to identify the respective protagonists with historical figures in the light of the subsequent explanations in the commentary section of the text. None of these glosses can be found in the other versions.[138] It is therefore certain that they are secondary and constitute a kind of commentary on text. From the nature of this commentary it becomes clear that the Peshitta has understood the vision as a kind of historical allegory – an approach which is predominant in modern scholarship as well. Moreover, the Peshitta labels the vision a *dream* (as does the Old Greek, see below on the visionary frame), even though the Hebrew text has no such specification.

More specific information concerning the date and milieu of the Peshitta of Daniel cannot be given at the moment, as it seems.[139] The text of Daniel 8 presents no evidence whatsoever for the old hypothesis, founded by P. Kahle and A. Baumstark and defended by A. Vööbus and B. J. Roberts,[140] that Septuagint, Targum and Peshitta go back to a common Aramaic ancestor, more precisely: a Palestinian Targum. On the contrary, it seems now certain that the Peshitta has been translated from

---

[138] Dan 8,5: "the he-goat, Alexander, son of Philip"; 8,7: "the ram is Darius the Mede"; 8,8: "the death of Alexander, son of Philip" (after the second clause), "Antiochus Epiphanes. The four servants of Alexander, son of Philip, who reigned after his death" (at the end of the verse); also: 8,20: "Darius the Mede"; 8,21: "Alexander" (both inserted at the beginning of the verse).

[139] So Taylor, "Origin," in *VI Symposium Syriacum*, ed. Lavenant, 1994: 31-42.

[140] For references see Morrison, *Syriac Version*, 2001, 1-3.

the Hebrew (and maybe even the Masoretic) text,[141] even though it is
fairly likely that certain techniques which tackle the question how to
translate a Hebrew text into Aramaic have been taken over from the earlier Targumim.

At this point one may note that specific historical allusions, which
have been used with some success by some scholars in giving a precise
date to the Peshitta of Isaiah,[142] have not yet been detected in the Syriac
Daniel. The same is true for several unambiguous "theological" renderings which could in theory point to a specific Jewish or Christian origin.[143]

---

[141] Cf. Dirksen, "Peshitta", in *Mikra*, eds. Mulder and Sysling, 1988, 258-259.

[142] See van der Kooij, *Textzeugen*, 1981, 295; Weitzman, "Lexical Clues," in *Studia Aramaica*, eds. Geller et al., 1995: 245.

[143] Again, there are some passages in the Peshitta of Isaiah which have been thought to betray genuinely Christian thought, although none of these cases has been universally accepted. See Gelston, "Christian Origin," in *Writing and Reading*, eds. Broyles
and Evans, 1997: 563-582. The fact that the Old Testament Peshitta was directly
translated from the MT and not from the LXX (as many other Christian versions,
such as the Armenian translation), may in fact bear on its origin (581).

3
The Visionary Frame

The main part of Daniel 8, which can be divided into the report of a vision and its explanation (again in a visionary setting), is framed by an introduction and a conclusion. This frame determines the literary form of what follows, provides information on its fictional setting and so gives certain important clues which lead the reader to intuitively anticipate some major issues of the subsequent text.

The widely-accepted classification of Daniel 8 as a "symbolic dream" (although the Hebrew text does not say that it was a dream; this is an interpretation of the Greek and the Peshitta), together with its "allegorical" meaning, will first of all have to be tested against the internal criteria of the underlying literary form. Since details about the setting of the vision are strictly functional and establish a link between this chapter and the rest of the Book of Daniel, they will be discussed separately here.

1. The Vision Report as a Literary Form

The vision report given in Daniel 8 follows a specific literary form. A literary form is nothing else than an accumulation of certain traditional features which constitute a "container" that can be filled with individual information. The genre is explicitly identified by the remark that the narrator saw (רָאה) a vision (חָזוֹן). Apparently, this is by the time of the final redaction of the Book of Daniel already a fixed opening formula, just like lifting up the eyes belongs to the visionary style: Dan 8,3; cf. 10,5 and Zech 2,1; in Gen 31,10, however, it introduces a dream. וְהִנֵּה introduces the content of a vision or a dream.[144] חָזוֹן is a technical term

---

[144] Richter, "Traum," *BZ* 7 (1963): 204.

for a mysterious visual perception similar to a dream, but more intense,[145] and a typical means of God's revelation to human beings (cf. Num 12,6-8). From a more psychological point of view, it implies a state of mind in which the subject is no longer in control of his own thoughts and will.[146]

When the narrator, in addition to these stereotypical lexemes, provides information on the time and the place of his vision, he puts himself into the footsteps of various literary predecessors. By following such a literary convention, he establishes a kind of "contract" with the reader, through which he gives rise to certain expectations.[147] The reader will soon presuppose that the indications of time and place will be followed first by a description of the contents of the vision, then by its interpretation. However, not all vision reports have such indications.

As the technical terminology for dreams in Ancient Near Eastern literature, in particular in Akkadian,[148] indicates, something comparable to the modern basic distinction[149] between "message dreams"[150] and "symbolic dreams"[151] was already felt. The report of such a dream in various literatures throughout the Ancient Near East sticks to a conventionalized frame which provides information on the dreamer, the locality, and eventual other circumstances. The frame is followed by the actual narration of the dream-content and a final reference to the end of the

---

[145] Jeffers, *Magic*, 1996, 125-126.

[146] On the phenomenology of visions and their anthropological and psychological implications cf. also Heininger, *Paulus*, 1995, 32-43.

[147] Cf. Burridge, *Gospels*, 1992, 32-38; so, too (from the point of view of a literary critic), Hirsch, *Validity*, 1967, 68-102.

[148] Butler, *Conceptions*, 1998, 15-41.

[149] It goes back to A. Leo Oppenheim (Oppenheim, *Interpretation*, 1956). There are other models of systematically grouping ancient dream reports, but the division between "message dreams" and "symbolic dreams" has recently been taken up again by Husser, *Dreams*, 1999, 99-103.

[150] They contain a mostly self-evident communication from a deity, such as an exhortation to a certain kind of moral behaviour. Very often they are purely auditive. See Oppenheim, *Interpretation*, 1956, 197ff.

[151] Usually this refers to the vision of something which represents reality in an encrypted way and requires professional explanation, cf. Oppenheim, *Interpretation*, 1956, 204ff.

dream and the dreamer's reaction.[152] The visions in Daniel, and many other apocalyptic revelations, are particularly close to this form of a dream-report.[153] They may have originated as transformations of prophetic visions,[154] but from the point of view of the contents and the *Sitz im Leben* there are significant differences,[155] insofar as, for instance, the effect of the vision on the seer[156] or a hierarchically structured angelic world are distinct features of the apocalyptic genre.

It is precisely this basic pattern of a vision or dream report which can be found in Daniel 8. The actual vision (vv. 3-12) is prepared by a short introduction giving the genre and setting (vv. 1-2), followed by an interpretation (vv. 13-26) and the description of the psychological effect (v. 27). Both, the vision itself and its interpretation, make use of a kind of hierarchic and developed angelology, in which the members of the divine council have their individual names, and the effects of the vision are described at length, so several fundamental formal conventions of the apocalyptic genre in particular are fulfilled here.

The content of the vision has often been thought to be "symbolic"[157] in the strict sense, namely as featuring symbols construed and arranged *ad hoc* to a scene in order to illustrate reality (e.g., the dreams in the context of the Joseph story in Gen 37 and 40-41), as if they had no independent value apart from their didactic purpose and were meant to represent in fact something else.

While it is true that the animals in Daniel 8 transcend everyday-experience (the ram has two unequal horns, it dominates all the other animate beings, the horn of the he-goat breaks and gives rise to other horns, the last of which makes some of the stars fall down to earth), it is not clear why they should be mere allegories for specific political powers, invented *ad hoc* for the sake of illustration.

---

[152] Oppenheim, *Interpretation*, 1956, 187.

[153] Collins, *Daniel with an Introduction*, 1984, 6-14; Gnuse, *Dreams,* 1996, 73-78.

[154] Koch, "Visionsbericht," in: *Apocalypticism*, ed. Hellholm, 1989: 413-441.

[155] Ibid., 428-430.

[156] Panic as a result of the vision is, however, also mentioned at the end of the Akkadian *Vision of the Netherworld* (cf. Kvanvig, *Roots*, 1988).

[157] Collins, *Daniel with an Introduction*, 1984, 6-14 and id., *Daniel*, 1993, 54-56; Koch, "Visionsbericht," in: *Apocalypticism*, ed. Hellholm, 1989: 428ff.

There are several elements in Daniel 8 which twist the genre of the "symbolic dream" considerably. The presence of the angels, who in vv. 13-14 are described as independent beholders of the same vision and linguistically explicitly connected to the mainline story (*wayyiqtol*), makes it clear that the visionary gains an insight into the "real" supernatural world. The auditive elements, also present at Dan 7,16, introduced through the visionary's listening to the angelic conversation add to the "realism", while "symbolic dreams" according to the traditional pattern are in general silent. But Daniel sees and hears what the angels, too, can see and hear, and the specific interpretation given afterwards is part of the vision – again a strikingly non-conformist feature.[158]

From this evidence it emerges that the vision described is less a theoretical constellation made up for the visionary than a reality with its own objectivity, consisting in a combination of both visible and auditive elements accessible only to spiritual beings. When the angels in the vision are not allegorical for the narrator (and it would be risky to assume that they are), it is likely that the other elements, to which they are so closely linked by the text, are not allegorical either. Nonetheless one can of course not determine with certainty *what* actually has inspired the visionary's imagination – it might just have been clouds in a red evening sky.

The narrative presentation that will be analyzed in the following chapter confirms these rather formal observations, since it betrays a multi-layered logical and chronological sequence of events and repeatedly stresses the idea that everything told there is in fact rooted in personal experience. It is thus the "cosmic meta pattern", the ongoing and very "real" struggle between the forces of good and evil in the supernatural realm, in the light of which the whole contemporary history can be explained.

Hence, the literary genre specified in the beginning as a חָזוֹן should be taken literally. It is a formal marker saying the text reports what Daniel has seen during a mystic experience. During such an experience, he was in fact able to see the universal reality in the way the angels do. There is nothing in the text which indicates why for Daniel this incident should have been any less "real" than the locusts rising from the end

---

[158] Although a dream interpreted within a dream was recognized as a specific type of dreams in Rabbinic Judaism, cf. bBerakhot 55b.

of the world and the enigmatic figure in Amos or the prophetic throne vision in Isaiah.[159]

As in Ezekiel (11,13), there is also an immediate point of contact between the realm of the vision and some historical reality, especially when the sanctuary is involved in the cosmic battle. Such a decisive point of contact is very unallegorical, as is indeed an angelic dialogue and a *pešer* of the vision that is part of the same vision. All this appears to constitute at least cumulative evidence for the conclusion that Daniel 8 is *not* a "symbolic dream" or an "allegory", as continuously stated in secondary literature, but a revelation of a transcendent reality, much in the way prophetic revelations are.[160]

2. The Significance of Time and Place (8,1-2)

Besides clarifying the literary genre of the subsequent textual unit, the two introductory verses of Daniel 8 also provide information on the absolute and relative time of the vision, its place and the personality of the visionary. These pieces of information are typical for the genre of the vision report; especially the reminiscences of Ezekiel's inaugural vision have been duly noted by commentators.[161] Yet these indications do not seem to be given for their own sake, but have a bidirectional literary function in that they 1) illuminate the reliability of the report by collocating it fictionally in time and space, and 2) contain intertextual references which are pertinent to the literary setting of the book:

---

[159] Koch, "Visionsbericht," in: *Apocalypticism*, ed. Hellholm, 1989: 428-429, remarks that these experiences are real for the prophetic visionaries, they are a "Tiefenschau" of what lies behind the world as it can be perceived with man's elementary senses.

[160] Even Niditch, *Symbolic Vision*, 1983, who correctly observes that the vision "serves as medium which joins divine and human realm" (216), still analyzes the animal fight alongside categories like "symbols" and "references" (226-233) and so does not distinguish between an *interpretation* of the vision and an *application*: "Whatever the background for these animal types, they have been adapted and described specifically in order to portray certain historical figures and events" (227). She, too, may have been misguided by the astrological explanations which she accepts (ibid.).

[161] Bentzen, *Daniel*, 1952, 69; Collins, *Daniel*, 1993, 329.

בִּשְׁנַת שָׁלוֹשׁ לְמַלְכוּת בֵּלְאשַׁצַּר הַמֶּלֶךְ
חָזוֹן נִרְאָה אֵלַי אֲנִי דָנִיֵּאל אַחֲרֵי הַנִּרְאָה אֵלַי בַּתְּחִלָּה׃
וָאֶרְאֶה בֶּחָזוֹן וַיְהִי בִּרְאֹתִי
וַאֲנִי בְּשׁוּשַׁן הַבִּירָה אֲשֶׁר בְּעֵילָם הַמְּדִינָה
וָאֶרְאֶה בֶּחָזוֹן וַאֲנִי הָיִיתִי עַל־אוּבַל אוּלָי׃

In the third year of the reign of King Belshazzar a vision ap-
peared to me, yes, to me, Daniel, after the one which had ap-
peared to me before.
Then I concentrated on the vision and saw, while I was looking,
that I was in Susa the fortress, which is in the satrapy of Elam. I
concentrated on the vision and was by the river Ulai.

a. Creating an Impression of Reliability

The primary and matter-of-fact dating formula is fairly easy to
grasp. When the narrator stresses at the very outset (v. 1) that his vision
took place exactly in the third year of the reign of King[162] Belshazzar
(בִּשְׁנַת שָׁלוֹשׁ לְמַלְכוּת בֵּלְאשַׁצַּר הַמֶּלֶךְ), he commits himself to an objective
and absolute collocation in time.[163] The wording itself corresponds to the
normal way of numbering years in the Ancient Near East and so provides
an immediate link between the vision and the "real" world which sur-
rounds it.

Then the narrator specifies the genre he adopts (חָזוֹן) and identi-
fies himself explicitly by his name (אֵלַי אֲנִי דָנִיֵּאל). The construction employed, an additional independent pronoun which refers back to the suffix attached to a preposition, is generally considered to be strongly emphatic by grammarians.[164] The function of this extra information here is
that the seer unambiguously points out that he is indeed an eye-witness,

---

[162] The title has been omitted by the Old Greek, see the corresponding textual note
above.

[163] See the next chapter for further-reaching implications of this formula.

[164] See GK §135g (the examples are subsumed under "starke Hervorhebung", cf.
§135d-e); JM §146d.7 (with Muraoka's note).

a living and "real" person who has himself beheld all the things he is going to tell.[165] He is thus a witness to future generations.

This piece of personal information is rudimentary, since Daniel is already known to the reader of the text, so the narrator can be brief here. It is followed by a piece of relative chronology. The absolute one is clear by now, the relative one dates the vision of Daniel 8 precisely "after the one which had appeared to me before"[166] (אַחֲרֵי [167] הַנִּרְאָה אֵלַי בַּתְּחִלָּה), namely the one described at great length in Daniel 7. The latter vision is said to have occurred in the first year of Belshazzar and whose general pattern of presentation the narrator follows in Daniel 8. Again, this may have something to do with trustworthiness, for the statement implies that the seer is in fact someone accustomed to visions, not only a real person, but also an expert. As such he has been continuously described in the court tales.

In v. 2, the narrator switches from the chronological to the geographical collocation of the vision, using the same lexemes, ראה and חָזוֹן, as in v. 1. He points out that he was in Susa[168] (one of the residences of

---

[165] On this topos and its use for establishing credibility in general see Speyer, *Literarische Fälschung*, 1971, 50-56.

[166] This must be the meaning of בַּתְּחִלָּה, cf. Gen 13,3; 43,18 and esp. 20, *pace* Zevit, "Exegetical Implications," *VT* 28 (1978): 488-492, who thinks this word indicates "the vision at the beginning", namely the first vision Daniel had, or rather: the first vision of Daniel known to the reader (this would still be the one in Daniel 7, since the ones in Daniel 2 and 4 appeared to Nebuchadnezzar).

[167] The ה is a relative particle here, as it tends to occur in post-classical usage. Most examples come from Chronicles and Ezra, cf. JM §145d-e. נִרְאָה is presumably a 3rd masc. sg. *qatal*, since this usage of the article as a relative particle regularly occurs with the *qatal*, while instances from the older books appear to be originally participles, even if they have been reanalyzed as *qatal* forms by the Masoretic accentuation (GK §138i-k).

[168] הַבִּירָה is a traditional designation of the city of Susa ("the fortified city"), cf. Esth 1,2.5; 2,3.5 (Esth 3,15 is probably synonymous); Neh 1,1. It is presumably not a reference to a citadel within the city (so Marti, *Daniel*, 1901, 56: "*die Burg*, die im Altertum berühmte [...] Citadelle von Susa im Unterschied von der übrigen ausgedehnten Stadt"), just as יב בירתא together means "Elephantine" in the Elephantine papyri, as has been correctly pointed out by Collins, *Daniel*, 1993, 329. The use of a geographical name plus "city" etc. is very frequent in Aramaic and later in Syriac (cf. also *la ville de Paris* in French).

the Achaemenid kings), in the province ("satrapy")[169] of Elam, at the canal[170] Ulai.[171] This rather accurate description is not redundant, but appropriate in that it makes clear that Daniel refers to Susa in Elam. Without such additional information, one could think he intended the district of Babylon bearing the same name in Achaemenid times.[172] By aiming at geographical precision, the narrator increases his trustworthiness significantly.

The question whether Daniel was physically in Susa or whether the geographical setting is imaginary, the latter being favoured by the *communis opinio*,[173] does not seem to be of greater importance. However, a "spiritual" presence in Susa is in any case more likely, because it

---

[169] For the satrapies as administrative units in the Achaemenid Empire cf. Petit, *Satrapes*, 1990.

[170] Taking אוּבָל as a synonym (or maybe even just a phonetic variation) of יוּבָל (cf. Jer 17,8 = יָבָל, "stream, watercourse") and thus following Bevan, *Daniel*, 1929, 129; see also Montgomery, *Daniel*, 1927, 327. The Old Greek, the Peshitta and the Vulgate, on the other hand, derive this word from the Akkadian *abullu*, which had by then entered Mishnaic Hebrew, Targumic Aramaic and Syriac, and so translate it as "gate". The sense would then be precisely the city gate, the road from which led to the Ulai. This interpretation is followed by Hartman and Di Lella, *Daniel*, 1978, 224, but since contact with the divine often took place at rivers in exilic times, the collocation at the river itself may be a significant feature of the diaspora setting and hence original.

[171] This is the Akkadian name (*Eulaeus* in the Classical sources); in Middle Babylonian it is spelled Ú-la-a, in Neo Assyrian U-la-a-a.

[172] Cf. Dandamaev, "Diaspora. A: Babylonia in the Persian Age," in *CHJ*, Vol. 1, eds. Davies and Finkelstein, 1984: 339, and Unger, *Babylon*, 1931, 81-82, for this district; the distinction (yet not its ulterior motivation in the text) is also pointed out by Collins, *Daniel*, 1993, 329.

[173] Marti, *Daniel*, 1901, 55; Montgomery, *Daniel*, 1927, 325-326; Hartman and Di Lella, *Daniel*, 1978, 233; Collins, *Daniel*, 1993, 329 etc. This interpretation corresponds to the Syriac version which makes it clear by translating חָזוֹן with ܣܠܕ twice in v. 2 (although it has ܫܢܐ elsewhere) that Daniel saw *in his dream* that he was in Susa. The Vulgate goes into the same direction (*vidi autem in visione esse me super portam Ulai*). The Old Greek understands the vision as a dream as well (ἐν τῷ ὁράματι τοῦ ἐνυπνίου μου ἐμοῦ ὄντος ἐν Σούσοις κτλ.), contrary to the MT (maybe in analogy to Dan 7,1, where dream and nocturnal are vision equated, see below), but the wording does not clearly say whether Daniel dreamt *that* he was in Susa or *while* he was in Susa.

belongs to the typology of such narratives.[174] Maybe the repeated phrase
וָאֶרְאֶה בֶחָזוֹן just before the reference to the Ulai can be taken as an indication that the geographical context belongs to the vision as well,[175] but
it is unclear whether these two words were part of the original text.[176]
Moreover, there is another reinforced insistence on the speaker's ego
due to the double וַאֲנִי in this verse (cf. 7,15.28; 8,27), which may go further than a mere pseudonymous habit and point to the speaker's self-
consciousness when he receives the vision.[177]

b. Foreign Setting and Diaspora Life-Style

Apart from the use of external information of the kind just described as a device to point out the reliability of the account to follow,
there is a more literary dimension of the frame. This second dimension
goes far beyond the generic conventions of the vision report and alludes
to a crucial theme in the Book of Daniel as such. This fact has generally
been ignored by commentators, although it occupies an important place
among the various attempts of the Book of Daniel to establish a specific,
coherent setting. For this reason, it shall be treated a bit more extensively
here.

First of all, the repetition of a formula quite similar to the one
that was used for the – absolute – date of the vision already in Dan 7,1
(בִּשְׁנַת חֲדָה לְבֵלְאשַׁצַּר מֶלֶךְ בָּבֶל, that is, without לְמַלְכוּת) creates a sense
of unity[178] and indicates that both chapters are very similar in outlook.

---

[174] See esp. Ez 8,3; 11,24; 40,2 (particularly pertinent, because there seems to be
some influence of Ez on Daniel 8).

[175] So the acute observation by Behrmann, *Daniel*, 1894, 51, not taken up by the other
commentators: by the pleonastic expression in v. 2 "soll ohne Zweifel ausgedrückt
werden, dass Dan nur in der Vision sich in Susa und am Ulai befand."

[176] The MT's reading is confirmed by 4QDan[a], the Peshitta and the Vulgate, while
these words are lacking in Theodotion; the Old Greek has a conflation of two variant
readings. They could result from a dittography, but the support from the versions is
rather strong. Niditch, *Symbolic Vision*, 1983, 218, sees in the MT itself a conflation
of two readings.

[177] See Montgomery, *Daniel*, 1927, 305.317 (ad 7,15.28).

[178] Cf. Hartman and Di Lella, *Daniel*, 1978, 223: "The purpose of this verse is to
connect ch. 8 with ch. 7." But it will be seen in the course of this chapter that such a

Both portray a supernatural battle in the form of an animal vision which becomes more and more surreal and is then applied to a specific historical situation. From another point of view, Daniel 8 is a kind of answer of and a complement to Daniel 7.[179] While Daniel 7 ends with humanity as a place where the sacred manifests itself (this appears to be the function of the figure of the "Son of Man" who receives dominion), Daniel 8 is concerned with the violation of the sacred in the human sphere, but also with the idea that such a violation is determined to end after an appointed period of time (8,13f). Therefore chronological precision is important not only in principle, because a vision which conveys a message generally has to be rendered as trustworthy, but also for the specific topic of Daniel 8, that is, consolation.

However, there is much more to that than just an allusion to Daniel 7. The dating pattern [name of the king] לְמַלְכוּת [year] בִּשְׁנַת apparently looks explicitly back to the court tales, since both chapter headings in the preceding Hebrew sections of Daniel (1,1 and 2,1) follow this pattern. This subtle connection is lost in the Old Greek translation, which fully concentrates on the connection with Dan 7,1 by assimilating both formulae in the Greek text. In doing so, the translator turns Dan 8,1 into a kind of chapter heading of the "book" Daniel is said to have written in Dan 7,1. Moreover, Daniel 8 is explicitly understood as a *dream* (ἐνύπνιον) in the Old Greek (the Hebrew only calls it a *vision*), just like the "dream" (חֵלֶם)[180] Daniel had on his bed according to 7,1.[181]

After Daniel 8, the pattern of dating changes markedly, since in 9,1, 10,1 and 11,1 it is consistently [name of the king] לְ [year] בִּשְׁנַת. Other evidence confirms the impression that the introduction in Dan 8,1-

---

statement explains too little, since it does not do justice to the fact that Dan 8,1 and Dan 7,1 use *different* formulae of dating.

[179] See Goldingay, *Daniel*, 1989, 195, who remarks that אַחֲרֵי implies that the vision in Daniel 8 "was different yet related to" the one in Daniel 7 "in form and content".

[180] The Old Greek translates this word with ὅραμα, "vision", but surely it will have seen that it is clear from the context (Daniel is on his bed) that the vision takes place in a dream situation. It is quite feasible that the translator thought the situation in Daniel 8 was analogous.

[181] See the corresponding textual notes on Dan 8,1 and 8,2 above.

2 wants to look back beyond, but including, Daniel 7 to the very beginning of the court setting, namely to the material in Daniel 1 and 2. There
are indeed numerous instances of Persian colouring found in these two
verses, which also appear to serve a literary function.

Commentators sensitive to a meaning behind these factual state-
ments point out that "the ancient land of Medo-Persia" is appropriate
"for the setting of the drama of the symbolical contest between that Oriental empire and Greece."[182] Yet such a supposition rests on the assumption that the vision is indeed a "symbolical contest" concerning the Persian Empire, which is subjected to criticism in the present study.[183] It is,
in any case, not necessary to look for a specific connection between the
Persian allusions in vv. 1-2 and the vision itself, as they fit in well with
the overall concern of the Book of Daniel to create a vivid literary setting in the Persian diaspora. They are not meant to elaborate on the "Persian" connotation in the vision, but contribute to the overall depiction of
the setting which has been inaugurated very effectively in Daniel 1.

So the application of the reign of Belshazzar as a basis for dating
and the precise geographical information, employing not only the names
of the capital Susa, the region Elam and the river Ulai, but also the correct Aramaic technical term for an administrative unit in the Persian Em-

---

[182] Montgomery, *Daniel*, 1927, 326. In the same vein then later on Bevan, *Daniel*,
1929, 129; Collins, *Daniel*, 1993, 329: "The location of the vision in Susa, while still
in the reign of a Babylonian king, is a clue from the author that the vision concerns
the Persian Empire." But the author of the text does not establish any explicit connection between the setting of the vision and its content, and even if this were true, the
Persian Empire would only be in the background in the first couple verses in the vision. The ram, which is supposed to represent it, disappears after the victory of the
he-goat, and it has nothing to do with the real climax of the text in vv. 8ff! Hence it
seems quite unsatisfactory to assume that the setting in Susa is connected with the
animal fight in the vision in more than a very superficial way. On the contrary, the
geographical setting in the strict sense is rather an apocalyptic wasteland.

[183] At the remotest, the choice of this site may have been influenced by an eventual
memory of a battle fought during Nebuchadnezzar I's campaign against the Elamites,
as recorded by a Middle Babylonian *kudurru* (boundary-stone): King, *Boundary-
Stones*, 1912, no. 6, col. i, ll. 14-43 and esp. l. 28; for the historical background cf.
Brinkman, *Political History*, 1968, 105-110. This idea has not been mentioned by
commentators so far and it is true that it might be too speculative.

pire (מְדִינָה, a "satrapy"),[184] collocate ch. 8 explicitly within the *cultural* milieu of the whole Book of Daniel. Especially the use of foreign words (that is, in the first place geographical terms) is a linguistic means consciously applied here in order to create a "foreign" setting. The geographical terms in Daniel 8 perform just the same function as the Persian loan-words in Daniel 1.[185] Taking up the dating pattern from 1,1 and 2,1 again in 8,1 provides a formal bridge between the two halves of the Book of Daniel.

There are other literary devices which corroborate the idea that the chronological and geographical information in Dan 8,1-2 alludes to the court tales. In particular the detail of the river Ulai could point to the diaspora setting and the resulting theological problems which it reflects, beyond the intertextual reference to Ez 1,1. Revelations were often received at the banks of rivers in the exile, and this feature is especially prominent in the Book of Daniel – besides the Ulai in ch. 8, the Tigris is the setting of the vision in ch. 10 (cf. 10,4), and also in 12,5 the bank of a river is mentioned.

The origin of this belief is presumably that foreign lands were considered unclean,[186] so Israelite exiles would choose the proximity to running water[187] for their private devotions,[188] probably even up to the time of the New Testament: Acts 16,13 is a later reflection of the same practice. In Dan 9,3 a vision is explicitly described as subsequent to devotional practice, that is, prayer and fasting, and a similar idea may be implicitly present here.

---

[184] Cf. Vogt, *Lexicon*, 1994, s.v. (97) and Fitzmyer, *Genesis Apocryphon*, 1971, 137-138. The original meaning appears to have been a district over which a "judge" (root *dīn*) ruled; the shift to the meaning "city", normal in Syriac and Arabic, appears to be only secondary.

[185] Cf. הַפַּרְתְּמִים (v. 3), פַּת־בַּג (vv. 5.8.13.15.16; 11,26).

[186] See Am 7, 17 (אֲדָמָה טְמֵאָה)

[187] Running water was thought to be purifying, cf. Lev 14,5.50; 15,13; Num 19,17.

[188] Cf. also Greenberg, *Ezekiel*, 1983, 40, with further references and some remarks on traditions in medieval Jewish mysticism, according to which the reflection of the celestial vision in the water would avoid the immediate sight of divine beings. The lament about the exilic situation in Ps 137, too, takes place at "at the rivers of Babylon".

It is true that the author of Daniel 8 does not elaborate further on this point. The reference also seems to be rather casual, even to the extent that it does not really matter whether Daniel was physically present at the Ulai or only transported there in his vision. Nonetheless, this typical element of Jewish religious custom in the diaspora reflects a theological dimension which has a special significance in the first half of the text. It hints at the possibility to develop a new religious identity after the traditional institutions of King and Temple have disappeared and to maintain this identity in a foreign environment without making compromises concerning one's religious beliefs and practices.

This is the sense behind more amplified instances of keeping the Jewish faith in the diaspora throughout the Book of Daniel, such as the refusal of gentile food in Dan 1,8-14,[189] the unwillingness to worship the statue of the king in Dan 3,12ff, or the prayer towards Jerusalem in Dan 6,11ff. W. Lee Humphreys[190] has pointed out in a concise, but nonetheless ground-breaking, study that especially the tales in Daniel 1-6 suggest a life-style for living as a Jew in the diaspora, an environment which, as one might add, becomes more and more hostile in the course of the latter half.[191] Within the visionary part, Daniel 7-12, the significance of the historical dimension changes insofar as it becomes the visible stage for the effects of a cosmic drama.

3. The Effect of the Vision (8,27)

The application of the vision and hence the vision report as a whole ends with a comment on the physical effect this experience has caused on the seer:

---

[189] Food customs are a strong means of affirming a particular personal identity and dignity. One may compare the, at least in a certain period, rigorous observance of the Friday rule by Irish Catholics in London.

[190] Humphreys, "Life-Style," *JBL* 92 (1973): 211-223.

[191] There has been no lack of contributions which outline the negative side of the diaspora as it is presented in Daniel 1-6, most notably the constant danger to become a victim of slander and the king's temper, cf. Henze, "Ideology," *SBL Seminar Papers* (1999): 527-539.

וַאֲנִי דָנִיֵּאל נִהְיֵיתִי וְנֶחֱלֵיתִי יָמִים
וָאָקוּם וָאֶעֱשֶׂה אֶת־מְלֶאכֶת הַמֶּלֶךְ
וָאֶשְׁתּוֹמֵם עַל־הַמַּרְאֶה וְאֵין מֵבִין:

But I, Daniel, was undone and sick for a number of days. Then I arose and did the king's business. But I was dismayed by the vision, and there was nobody who could gain insight.

The focus therefore turns to the visionary again, who attracts all the attention by means of the forcefully contrastive וַאֲנִי. This concluding remark is in principle part of the conventional frame (cf. Dan 5,6; 7,28; Ez 3,15; 2 Esdr 5,14 etc.), but here the almost pleonastic wording leaves a particularly strong impression: וַאֲנִי דָנִיֵּאל נִהְיֵיתִי וְנֶחֱלֵיתִי יָמִים. Daniel confesses that he was undone and sick for several[192] days. There is hardly a need for textual emendation,[193] and נִהְיֵיתִי presumably derives from הוה, "to ruin".[194]

The subsequent statement is in various ways interesting, for it does *not*, as the reader might have guessed from the genre, describe the *fulfillment* of the prophecy, as often in dream reports, but Daniel's return to *normality*: וָאָקוּם וָאֶעֱשֶׂה אֶת־מְלֶאכֶת הַמֶּלֶךְ,[195] "and I arose and did the

---

[192] See the textual note above.

[193] Cf. the discussion in the annotated reading text above.

[194] This etymology has already been made by Rashi and Qimchi. In recent times it has been accepted by most commentaries (incl. the most comprehensive modern treatment by Collins, *Daniel*, 1993, 328), even by those written by philological authorities like Montgomery (cf. *Daniel*, 1927, 355).

[195] The spelling practice וָאָקוּם (a long form with full consonantal orthography) is relatively late. The consonantal orthography of earlier compositions, such as וָאָקֻם (1 Kgs 3,21), strongly suggests that the last syllable was originally short (*$wā\,{}^{\prime}āq\breve{o}m$). Hence the Masoretic pointing and accentuation (the stress is on the second syllable) $wā\,{}^{\prime}āq\hat{u}m$ is a compromise, because the Masoretes did not want to insert a *waw* in the consonantal text there, while the pronunciation had already changed by the time Daniel 8 was written. The diachronic development will have been a process from the original short form to the seconded cohortative and finally to the full long form. See Rainey, "Mesha' and Syntax," in *The Land*, eds. Dearman and Graham, 2001: 290.

king's business". This comment has a literary function in that it provides a caesura and so marks the end of the content of this chapter, since it is a return to the mainline story, namely the Daniel narrative, whose principal setting is the royal court. It therefore establishes a bridge between the "tales" in Daniel 1-6 and the visions in 7-12,[196] pointing out that the setting is still the same: The visionary is an influential official in the service of the king. One may theoretically compare Dan 2,48, although this does not square very well with the fact that Daniel was unknown to Belshazzar in ch. 5.

The introduction of a new theme, however, is mirrored by the change of the linguistic code. While the preceding section was a visionary dialogue commenting on the visionary animal fight and concluding with an imperative (8,26), v. 27 switches to plain and straightforward narrative again. After the angel's discourse, the focus is on Daniel again (וַאֲנִי דָנִיֵּאל), his initial situation is described by means of two *qatal* forms, which are followed by a sequence of three *wayyiqtols* expressing successive events and a final evaluation of the situation by means of a participle construction.

Moreover, the clause describing Daniel's return to "business as usual" adds an important nuance to the vision precisely by suggesting that the fulfillment of its message is still far away. The foreign environment has not yet become so oppressive as not to grant an Israelite the possibility of a career at the court of a foreign king. Hence, the main theme of Daniel 1-6, the "diaspora life-style", is here taken up again, and it provides an extremely forceful contrast with the gloomy situation foretold in the vision where the foreign powers have become so hostile as to defile the Temple, whose purification and restauration would be the ultimate desire of a pious Jew in exile.

As an abomination of this kind is so utterly remote from any imagination, the narrator adds a further comment stating the bewildering lack of understanding of the vision on his part even after his recovery:

---

[196] Cf. Davies, "Eschatology," *JSOT* 17 (1980): 33-53, for an appreciation of the unity between the tales and the visions. Despite the shortcomings of his own approach which tries to derive the eschatology of the visions from the earlier chapters, his concern for interpreting the visions within their narrative context remains valid. See Gane, "Genre Awareness," in *To Understand*, ed. Merling, 1997: 138.

וָאֶשְׁתּוֹמֵם עַל־הַמַּרְאֶה וְאֵין מֵבִין.[197] The final וְאֵין מֵבִין, which rounds off the narrative, is particularly disconcerting, since it characterizes the whole state of affairs. Compare with Dan 12,8, where it is said that Daniel did not understand what he had heard. This is one of the characteristics of apocalyptic style.

---

[197] וְאֵין מֵבִין supposedly refers to Daniel's own failure to grasp the meaning, because he was told not to talk about the vision. Both the Old Greek and Theodotion take this in a general sense: "there was nobody who understood". In this case, the Classical Hebrew construction would be אֵינֶנִּי, see below on Dan 8,5.

4
The Battle Narrative

The core part of Daniel 8 is the description of the battle between the ram and the he-goat. This battle is reported as a vision and then explained in a *pešer*-like fashion by angelic mediator figures. Contrary to scholarly orthodoxy, it can be appreciated on different levels, even as an artful piece of narrative prose. A symbolic interpretation in the sense of a kind of allegory of the struggle between Persia and Greece has too often been taken for granted as the exclusive possibility to understand this text.[198]

Since this assumption will presumably influence the understanding of the vision narrative, it is useful to delineate here the different hermeneutical approach taken here. Then there will be an outline of the literary presentation of the narrative as it stands and the various linguistic means which it employs. This literary analysis will then be followed by a discussion of the biblical and (supposedly) Ancient Near Eastern background of the imagery and its implications. The outline of this chapter thus corresponds to the clear distinction between the battle scene and its

---

[198] Cf. Porteous, *Daniel*, 1978, 97, whose judgment is characteristic for this kind of interpreting Daniel 8: "[...] ist der Verfasser in diesen Schlußkapiteln hauptsächlich mit der wirklichen Geschichte beschäftigt, vor allem mit der zeitgenössischen Geschichte, die, selbst dann, wenn die Deutung nicht beigegeben worden wäre, der Leserschaft wohl vertraut gewesen wäre; und es hätte kaum auch Schwierigkeiten bereitet, die ziemlich durchsichtige Verkleidung der Tiersymbolik des 8.Kap. zu durchschauen." Note also his use of "symbolisieren" and "darstellen" on pp. 99-103. So, too, Hartman and Di Lella, *Daniel*, 1978, 233: "The symbolism of the ram and the he-goat is so patent that the reader would have no difficulty in identifying the two-horned ram with the kingdom of the Medes and the Persians, and the one-horned he-goat with the kingdom of Alexander the Great, even if the interpreting angel had not explicitly made this identification (vss. 20-21)." Consequently, Hartman and Di Lella treat the respective parts in the vision and their explanation in the second part of Daniel 8 together in their commentary section. See also the epigrammatic judgment of Goldingay, *Daniel*, 1989, 201: "chap. 7 is myth, chap. 8 is allegory".

subsequent application to the historical situation of the original addressees of the Book of Daniel made by the text itself.

1. The Hermeneutical Perspective

Since the battle between the ram and the he-goat is in scholarly
literature generally considered to be a *symbolic* representation of the
struggle between Persia and Greece, much effort has been put into the
question why these animals must represent their respective nations. Solutions usually draw on astral symbolism or the role of the ram and the he-
goat in Persian and Macedonian royal iconography. This approach, however, may end up in reducing the vision to some sort of historical allegory which is adduced only in order to explain that which allegedly matters, namely contemporary history. But the choice of these particular
animals for Persia and Greece is not at all obvious, since neither the astral symbolism nor the connection with royal iconography rests on firm
ground, as will be seen.

Accordingly, the battle narrative itself does not from the outset
push the reader into one or the other direction. It simply starts off as an
animal fight, a scene very familiar throughout Ancient Near Eastern iconography.[199] Nothing in the text suggests that it has to be read with a
prior identification of its supposedly symbolic protagonists in mind, as
the mainstream of interpretational history of this chapter from antiquity
up to the present day wants to lead one to believe. Some explicit historical identifications in the vision itself appear in the Syriac version,[200] but
they only show that the translator has taken exactly this approach and so
emphasize its antiquity. They say nothing about the original meaning of
the Hebrew text.

A rather sceptical perspective in this respect does justice to the
macrostructure of the Book of Daniel, since the animal fight is by no
means presented as a metaphor. It just begins to evolve before Daniel's
eyes without too much explanation. In fact, the frame of the report
clearly determines the literary genre of the text as a faithfully communi-

---

[199] See Keel, *Recht der Bilder*, 1992, 1-59.

[200] Cf. the additions in vv. 5.7.8 (*bis*).

cated vision and not as a parable. In the latter case one would expect an introduction like "Worldly powers are like a ram and a he-goat...", as often in the New Testament. The subsequent application of the vision takes place within the visionary setting itself, while it is made explicit in vv. 13-14 that the angels see just what Daniel sees, even independently of him: he is a silent listener to their conversation.

As the text shows, the connection of the animals with specific nations briefly made in three short verses (v. 20 for the ram, v. 21 for the he-goat, v. 23 for the horns) in the second part of the chapter is as a matter of fact a *pešer*-like application of the distressing things beheld before by the visionary and the angels. It establishes a *connection* between the transcendent, cosmic pattern and a specific historical situation, much like the actualizing *pešarim* on prophetic texts. In fact, the second half of the Book of Daniel is very similar to the vocabulary and style of ancient Jewish commentaries. But it is not the same thing which is said in different words, as becomes clear from the next chapter which will point out that the "commentary" part in Daniel 8 introduces a number of elements which are not part of the vision. So the vision itself does not depend on some justifiable "decipherment" of the symbolism.[201] On the contrary, it represents an objective form of reality, that is, the world seen with angels' eyes.

This is also true for other visions found in the Book of Daniel, such as the one given in ch. 7. They, too, provide insights into hidden universal realities, of which contemporary history is but a visible part. The true combat takes place in the supernatural world, between the princes (i.e., the divine or demoniac champions) of the earthly kingdoms, while God-given wisdom provides a bridge between the supernatural and the historical. One may note that exclusively the detailed account of Hellenistic political history in Daniel 11 is not in itself presented by means of a visionary backdrop, but as a transparent, and indeed very worldly, historical account. It is therefore not only unnecessary to assume from the

---

[201] The tension between an image and its referent bears on questions of hermeneutics far beyond the immediate concerns of literary scholarship. It has been tackled extensively in the discussion concerning the "iconology", a specialized branch of art history. This branch was originally founded by Erwin Panofsky (Panofsky, "Zum Problem der Beschreibung und Inhaltsdeutung von Werken der bildenden Kunst," *Logos* 21 [1932]: 103-119), but its techniques have entered literary scholarship as well.

outset that the visions are historical allegory, it is even grossly mislead-
ing, since the Book of Daniel itself distinguishes sharply between the "visionary" and the "historical" genre. The author makes it clear by contextual means which genre he applies.

On the level of the particular text of Dan 8,3-12, an approach
which tries to distinguish sharply between the vision and its *pešer* can derive support from the actual literary presentation. First of all, the animal
fight is, on the surface level, "mimetic". It can be appreciated as a sequence of events with a certain logic of their own, as various literary devices indicate: 1) the strong emphasis on the idea that everything is actually being *seen* (ראה: vv. 3.4.6.7; the repeated use of this verb in a reported narration is very noteworthy) and personally experienced by the
visionary as it unfolds before his mental eye; 2) the clear separation of
background circumstances and foregrounded action given in a chronological sequence against this background; 3) the subtle shift of focus to
highlight one particular element.

The fact that the characters (ram, he-goat, horns) as well as their
actions (fight, trampling, attack on the stars) are part of a continuum of
recurrent images permits an intertextually informed re-reading of the
"mimetic" narrative as a "tradition-bound" narrative.[202] As it stands, the
scene thus allows in the first place for a "naive literal reading", that is, a
transparent account of reality, and secondly "esoteric reading",[203] namely
a reading that considers further implications of the images and actions
described by trying to locate them into their cultural setting. A third step
would then consist in the historical application of the visionary material.
Similar theoretical view has been gaining ground in biblical studies most
notably in the distinction between a "first reader" (a reader looking at a
specific biblical text for the first time), a "second reader" (a reader medi-
tating on a text with the whole Hebrew Bible in his mind) and a "Christian Bible canonical reader" (a reader who has also access to the New
Testament). This approach has been developed by Georg Braulik and
Norbert Lohfink in their still ongoing research on the Pentateuch.

---

[202] Cf. Scholes and Kellogg, *Nature of Narrative*, 1966, ch. 4, for such a distinction
between "mimetic" and "tradition-bound" narrative.

[203] According to the terminology of Kermode, *Genesis of Secrecy*, 1980, ch. 1.

2. Literary Analysis

The present state of research on the literary presentation of the vision in Daniel 8 can be stated in just a few words. Scholarly literature has hardly exploited the relation between the syntax and the interpretation of the animal fight in Dan 8,3.[204] Commentators are often too quick in subscribing to the traditional view of Daniel 8 as a rather unexciting book written in bad and uninspired Hebrew.[205] Consequently, they pay little attention to linguistic subtleties in the text. A notable exception, however, is Klaus Koch, who offers on a couple of pages an excellent, but very brief and sketchy treatment of the "macrosyntax", that is, the syntax beyond sentence-level.[206] Yet not even he really goes into the details.

[204] The first analysis of the narrative in Daniel 8 ever has been presented by Bernhard Hasslberger in 1977 (Hasslberger, *Hoffnung*, 1977), but his treatment is for various reasons extremely unsatisfactory. Perhaps the most serious drawback is that Hasslberger does not tackle questions of macrosyntax at all. His application of "Textlinguistik", on the other hand, often lacks a sound philological basis, so he does not succeed in presenting a convincing picture of the Hebrew verbal syntax in this text. In fact, he hardly goes beyond a description of individual sentences on the surface-level.

[205] Porteous, *Daniel*, 1978, 97: "Auch ist die Diktion nun nicht mehr von demselben schöpferischen Rang." Hartman and Di Lella, *Daniel*, 1978, 230, have a similar statement: "From a literary viewpoint ch. 8 is inferior to ch. 7 and shows a less vivid imagination." More sober is the appreciation voiced by Pfeiffer, *Introduction*, 1952, 772: "The style of the Hebrew part of the book, particularly chs. 8-12, is deliberately mysterious, befitting the revelation of secrets as in chs. 2; 4; 5; 7, but (aside from ch. 8) less fantastically picturesque, more prosaic and abstract."

[206] Koch, "Visionsbericht," in: *Apocalypticism*, ed. Hellholm, 1989: 420, passes a very fine judgment indeed which deserves to be quoted extensively: "[...] so wird doch, wie ich hoffe, sichtbar, wie überlegt und kunstvoll Dan 8 aufgebaut ist. Kein einziges Tempus, kein Morfem ist nachlässig gesetzt, keine Wiederholung ohne Funktion. Ginge es nicht um den düsteren Ernst apokalyptischer Geschichtsschau, möchte man sich dem Aufbau geradezu mit ästhetischem Genuß hingeben." But he, too, understands the characters in Daniel 8 symbolically and sets them apart from the "real" experiences of prophetic visions (Koch, "Visionsbericht," in: *Apocalypticism*, ed. Hellholm, 1989: 423-424), a distinction which is unnecessary. Behrens, *Visionsschilderungen*, 2002, 320-321, rightly stresses that the interpretation is given outside the vision of the ram and the he-goat itself, even though he maintains that both cannot be separated. However, he does not really go into the linguistic details.

a. Central Issues, Method and Aim of the Narrative Analysis

Some of the central issues of this chapter have already been hinted at in the textual commentary, which is intended to introduce the reader into the finer points of meaning. The presentation of the material there may have given a first idea of how much there is still to be said on the conscious and at times surprising use of linguistic subtleties in the Hebrew Daniel. Indeed, a careful re-examination of the way distinctive syntactical and literary possibilities of the Hebrew verbal system are used in this passage in order to establish a quite complex and multi-layered narrative can perhaps question the mainstream verdict in favour of a more sympathetic view of the text. The Hebrew of Daniel certainly lacks the epic flavour of Deuteronomistic history, but the author consistently and successfully distinguishes between background setting, mainline action (events which keep the story moving) and the consequences of the action, leading to a new overall *status quo*.

The fundamental distinction between what has been described by some scholars in terms of "backgrounding mechanism" and "foreground" has become common various linguistic circles[207] and is now very fashionable in the analysis of Hebrew narratives. The association of each of them with certain verbal forms (*wayyiqtol* with the foreground; *qatal*, participles, nominal sentences with the background) is mainly due to the influence of Robert E. Longacre.[208] A similar approach which also associates certain tenses strictly with grounding features has been taken from the perspective of Romance Philology by Harald Weinrich in his highly controversial theory of tenses. Weinrich's approach has met more approval, as it seems, in Semitics than in other philological disciplines.[209]

---

[207] For a general overview cf. Fleischman, *Tense*, 1990. There are several terminologies in use; some scholars prefer "figure" and "ground" instead of "foreground" and "background".

[208] Longacre, *Joseph*, 1989, 64.80-82. The application of the categories "background" and "foreground" to Old Testament texts has been anticipated, several decades before Longacre, by Erich Auerbach in his famous essay on the Sacrifice of Isaac (in: Auerbach, *Mimesis*, 1946).

[209] Weinrich, *Tempus*, 2001. The main problem with Weinrich's theory seems to be the fact that a certain *application* of "tenses" in various literary contexts in order to

Grounding will play in any case a major role in the present analysis, because it is certainly one of the most important devices through which the narrator guides the reader through the text. Since the corresponding terminology has been accepted by many scholars, it shall be adopted here as well, despite the fact that it is based on metaphors from the world of theatre which break down at some stage. Therefore it has to be borne in mind that terms like "setting" and "mainline story" may be more appropriate to the analysis of narrative. The linguistic facts, however, are there.

Although the underlying text-linguistic model has not found unanimous acceptance,[210] its basic categories and their effects on the text appear to be valid at least for Daniel 8, as will be seen, even if they are not exhaustive. The distinction between *wayyiqtol* which moves on the narrative and other forms which cannot be easily included into the chronological sequence of events is in any case very strict here. Moreover, the mainline story is also highlighted by other grammatical and pragmatic features, such as topicalization, determination, the presence and absence of the narrator etc. Thus "grounding" apparently correlates with more than just one single grammatical category. Consequently, these concepts will be taken up here, regardless whether they are universally applicable or not.

The sophisticated presentation of the vision in its self-sufficiency as a narrative[211] contains in turn valuable hints as to how it is intended to

---

distinguish between narration and description does not really say very much about the *nature* of theses "tenses" (although this is exactly what Weinrich proposes). It is rather a question of contextual functions of "tenses", beyond mere time reference.

[210] See, for example, Heimerdinger, *Topic*, 1999, esp. ch. 2. Heimerdinger remarks that a division of the plot pattern into background and foreground is problematic, although he discusses isolated sentences rather than syntactical units. Furthermore, he challenges Longacre's assumption that *wayyiqtol* always refers to the foreground, claiming that it can also be used for flashbacks, situational descriptions etc. These observations are themselves subject to further investigation. They do not bear on Daniel 8, where the only function of *wayyiqtol* is to depict a series of successive events in the past.

[211] With the term "narrative" I mean the linguistic representation of a number of events reported in chronological sequence, but including flashbacks, digressions etc. So in this context, "narrative" is similar to *histoire* in French structuralism.

be understood by the author. The outcome of the following observations will militate strongly not only against the almost "canonical" scholarly verdict on the author's lack of linguistic competence in Hebrew, but also against the "symbolic dream" hypothesis which is no less widespread in secondary literature.

In order to reach this goal, it will be attempted to evaluate the function of the various verbal forms employed in the narrative not according to a unified view of the Hebrew verbal system, like the tense / aspect opposition,[212] but in the light of their function in the specific literary context. Nevertheless, this perspective will also consider the historical facts about Hebrew, such as stages of its development.[213]

This approach is at variance with the contradicting traditional theories on the nature and function of the Hebrew verbal system, which seek to determine absolute and context-independent functions of Hebrew "tenses".[214] However, a perspective which also takes into consideration the syntax beyond sentence level – and not just the supposedly intrinsic temporal or aspectual value of an isolated verbal form – appears to explain the choice of a specific form ("tense") in an individual case much better. As soon as a wider point of view is taken, it becomes clear that

---

[212] See McFall, *Enigma*, 1982, *passim*.

[213] On the problematic nature of the concept "Late Biblical Hebrew" and the relationship between the Hebrew Daniel and other obviously late texts see the chapter on language in the introduction. I use this term only *in fugam vacui*, since the language of, say, Daniel and Qohelet can hardly be put on the same level due to the great differences in literary genre. For the extent to which such a double perspective can contribute to historical linguistics as well as to the interpretation of specific textual units one may compare Gianto, "Moods and Modality," *IOS* 18 (1998): 183-198; Gianto, "Variations," *Bib* 77 (1996): 493-508.

[214] This is also true for one of the most popular (and most sophisticated) linguistic approaches to Semitics in Germany, namely the "noetische Sachverhaltsanalyse" developed by the Slavonic scholar E. Koschmieder. Koschmieder was concerned with the relationship between universal logical categories and the particular categories of individual languages. His methods have been applied to various ancient and modern Semitic languages by Adolf Denz and his Munich school. Their theory tries to individuate, with respect to verbal syntax, "das allen Verwendungsweisen kleinste gemeinsame Vielfache" and seeks to abstract from specific literary contexts. For a brief synopsis and bibliographical remarks cf. Weninger, *Verbalsystem*, 2001. Koschmieder himself has described his own approach succinctly in *Noetische Grundlagen*, 1952.

such a choice is motivated by various criteria, including literary devices, such as "grounding" (in the sense just outlined), change of perspective, topicalization, but also structural marking. In any case, one has to bear in mind that ancient written records have very few graphic means, such as punctuation marks, to indicate their logical structure.[215] Consequently, the grammar was of utmost importance.

Since the literary genre (and the linguistic coding for that matter) moves back and forth several times between narrative, commentary, and prophecy, Daniel 8 perhaps provides a model example for any study which tries to determine the influence of the literary context on the use of verbal forms.[216] The fact that this chapter consists in a rather limited amount of data and yet expresses a lot of meanings makes it useful as an illustration of the working of various unexplored features of Hebrew syntax, their function in a literary context, and their often surprisingly subtle interpretation by the ancient versions.

h. Individuation of Textual Unit, Literary Form, Structure

The first part of Daniel's vision in ch. 8, vv. 3-12, consists of an animal fight and its consequences, roughly along the same lines as in Daniel 7. It has been demonstrated at some length in the textual commentary that the Old Greek consciously assimilates the whole episode to the preceding one through various subtle changes unknown in any other textual witness, especially the harmonization of the dating formulae in 8,1 and 7,1. This way the Septuagint draws the reader's attention to the fact that it has seen something important; it points out the similarities between both accounts much more effectively than the Hebrew text or indeed the other versions. These similarities will always have to be remem-

---

[215] Cf. Justus, "Visible Sentences," *Visible Language* XV,4 (1981): 373-408, for further ideas how word order and particles can "punctuate" a clause.

[216] The introductory remarks on the character of the Hebrew of Daniel made in the first chapter should have pointed out why it is absolutely valid to draw such conclusions from a "Late Biblical Hebrew" text. The "Late Biblical Hebrew" of the Book of Daniel exhibits certain features of its own and has certain stylistic preferences, but its verbal syntax is not essentially different from Classical prose. What matters is rather the literary genre – "Late Biblical Hebrew" is not a structurally different language in the way Modern Hebrew is.

bered here. Daniel 8 is, although being formally distinct, not completely detached from the other chapters.

After the chronological and geographical specification in vv. 1-2, the vision sets in at once with v. 3.[217] This verse describes the lifting of the visionary's eyes as the prerequisite necessary in order to perceive what is going on. It finishes with the introduction of the "angelic" discourse in vv. 13-14, which serves as a kind of bridge from the vision itself to its interpretation proper.[218] On the one hand it is still linked with what comes before, since it explicitly takes up the last event mentioned in the vision report itself, the "transgression" caused by the horn. But on the other hand the introduction of two new characters not mentioned before and the shift back to an immediate focus on the visionary himself in the foreground action (again *wayyiqtol* in the 1st pers. sg. for the first time after v. 3, where it had already served as a structuring device, providing the bridge from the frame to the mainline story) are formal means hinting at a caesura which sets these two verses apart from vv. 3-12.[219] The much stronger caesura in v. 15, which begins the interpretation of the vision by means of the epiphany of the interpreter,[220] is formally indicated by a וַיְהִי as well as וְהִנֵּה and sets vv. 13-14 apart from what follows. Thus, Dan 8,3-12 is a textual unit distinct from the preceding and the following parts of the chapter.[221]

---

[217] So, too, Collins, *Daniel*, 1993, 328.

[218] Collins, ibid., takes vv. 13-14 as part of the vision report as such and lets the interpretation begin with v. 15. This is certainly possible, but the status of vv. 13-14 remains ambiguous.

[219] Cf. Hartman and Di Lella, *Daniel*, 1978, 230: "It is clear that the dialogue between the two angels in vss. 13-14 interrupts the sequence between vss. 1-12 and vs. 15; the 'vision' that Daniel wishes to understand (vs. 15) refers to the vision described in vss. 1-12 and has nothing to do with the conversation of the two holy ones in vss. 13-14, whom he hears speaking but whom he does not see." They conclude that vv. 13-14 are an insertion made by the author of Daniel 9 (p. 231).

[220] Correctly taken as a vision of its own by Marti, *Daniel*, 1901, 60, and Plöger, *Daniel*, 1965, 128; the interpreter is a new figure.

[221] For an alternative structural analysis cf. Koch, "Visionsbericht," in: *Apocalypticism*, ed. Hellholm, 1989: 415-417, who distinguishes between "Vorspann" (vv. 1-2aα), "1. Hauptteil" (vv. 2aβ-14), "2. Hauptteil" (vv. 15-26) and "Abschluß" (vv. 26b.27).

As has already been touched upon, from the form-critical perspective, the vision narrated in vv. 3-12 is, in a wider sense, a vision report.[222] This classification is also corroborated by the continued use of the verb ראה, already present in the introductory verses 1-2, in vv. 3-4.7. Still, one may try to go beyond this obvious as well as ubiquitous assertion to which secondary literature is confined up to the present day and note that, in the stricter sense, this unit takes up several features of the "single combat" in a "battle narrative". The "single combat" is a constitutive element of many pieces of epic literature.

In traditional epic, the story often follows a firm pattern, starting from a crisis and going on to elaborate on the corresponding vocation of the hero, at times his difficulties, his confrontation with the enemy, his victory, and finally his triumph.[223] This pattern is universal in epic literature and folk-tales throughout the world, and it is widely attested in the various literary traditions of the Ancient Near East as well, including the Bible.[224] It is, in effect, a "meta pattern" which can be realized in different "modes", such as the divine realm, the mainly human world, or a fairy tale setting.[225] In the case of Daniel 8, the setting does not seem to be completely clear, but it is certainly a world illustrating the powers at work behind reality as it can be perceived sensually.

The very confrontation with the enemy, too, generally follows a certain scheme, of which here only individual elements, without the wider framework of a hero's adventures, are present in Dan 8,3-12, namely the actual combat and the victory with the triumphant gesture of the winner. A paradigmatic model battle narrative, however, would also include a verbal confrontation of the two opponents prior to the actual fight, often characterized by provocative or even insulting remarks.[226]

---

[222] The formal typology of the "vision report" ("Visionsbericht") in prophetic and apocalyptic literature has been analyzed by Koch, "Visionsbericht," in: *Apocalypticism*, ed. Hellholm, 1989: 423-427, by means of a comparison mainly of Daniel 8, Am 7,7-13 and Apc 6,7f. Cf. also Behrens, *Visionsschilderungen*, 2002, 314-345.

[223] Cf. Jason, "Precursors of Propp," *Journal of Poetics and Theory of Literature* 3 (1977): 471-516, who refers in particular to A. Skaftymov's model.

[224] See Hagan, *Battle Narrative*, 1986, *passim*; West, *East Face*, 1997, 214-217.

[225] Cf. Jason, *Ethnopoetry*, 1977, 17-26.

[226] Hagan, *Battle Narrative*, 1986, 58.

Nonetheless, the "single combat" seems to be the literary form which is closest to the character of the textual unit in question here.

The vision report in vv. 3-12 can reasonably easily be divided into three parts. These contain a depiction of the initial situation and two combat scenes: first, the ram in vv. 3-4, which serves as a background for the mainline story (as becomes apparent from the use of the verbal forms), then, in vv. 5-7, the fight between the ram and the he-goat. The latter section can be distinguished from the preceding one due to the introduction of a new participant and the change of the predominant verbal form to *wayyiqtol*, not featuring before. The third part consists of vv. 8-12 and describes the consequences of the he-goat's victory; it is marked by the disappearance of one of the protagonists, the vanquished ram, and the appearance of several new ones, namely the horns of the he-goat. The horns take over the action, while the he-goat itself disappears to the background. Each unit finishes with a kind of summary, an overall evaluation of the situation.

These three units have in various respects a clear climactic structure. First of all, they steadily grow longer, as the first one contains two verses, the second one three and the final one five verses. Moreover, they become more detailed, because there is a notable increase of finite verbal forms describing the action going on. Lastly, they also become more dramatic, since they depict some continuous aggression in the first one, a proper animal fight in the second one, and in the final part the growing of several goat's horns, one of them throwing down even the stars of heaven. Due to their climactic character, the structure of these sections mirrors the rise of tension which the situation exhibits as it develops, finally leading up to the profanation of the sanctuary as the ultimate sacrilege. The battle narrative is therefore not a broad, continuously flowing epic account, like the Homeric poems or, if one may say so, the historical books of the Bible. It is rather a drama which unfolds rapidly in three brief acts and suddenly stops at its peak. Its outcome, however, can be derived by analogy from the end of Daniel 2 and Daniel 7: The message it seems to convey is that worldly powers are like chaff. This idea has already been analyzed in the section on the "theology of power" in the Book of Daniel.

The smooth succession of thoughts indicates that the final redaction of this chapter has abolished eventual egregious irregularities which would point to the identification of several redactional layers. It has been suggested that the motif of the "little horn" in Daniel 8 is a later addition,[227] but it will appear from the subsequent analysis that the textual evidence which provides the strongest arguments for this view (especially the change of gender in vv. 9-12 and the lack of exact agreement between vv. 8,9-10 and vv. 23-25) can also, and perhaps better, be explained by means of internal criteria. It is clear by now that similar phenomena of grammar, such as the well-known *Numeruswechsel* in Deuteronomy,[228] are stylistic features widely attested in many Ancient Near Eastern literary texts and cannot be used as evidence for distinguishing redactional layers. So it may in the end be possible that the "little horn" is a secondary addition, but it has been inserted rather neatly into the final text. In general, redactional criticism is seriously at a loss in Daniel 8 and appears to contribute very little to the explanation of this text.

c. The Background: A Charging Ram (vv. 3-4)

The verse linking the chronological and geographical frame to the vision itself, v. 3, and the following verse are dominated by the description of a ram. The description itself is twofold and consists of the outer appearance and the behaviour of the animal. The use of the verb ראה employed in each of these verses (*wayyiqtol* in v. 3 and *qatal* in v. 4) continues at first the very strong emphasis on *visual perception* already introduced in vv. 1-2, where the root ראה occurs as often as five times, stressing the conscious experience of the beholder. Also the only seemingly redundant וָאֶשָּׂא עֵינַי וָאֶרְאֶה suggests that the narrator is an eyewitness and invites the reader: "Look!" This wording makes it clear that what is being described is not presented as an allegory, a world only existing in imagination, but as an event which is depicted as taking place in the real world:[229]

---

[227] This is a reasonably old thesis recently advanced again by Kratz, "Visionen," in: *Schriftauslegung*, eds. Kratz, Krüger and Schmid, 2000: 219-236, esp. 226-230 (this view has already been prominent in past redactional criticism on the Book of Daniel).

[228] Related features occur, for example, in Jeremiah and, especially, in Isaiah.

[229] In this light, the comment by Porteous, *Daniel*, 1978, 98, is all the more strange, for he remarks that because of the, in comparison with ch. 7, "künstlich anmutende

וָאֶשָּׂא עֵינַי וָאֶרְאֶה וְהִנֵּה אַיִל אֶחָד ‹גָּדוֹל› עֹמֵד לִפְנֵי הָאֻבָל
וְלוֹ קְרָנָיִם וְהַקְּרָנַיִם גְּבֹהוֹת וְהָאַחַת גְּבֹהָה מִן־הַשֵּׁנִית
וְהַגְּבֹהָה עֹלָה בָּאַחֲרֹנָה:
רָאִיתִי אֶת־הָאַיִל מְנַגֵּחַ ‹מִזְרָחָה› יָמָּה וְצָפוֹנָה וָנֶגְבָּה
וְכָל־חַיּוֹת לֹא־יַעַמְדוּ לְפָנָיו וְאֵין מַצִּיל מִיָּדוֹ
וְעָשָׂה כִרְצֹנוֹ וְהִגְדִּיל:

*Then I looked up and saw a <great> ram standing in front of the
river. It had two Horns.*[230] *Both Horns were high, but one was
higher than the other, and the high one came up last.*
*I was seeing the ram charging <eastward,> westward, northward
and southward. No beast could withstand it, and there was no
one to rescue from its power. Thus, it did as it pleased and became great.*

Once the setting has been supplied, the visionary lifted up his
eyes (*wayyiqtol*: וָאֶשָּׂא עֵינַי) and, as an immediate consequence, "saw"
(*wayyiqtol*: וָאֶרְאֶה).[231] These verbal forms also clearly determine the
genre of what follows, namely a narrative of past events against the very
general background depicted in vv. 1-2. In fact, they confirm the reader's
expectations. It is now evident that the subsequent descriptions will all
refer to the past and take place in chronological order.

All the participles, nominal sentences and *qatal* forms which
dominate the rest of vv. 3f would be ambiguous regarding their temporal
reference without this contextual information, while the two *wayyiqtols*
introducing this scene can only refer to a narrative with explicit past

Symbolik" in ch. 8 one could suppose that "hinter dem letzteren eben keine solche
ekstatische Erfahrung steht, wie wir sie hinter dem ersteren wohl zu Recht suchen
dürfen."

[230] I have capitalized "Horns" in the translation in order to point out that this important keyword is visually highlighted in various ways in the Hebrew text as well (see
the narrative analysis for a full discussion).

[231] Cf. Gen 18,2: וַיִּשָּׂא עֵינָיו וַיַּרְא וְהִנֵּה שְׁלֹשָׁה אֲנָשִׁים נִצָּבִים עָלָיו.

tense meaning. Thus they determine the tense value of the ambiguous forms.

Moreover, the use of the 1st pers. *wayyiqtol* indicates that the visionary actively and consciously participates in the foreground action. Initially, the reader's attention is on him, as he is placed right within the dream landscape somehow associated with Susa in Elam and starts looking around. This is significant for the theological message, since the text is, despite its various claims to objectivity, not a purely descriptive account, but maintains a strong personal dimension.

The beginning of the vision in the strict sense, וְהִנֵּה, introduces something evident, a scene which evolves before the reader's eyes.[232] With a participial clause after a verb of perception (so, too, in vv. 4.5.7, of which v. 5 also has a וְהִנֵּה), it communicates *what* is actually being perceived, namely "a ram standing beside the river", and *that* it is perceived as immediately present. The use of וְהִנֵּה and the participle is a straightforward expression of the *content* of sensual perception and differs significantly from the וְהִנֵּה of "excited perception".[233] In the former case, the *waw* introduces the content of perception in the form of a הִנֵּה clause (that is, a complement clause); in the latter, וְהִנֵּה is a whole particle introducing what for most modern languages would appear as an adverbial clause.

Perhaps the Old Greek can be adduced as a witness to the polysemy of וְהִנֵּה. It is surely interesting that the וְהִנֵּה in v. 3 is not translated at all,[234] but the content of perception is given as the direct object in the accusative case, while וְהִנֵּה is translated with its usual equivalent καὶ ἰδού in v. 5. An otherwise unattested omission of וְהִנֵּה after a verb of perception does not occur elsewhere in the Septuagint, so it is hard to say whether the translators were generally aware of the distinction between

---

[232] It is a standard element of the dream report, cf. Richter, "Traum," *BZ* 7 (1963): 204.

[233] For a treatment of this particular use of the particle וְהִנֵּה see McCarthy, "*wᵉhin-nēh*," *Bib* 61 (1980): 332-333. But the וְהִנֵּה of "excited perception" functions like the presentative particle הִנֵּה (without the *waw*); its main function is the introduction of a new topic or subject-matter.

[234] There is no evidence for a Hebrew *Vorlage* without the וְהִנֵּה or a Septuagint text which, like Theodotion, has καὶ ἰδού in v. 3.

the "contents of sensual perception" and the "surprise" particle. However, it has to be borne in mind that the translator responsible for the Old Greek of Daniel 8 seems to have had a more thorough understanding of Hebrew syntax than most of his colleagues.

Here וְהִנֵּה has a particular literary effect, since it presents Daniel's personal experience as a visionary to the reader as if it were real and recurs in vv. 5 and 15. Interestingly, the particle וְהִנֵּה is missing in the "surreal" description of how the "little horn" attacks the stars (vv. 9ff). It seems that the visionary himself turns down his self-understanding as an eye-witness a bit as the story develops and as he makes progress in gaining understanding, while he is still a "naive" observer of the facts in vv. 3-5.

The main action, in turn, will not begin until v. 5. Hence, what comes after the וְהִנֵּה is a modification and amplification of the general background description of vv. 1-2. It also implies a shift in the point of view taken, as the narrator now disappears to the background. Such a shift is the normal, and indeed natural, function of the "presentative" particle וְהִנֵּה,[235] but it can cooccur with the וְהִנֵּה introducing the content of perception as well.[236] This seems to be the case here, for the main protagonist of vv. 3f, אַיִל אֶחָד, "a ram",[237] is introduced immediately after the presentative or focus particle וְהִנֵּה, it is the content of the visionary's first impression upon lifting his eyes. It did not enter the scene, but was simply there.

The numeral אֶחָד is used as an explicit marker of indetermination,[238] almost as in Syriac, where it frequently has the function of an in-

---

[235] For וְהִנֵּה as a main stylistic indicator of a shift in focalization cf. Ska, *"Our Fathers"*, 1990, 68 (with ample bibliography); Ska apparently in this context means the presentative וְהִנֵּה, but he makes no distinction between the two types.

[236] Another example is 1 Kgs 10,6-7.

[237] This juncture is common, cf. the numerous instances in Num 7,15ff. A close parallel is Gen 22,13 (the Sacrifice of Isaac): וַיִּשָּׂא אַבְרָהָם אֶת־עֵינָיו וַיַּרְא וְהִנֵּה־אַיִל אֶחָד (the MT reads אַחַר, but in the light of the expression and the Septuagint reading καὶ ἰδοὺ κριὸς εἷς, it is fairly clear that the text should be corrected to אֶחָד).

[238] Contrary to Marti, *Daniel*, 1901, 56, who thinks the meaning is "in der Gestalt eines *einzelnen* Widders" (basing himself on König, *Syntax*, 1897, §291d).

definite article.[239] The contrast with the attacking he-goat, which is rendered determinate through the definite article (see below), may already be foreshadowed here, hence the explicit use of אֶחָד, while אַיִל on its own would have sufficed.[240]

Moreover, the description of the ram is supplemented by an elaborate description of its long horns (וְלוֹ קְרָנַיִם וְהַקְּרָנַיִם גְּבֹהוֹת),[241] among which one is longer than the other (וְהָאַחַת גְּבֹהָה מִן־הַשֵּׁנִית). The longer horn came up after the other one (וְהַגְּבֹהָה עֹלָה בָּאַחֲרֹנָה). The Masoretic vocalization קְרָנַיִם is a (later?) byform of the dual formed presumably on the analogy of the plural of the segholate noun with its typical stress pattern.[242] This form is rare, especially with קֶרֶן, which generally prefers the dual formed from the monosyllabic singular,[243] and therefore more striking. It is hard to assess the particular nuance conveyed by the use of the much less regular form, but it cannot be ruled out that it has been applied intentionally. Such an interpretation is in particular supported by the observation that the whole point of this elaborate description consists in illuminating the horns of the ram,[244] just as its horn will be pointed out as a distinctive feature in the presentation of the he-goat. From vv. 8ff it becomes obvious that horns play a crucial role in the third part of this textual unit.

Furthermore, it can hardly be doubted that an unusual or even ungrammatical pointing does at times highlight a certain keyword in the MT and needs to be treated with more attention.[245] In this very place, the reader will also remember the sinister horn at the end of the vision in

---

[239] One may compare the appearance of the indefinite article in the Romance languages, which also derives from the numeral *unus*.

[240] See JM §137u.

[241] Cf. the textual note above.

[242] Cf. JM §91b.

[243] Cf. GK §93o; Meyer, *Grammatik*, 1992, §52.1c.

[244] Cf. Koch, "Visionsbericht," in: *Apocalypticism*, ed. Hellholm, 1989: 432: "Begonnen wird mit einem Widder V. 3, wobei die Aufmerksamkeit sich auf seine Hörner richtet."

[245] Scholars hardly pay any attention at all to the functional character of non-standard vocalizations as a kind of commentary, but see Gzella, *Lebenszeit*, 2002, 61, for some very revealing examples.

Daniel 7, which does not only exhibit a similar pattern, but is explicitly connected with Daniel 8 through the visionary introduction. There this connection is even more apparent in the Old Greek translation due to a subtle harmonization of the dating formula, as has been pointed out above.

This belongs all to the description of a situation, and before the arrival of the second protagonist, there will be no more foreground action. The ram is standing and acts from its firm position, as the visionary observes (רָאִיתִי). The verb possibly suggests mere visual perception of what is going on, with participles giving the content of the perception. The idea may be that this perception at first takes place without further reflection. Interestingly, the verb is replaced by בִּין in v. 5, see below. The use of this particular verb may also give a clue why the visionary does not yet see anything special in the ram which is qualified by the word אֶחָד here. But the switch from the 1st pers. *wayyiqtol* in v. 3 to the 1st pers. plain *qatal*, without a connecting conjunction, at the beginning of v. 4 is noteworthy. It seems to indicate that the visionary has now moved to the background (*qatal* is often used for backgrounding),[246] from which he will appear again in vv. 6 and 7 (both times by means of a 1st pers. *qatal*). He is not presented as the principal agent anymore, but as an observer in the state of expectation whose attention is fixed on the general situation. Step by step the reader's attention is directed towards what is going on. The *qatal* may here have its full stative force,[247] while the tense value had already been clarified by the *wayyiqtol* forms. So it does not indicate a subsequent action, rather it presents an event that takes place simultaneously with the rest.

The syntactical difficulty in v. 4 has not escaped the ancient translators. As already indicated in the textual commentary above, the Old Greek gives a markedly different interpretation of this passage. The clue to its understanding of vv. 3 and 4 is the rendering μετὰ δὲ ταῦτα for the MT's בָּאַחֲרֹנָה in v. 3 and the connection of this phrase with what follows rather than with the preceding וְהַגְּבֹהָה עֹלָה. So the translator avoids the

---

[246] See Hatav, *Semantics*, 1997, 186-187. Cf. Dan 1,1; 2,1; 8,1ff; Est 4,1; 6,1; 8,1; Ezr 10, 1 for post-exilic narrative texts in which a background is depicted against which the main action evolves.

[247] Eskhult, *Verbal Aspect*, 1990, 110. *Qatal* has of course originated as a stative.

asyndetic beginning of v. 4 and links both verses with the connecting particle δέ, thus introducing a new section. He may have seen that the asyndeton in the Hebrew of v. 4 is exceptional, since all the other clauses in
vv. 3-12 are connected among themselves, and fell back on an interpretative technique common to other books of the Septuagint as well in order
to resolve this difficulty.[248] He may have been guided in his choice by the
observation that v. 4 effectuates a change from the outer appearance of
the ram towards its behaviour, so there is in fact something new beginning with v. 4, formally indicated by the repeated use of the verb "to see"
which had already introduced the description in v. 3.

The effect of the rendering in the Old Greek is that vv. 3 and 4
are now a narrative sequence of their own which is constituted by successive events, that is, the visionary's observation of the charging of the
ram follows chronologically on the growing of the animal's horns.[249]
Consequently, the translator of the Old Greek has rendered the surprisingly durative רָאִיתִי (here expressing an ongoing state) with an aorist
(εἶδον, that is, a single past event), whereas in v. 3 the same translator
uses the imperfect ἀνέβαινε for the participle עֹלֶה with a stative sense.

While the growing of the horn and the visionary's observation are
contemporaneous and part of the overall setting in the Hebrew, the Old
Greek ends up with a continuous narrative sequence from v. 2 onwards
throughout the whole of Daniel 8. So vv. 3 and 4, too, are part of the
mainline story which in the Hebrew only begins with v. 6. This results in
a less marked contrast between the ram and the he-goat in favour of a
more straightforward development of the narrative. The linear sequence
in the Greek even overrides the Hebrew "anterior constructions" found
in v. 8 (see below) by translating the corresponding *qatal* forms with aorists and thus presents a plain series of successive events without the oc-
casional "flashbacks" of the Hebrew original.

The solution of the Old Greek is all the more striking, because its

---

[248] Especially the Septuagint Psalter has a strong tendency to solve problems of text
and interpretation or to introduce its own ideas by means of *enjambement*, cf. Gzella,
Lebenszeit, 2002, 44.174.287-288.309.313 for a discussion of various examples.

[249] Contrary to Jeansonne, *Old Greek*, 1988, 81, who does not see this subtlety and
dismisses the evidence by stating "that the OG [= Old Greek, H.G.] has not introduced any new levels of meaning to the text by the misplacing of this phrase."

translator exhibits a clear understanding of the difference between durative and punctual, at times combined with a differentiation between
background and mainline story. Such a differentiation is already implicit
in the switch from the imperfect in ἀνέβαινε v. 3 to the aorist εἶδον in v.
4. One may additionally compare the contrast between the imperfect
forms διενοούμην and οὐχ ἥπτετο τῆς γῆς (for a periphrastic tense and a
participle) in v. 5 and the sequence of aorists in vv. 6 and 7, the prase καὶ
ἐποίει ὡς ἤθελε for the *weqatal* plus infinitive וְעָשָׂה כִרְצֹנוֹ in v. 4 and the
imperfect ἤρχετο for בָּא in v. 5, presumably understood as a *qatal* form
(and not as a participle) by the translator. The latter examples show that
by no means every *qatal* form has been translated with an aorist in the
Greek.[250]

The outcome has thus not been determined by the mechanical application of a certain translation technique, but betrays a particular, reflected understanding of the syntax of the Hebrew text. The asyndeton in
v. 4 must therefore have appeared anomalous to the attentive translator.
He tried to resolve the resulting syntactical difficulty in the light of his
overall understanding of the syntax of Daniel 8. The Old Greek, although
it does not correspond to the Hebrew, does not betray carelessness, but a
certain feeling for syntactical subtleties.

In any case, the Old Greek correctly understands the shift from a
description of the ram's outer appearance to its intentions. More precisely, the situation is that the ram is now charging into the four (if one
corrects the MT) principal directions east, west, north, south (8,4); nothing can withstand it, it does whatever it wants and grows great. The
rather "static" character of the ram,[251] which keeps on charging into different directions, but appears to remain on its own position, is vividly
represented by the use of participles (אַיִל אֶחָד עֹמֵד and – said of the horn
– וְהִגְבִּהָה עָלָה in v. 3 and הָאַיִל מְנַגֵּחַ in v. 4), nominal sentences (v. 3b

---

[250] This would indeed be the usual procedure, cf. Barr, "Handling of Verb Tense," in
VI Congress, ed. Cox, 1987: 388. Barr has sharply pointed out a crucial question
which most other scholars have overlooked, but he attributes deviations from the
translators' standard choices of Greek tenses to *ad hoc* decisions without further reflection; for a critique of his views cf. Gzella, *Lebenszeit*, 2002, 126ff (with examples
for theologically motivated non-standard translations of Hebrew verbal forms).

[251] Emphasized by Hasslberger, *Hoffnung*, 1977, 73.

and וְאֵין מַצִּיל מִיָּדוֹ in v. 4b) and two *wᵉqatal* forms (וְעָשָׂה כִרְצֹנוֹ וְהִגְדִּיל) at the end of v. 4). They, too, may still convey the essentially stative character of *qatal*, though here they depict above all a consequence (see below).

Hence the process is presented matter-of-factly before the eye of the beholder.[252] The end of this process is still unknown, but certainly its progress is not presented as evolving in a linear fashion. Everything the ram does is given as a general condition of the situation as it is. Particularly the rendering of the "charging" by means of the participle מְנַגֵּחַ puts it on the same level as the "standing" of the ram (עֹמֵד) and delineates it as some sort of background which does not move on the story.

This specific setting also determines the meaning of the finite verbal forms. The *yiqtol* form in וְכָל־חַיּוֹת לֹא־יַעַמְדוּ לְפָנָיו (v. 4) is in the *narrative prose* context in which it is employed clearly and principally *modal*, meaning "they *could* not stand".[253] Its temporal value is obvious due to the whole setting in the past, while its imperfective aspect and its durative *Aktionsart* are clear from the participles surrounding it. So the modal meaning is dominant.[254] When the linguistic coding switches to *prophecy* in vv. 20ff, it will be seen that the *yiqtol* forms there have a non-modal future time meaning. In this case the temporal value becomes preeminent. Hence the principal value of a *yiqtol* form is determined by the literary genre of the text, but against the background of a set of respective linguistic conventions the meaning of this verbal form can be determined with precision.[255]

The marked contrast with the verbal forms used in the description of the behaviour of the he-goat, such as the chains of *wayyiqtol* completely absent in the portrayal of the ram, makes it clear that the partici-

---

[252] Cf. Koch, "Visionsbericht," in: *Apocalypticism*, ed. Hellholm, 1989: 418, who calls this a "verweilender Zustand" and a "Dauergeschehen".

[253] Following Collins, *Daniel*, 1993, 325. For the modal meaning of *yiqtol* in narrative texts see Gianto, "Moods and Modality," *IOS* 18 (1998): 187-191.

[254] For the interaction of tense, aspect and modality cf. Gzella, "Verbformen," in *Beiträge*, ed. Lehmann, 2003 (forthcoming).

[255] In archaic (or archaizing) poetry, such as Exodus 15, *yiqtol* is primarily temporal and indicates past tense. Within *dialogues*, its function may be different again, but this phenomenon has not yet been studied in detail.

ples in vv. 3f do *not* function as substitutes for finite verbs, as they on principle can do in "Late Biblical" (cf. Est 3,2)[256] and Mishnaic Hebrew,[257] perhaps under the influence of Aramaic.[258] Instead, they keep their traditional function in Classical Hebrew *narrative* with reference to a past state of affairs, namely circumstances of a principal event or, which is the case here, the description of repeated or continuous actions in the background.[259] It has to be borne in mind, however, that things are different for *dialogues*. It is exactly this contrast which indicates that the author of Daniel 8 makes use of the actual difference between participles and *wayyiqtol* forms in narrative without treating them as two different verbal registers for practically the same thing, as does the author of Prov 31,10-31: the sections in vv. 12-18 and 19-27 are both narrative,[260] but the former employs predominantly *wayyiqtol* forms, the latter participles. The difference there is likely due to structural marking rather than anything else, for while the theme changes at v. 19, the overall pattern remains the same.

Like the other two sections of the vision, this scene finishes with two *wᵉqatal* forms (וְעָשָׂה כִּרְצֹנוֹ וְהִגְדִּיל) which seem to sum up the content of the two preceding verses: the ram's victorious aggression into all directions leads to its complete mastery of the situation. It can do whatever it wants and "be great". The wording עָשָׂה כִּרְצֹנוֹ may even evoke the idea of brutal force.[261] This is, from the narrator's point of view, the strict logical consequence of the elimination of its enemies. Not featured

---

[256] Cf. Eskhult, *Verbal Aspect*, 1990, 113.

[257] See Segal, *Grammar*, 1958, §§322ff, and Gordon, "Participle," *Afroasiatic Linguistics* 8 (1982): 121-179 (he does not distinguish between prose and poetry, however).

[258] Cf. Rosenthal, *Grammar*, 1995, §177. But it is not absolutely necessary to assume an Aramaic influence here; there may well be a different reason for this usage of participles in later stages of Hebrew.

[259] See 1 Kgs 10,1 (the principal event is the Queen of Saba's coming to Salomon, but the background to this action is her continuous hearing of the king's fame); Waltke and O'Connor, *Syntax*, 1990, §37.6d.

[260] The narrative character of the second half is clear from the fact that the theme remains the same and that *wayyiqtol* forms are used inbetween with no apparent difference (for example in v. 25).

[261] Cf. Gen 49,6; Est 9,5.

elsewhere, the $w^e qatal$ appears to be reserved for a narrator's comment on the factual outcome of each section, a summary of the new *status quo*. This corresponds to the principal function of $w^e qatal$ in narrative, namely to express an event as consecutive to what comes before.[262] Precisely this is the function of the *waw*, which complementarily relates $w^e qatal$ to *wayyiqtol*,[263] though the former points more strongly to the future. It is the logical relation which is predominant, and the temporal and aspectual relations derive from it.[264] Here the use of $w^e qatal$ does not, however, express merely a successive *event*, but a resulting and, for the time being, ongoing general condition. One may note that the frequentative character can at times be the principal meaning of $w^e qatal$ in a narrative context, cf. 1 Sam 16,23; 2 Chr 24,11.[265] This condition, in turn, provides the background for a new stage in the development of the mainline story.

Following a series of *wayyiqtol* forms, $w^e qatal$ also marks the interruption of a chronological sequence, expressing "non-progress" ("*Stillstand*").[266] This is exactly how $w^e qatal$ is employed here – its value is largely determined by the surrounding verbal forms and the literary genre, namely a third-person narrative of past events, to which it stands

---

[262] See GK §112.1. Lipiński, *Semitic Languages*, 2001, §54.8, distinguishes in the use of $w^e qatal$ between expressing a desirable or expected situation (analogous to the optative use of the perfect in Classical Arabic; for instances of modal *qatal* forms in Hebrew cf. Gzella, "Verbformen," in *Beiträge*, ed. Lehmann, 2003 [forthcoming]) and merely ascertaining a fact. He does not put as much emphasis on the consecutive character of this usage as other grammarians do. But in any case the use of $w^e qatal$ in Dan 8,3-12 is clearly non-modal.

[263] Goldfajn, *Word Order*, 1998, 128.

[264] Many examples for the telic or consequental use of this form (cf. Gen 3,5; 6,14; 7,4; 24,4) are presented and discussed by Zevit, *Anterior Construction*, 1998, 59-61.

[265] Cf. Niccacci, *Sintassi*, 1986, §35.

[266] Cf. Bombeck, "w-Perf. für Gegenwart und Vergangenheit," in *Sachverhalt und Zeitbezug*, eds. Bartelmus and Nebes, 2001, 21-34. Such an interruption of the mainline story by means of one of the *qatal* forms is also attested for other adjacent dialects (cf. the Mesha inscription, ll. 7.10.18). In several other languages, such a "non-progress" would be marked with an adverb ("... where he *eventually* died", "... e *finalmente* morì"), while German can get close to a grammaticalization of this feature by a switch from the past tense to the perfect ("er *zog* sich auf das Land zurück, *lebte* dort noch einige Zeit, dann *ist* er *gestorben*").

in opposition. It is the exact counterpart of the plain *qatal* form initiating a narrative sequence. For this reason, *wᵉqatal* is in such circumstances obviously an important structural marker, because it reinforces the idea that the reader has in fact reached the closure of a series of events.

It is arguable that there is some "subjective" nuance in that *wᵉ-qatal* occurring in a narrative framework could theoretically be seen as highlighting a climactic or at least pivotal situation,[267] as Longacre has suggested. This forms indeed occurs at the very end of the climax of the series of actions in v. 12.[268] However, in general his examples refer to an *isolated* instance of *wᵉqatal* where normally a *wayyiqtol* would be expected,[269] while several instances of *wᵉqatal* in Dan 8,3-12 are clearly not climactic, but belong to the third level of narration, namely its evaluation. The specific use of *wᵉqatal* in Daniel 8 is thus in any case highly distinctive. Other formal means, such as the introduction of a new participant in v. 5, corroborate the view that, from a wider contextual point of view, *wᵉqatal* is also at least a structuring device which marks the end of a subsection. But it does not neccesarily mark the peak of a section.

d. The Foreground Action: The Attack of the Goat (vv. 5-7)

The purely visual perception leads the visionary to a reflection (v. 5), for as time passes the narrator appears to begin to think about the scene he witnesses, he becomes conscious. The use of the participles in the description of the ram's actions indicate something that is still in progress:

וַאֲנִי הָיִיתִי מֵבִין
וְהִנֵּה צְפִיר־הָעִזִּים בָּא מִן־הַמַּעֲרָב עַל ־פְּנֵי כָל־הָאָרֶץ
וְאֵין נוֹגֵעַ בָּאָרֶץ וְהַצָּפִיר קֶרֶן חָזוּת בֵּין עֵינָיו:

---

[267] Cf. the use of the Akkadian perfect in Old Babylonian letters as a device to mark the crucial point of the letter: Huehnergard, *Grammar*, 1997, 157-158. Although the Akkadian perfect is not genetically related to the West Semitic *qatal*, this could be a structural analogy for a similar application of a particular verbal form for emphasis according to certain literary conventions.

[268] Longacre, "Weqatal Forms," in *Biblical Hebrew*, ed. Bergen, 1994: 66-91.

[269] Cf. Judg 3,20-23.

וַיָּבֹא עַד־הָאַיִל בַּעַל הַקְּרָנַיִם אֲשֶׁר רָאִיתִי עֹמֵד לִפְנֵי הָאֻבָל
וַיָּרָץ אֵלָיו בַּחֲמַת כֹּחוֹ:
וּרְאִיתִיו מַגִּיעַ אֵצֶל הָאַיִל
וַיִּתְמַרְמַר אֵלָיו וַיַּךְ אֶת־הָאַיִל וַיְשַׁבֵּר אֶת־שְׁתֵּי קְרָנָיו
וְלֹא־הָיָה כֹחַ בָּאַיִל לַעֲמֹד לְפָנָיו
וַיַּשְׁלִיכֵהוּ אַרְצָה וַיִּרְמְסֵהוּ

And I was reflecting – yes, it is the he-goat! It came from the west upon the face of all the earth without touching the ground. As for the he-goat, there was a conspicuous horn between its eyes.
Then it came toward the ram, the one with the two Horns that I had seen standing in front of the river, and ran at it with burning anger.
And I was seeing it approaching the ram: it was enraged against it, hit the ram and broke its two Horns, so that there was no strength in the ram to withstand it. Then it threw it down to the ground and trampled upon it. There was no one to rescue the ram from its power.

Since it functions as an introduction to the whole subsequent section, the expression וַאֲנִי הָיִיתִי מֵבִין is presumably not a periphrastic construction with narrative meaning introducing a subsequent event as in Aramaic and, maybe under the influence of Aramaic, also at times in later Biblical Hebrew.[270] Instead, as can be seen in the shift of the key verb from seeing to reflecting, it expresses the *change* that takes place at a particular *moment*. The sense is rather "and *at just that time I became*

---

[270] Cf. Waltke and O'Connor, *Syntax*, 1990, §37.7.1c. Rendsburg, *Northern Origin*, 1990, 26, attributes the periphrastic perfects in Daniel to Aramaic influence. The Aramaic periphrastic perfect, however, is not strictly analogous, since the instances of היה plus participle in Daniel 8 are presumably *not* used as narrative tenses (this is exclusively the function of *wayyiqtol*, which the author of Daniel 8 distinguishes from all other verbal forms; in the light of such a consistency, the presence of a second narrative tense appears improbable).

someone who was reflecting", that is, "I began to reflect".[271] The *Aktion-sart* is thus ingressive, as the strange situation motivates the visionary to start to reflect on it. On the structural level, the use of this form creates a caesura.[272] Semantically, the Hiphil of בִּין expresses the idea of reflection and meditation; the participle, in turn, suggests that the author wants to illuminate the beginning of a whole *process* of thinking about this miraculous scene. This is similar to the change from חזה (visual perception) to שׂכל, itself another wisdom term, in Dan 7,8. There, too, the change of the verb marks a shift from passive beholding to active meditation. The reader may infer that the events beheld do not only have an aesthetic dimension, they also have a particular significance.

Then another instance of the focus particle וְהִנֵּה turns the reader's attention from the visionary's inward reflection back to the action on stage; after a verb of perception, this וְהִנֵּה functions almost like a colon, that is, a punctuation mark. The following participial clause is likely to express sensual perception again (see above), as a new actor appears who is at first introduced in the very same topicalizing manner as the ram in v. 3: וְהִנֵּה צְפִיר־הָעִזִּים.

The most uncommon double designation as צְפִיר־הָעִזִּים (literally "the goat of he-goats") is particularly striking and may indicate that there is something special about the he-goat. Since the proposal to delete הָעִזִּים, which has been made by some commentators (see the apparatus of the BHS), is purely conjectural and receives no support from the textual tradition, the expression צְפִיר־הָעִזִּים (*lectio difficilior*) is better left in the text, especially since it fits in very well with the finer nuances of the narrative.

The definite article in the MT, left out by the Old Greek as well as Theodotion (on this basis the editor of the BHS, too, proposes to delete it in the Hebrew[273]), also has a specific function in this context. It suggests that the he-goat is not completely new, although it has not been

---

[271] Waltke and O'Connor, *Syntax*, 1990, §37.7.1b, examples ##13-15. The temporal meaning would be past tense, the *Aktionsart* meaning inchoative, marking the beginning of a longer process. Cf. also Dan 10,2 (אֲנִי דָנִיֵּאל הָיִיתִי מִתְאַבֵּל).

[272] So, too, Koch, "Visionsbericht," in: *Apocalypticism*, ed. Hellholm, 1989: 417.

[273] Such an emendation is also contemplated by Montgomery, *Daniel*, 1927, 331, who labels the wording in the MT as "inexplicable", but this is not quite true, see below.

mentioned so far,[274] but already familiar to the storyteller and perhaps also his audience, maybe because of its specific demoniac connotation. Such a connotation is of crucial importance for the theological message of the passage, see below on the connotations of the imagery.[275]

In any case the presentation of a new entity as determined renders the narrative more vivid and dramatic, especially at the beginning of a new textual unit, because it immediately absorbs the reader into the action.[276] Moreover, on a rather pragmatic surface-level, the definite article also provides a marked contrast to the explicitly indeterminate rendering of the ram (אַיִל אֶחָד) in v. 3 and thus may increase the distinction between foreground and background, that is, between the general situation and significant events. This does of course not preclude the play with indetermination and determination from having a more profound meaning.

The narrator's reflection on the entire vision (בין in the Hiphil) may give rise to the idea that the he-goat becomes more distinct and its antagonism with the ram grows stronger. It is worth noticing that in Hebrew a person, though not formerly mentioned, can be determined by the article, if the circumstances in the course of narration render it particularly significant.[277] Here the visionary's attention would be such a circumstance, which would have been missing in v. 3, since there the narrator was not yet מֵבִין, but only applying sensual perception (ראה).

Thus the ram was perhaps not yet considered significant enough to be determined by the article. One may note that the ram, too, takes the definite article after v. 5, when it enters the foreground action due to its fight with the he-goat (הָאַיִל בַּעַל הַקְּרָנַיִם, v. 6)! It is thus very likely

---

[274] This has already been noted by Marti, *Daniel*, 1901, 57: "Der Artikel [...] fasst das Tier als ein schon bekanntes, obschon es erst hier auftritt."

[275] The identification made by the Peshitta ("the he-goat, Alexander, the son of Philip") is not only out-of-place (the animal fight is at first left uncommented, its relationship to actual history is only made explicit in the "commentary" which follows it), but also mistaken, since, according to the second half of Daniel 8, Alexander is the great horn (cf. 8,21 with 8,8), not the he-goat.

[276] Cf. (with respect to a different context) Weninger, *Verbalsystem*, 2001, 96 with n. 130, who also gives an example for the ample use of this feature at the beginning of a modern novel.

[277] See GK §126q-r; JM §137n; Joüon, *Ruth*, 1986, 47 (ad 2,3).

that the article reflects the original reading, for it corresponds to a distinctive feature of Hebrew grammar, but is nonetheless rare enough to drop out in the course of textual tradition, because "*a* he-goat" is in any case the *lectio facilior*.

The presence of the definite article would be an argument in favour of the idea that the storyteller deliberately presupposes certain connotations of the animal protagonists; this idea will be taken up later on. Moreover, this view goes together very well with the verb בין, which is a technical term in wisdom literature and in its context probably stresses the idea that the visionary, as presented by the storyteller, is looking for explanations in the cultural and religious heritage of his people. In this very case marking the he-goat as definite would be a subtle invitation to a "tradition-bound" re-reading of the text.

At the same time the he-goat's "dynamic" character is highlighted by the specification of its origin in the west and its rapid advance by means of hovering above the earth: בָּא מִן־הַמַּעֲרָב עַל־פְּנֵי כָל־הָאָרֶץ. Again, its coming into the scene is, like the ram, ushered by a participle, which suggests that its arrival is a process that is becoming more and more dramatic, but whose end cannot be determined at the moment. This process serves as a background to the he-goat's attacking the ram that is described in the subsequent verse by means of a chain of *wayyiqtol* forms, because a narrative cannot begin with *wayyiqtol*, but must follow a prior depiction of time, place, situation, circumstances etc. Such information is normally given without the use of *wayyiqtol*.[278]

The difference between the participle describing the he-goat's arrival and the *wayyiqtol* forms describing its attack illuminates the idea that the author wants to present the actual fight as exactly the foreground action which matters. It is only then that the he-goat enters the scene. The use of different verbal aspects is often applied for such literary distinctions.[279]

---

[278] Cf. Schüle, "Zur Bedeutung," in: *Studien zur hebräischen Grammatik*, ed. Wagner, 1997: 118. The only *wayyiqtol* form which can stand at the beginning of a narrative sequence is וַיְהִי, but this is rather a special case, since וַיְהִי on its own is semantically void (see below on v. 15 for a discussion of this phenomenon).

[279] See in general Pollak, *Verbalaspekt*, 1988, 109, who summarizes this kind of change, the so-called "Inzidenzschema", in abstract: "Ein Zustand war gegeben, oder eine Handlung im Gange, als etwas Bestimmtes eintrat."

It appears therefore justifiable to construe the form בָּא with the following clause ("it came from the west over against every land"),[280] because this is more forceful than "the he-goat came from..." and points out the momentary character of the visionary's insight. Almost like an intuition he realizes: "Yes, it is the he-goat!", then he turns to the description of the action again. The additional comment that the feet of the goat did not touch the ground (וְאֵין נוֹגֵעַ בָּאָרֶץ)[281] gives a vivid impression of its breathtakingly fast movement, just like the description of Cyrus in Isa 41,3:[282] אֹרַח בְּרַגְלָיו לֹא יָבוֹא (see below for eventual royal connotations of this idea).

The fact that the LXX renders that passage in a different fashion may be caused by the different connotations this metaphor evokes in a Hellenistic context.[283] The Greek text eliminates the idea of moving without touching the ground by taking the last word of the preceding stichos, שָׁלוֹם (where it functions as an adverbial accusative of the verb

---

[280] See the textual note above.

[281] In Classical Hebrew one would expect אֵינֶנּוּ, but אֵין can be used for merely negating a statement (Job 35,15 and Jer 38,5, for instance, are two extreme cases) and not only for indicating non-existence or absence. This former use is supposedly a development out of the latter, cf. Muraoka, *Emphatic words*, 1985, 102-111, esp. 109; see also Carmignac, "Négation," *RevQ* 8 (1972-1975): 401-411. However, this specific use of אֵין without expressing the subject, occasionally to be found in Mishnaic Hebrew, is unique in the Hebrew Bible (van der Peursen, "Negation," in *Sirach, Scrolls, and Sages*, eds. Muraoka and Elwolde, 1997: 224). The same feature reappears in Dan 8,27 (see above on the visionary frame), so a corruption of the text here due to haplography is most implausible.

[282] Marti, *Daniel*, 1901, 57. Baltzer, *Deutero-Isaiah*, 2001, 89, also mentions the idea that this description could refer to Cyrus as a rider. For a depiction of the speed of Chaldaean riders see Hab 1,6-8.

[283] For in Graeco-Roman literature and art the topos of moving slighty above the earth with the feet not touching the ground does not seem to indicate so much the mere *speed* of movement, but functions as a *divine* attribute, cf. Gzella's note on Lucian, *Philopseudes* 13, in: Ebner, Gzella, Nesselrath and Ribbat, *Lukian*, 2001, 120, n. 70 (with references). It has been pointed out successfully by Seeligmann, *Septuagint Translation*, 1948, that the Septuagint version of Isaiah generally betrays a strong influence of Hellenistic culture (which is not true for all books of the LXX), so it appears quite feasible to interpret the Greek translation as a kind of "anti-paganism".

יַעֲבוֹר, "he passes on safely"), as an adverb of manner of a nominal clause (ἐν εἰρήνῃ ἡ ὁδὸς τῶν ποδῶν αὐτοῦ) and omits לֹא יָבוֹא.

The description of the he-goat's outer appearance winds up with a comment that it, too, has "a conspicuous horn between its eyes". A topicalization by means of the *casus pendens* וְהַצָּפִיר ("and as for the he-goat ...") makes it explicit that the focus is now totally on the he-goat; it is the topic to be commented upon.[284] Grammatically, the comment takes the form of a nominal sentence, which is normal for this kind of description: קֶרֶן חָזוּת בֵּין עֵינָיו. Postponing this detail as far as the end of the verse adds imaginative force to the scene: while the he-goat was still far away, the horn would perhaps not have been visible from the outset. Moreover, it also effectuates a shift in perspective from the general depiction of the he-goat's arrival to the most salient feature of its appearance.[285] So the *casus pendens* is again a grammatical detail which points to the particular significance which horns have in this vision (see above for the unusual rendering of the ram in this respect), especially in vv. 8-12. The strong emphasis by means of a topicalizing *casus pendens* is thus strictly functional and forecasts already the theme of the subsequent section.

The description of the ram in v. 3 and the he-goat in v. 5 is therefore largely parallel, namely a construction with וְהִנֵּה after a verb of perception (ראה in v. 3, בין in v. 5) with subject-fronting for topicalization of אַיִל אֶחָד עֹמֵד (v. 3) and וְהַצָּפִיר (v. 5). But the additional information concerning the he-goat's arrival on stage, adding a dynamic moment, its unusual designation as צְפִיר־הָעִזִּים and the emphasis on the idea that all this is already a result of reflection (בין) rather than mere watching, however, suggest that there is a climax from v. 3 to v. 5. The function of this climax may be to prepare the reader for the foreground action soon to evolve, after the he-goat has almost dramatically entered the stage; it is thus pointed out clearly that the he-goat is really the more interesting participant.

---

[284] See JM §156 with further bibliography. The classic study is Gross, *Pendenskonstruktion*, 1987.

[285] This can be a regular function of a pronominal agreement construction with resumptive pronoun in an extrapositional sentence, cf. Khan, *Studies*, 1988, 82-83 (with reference to Dan 8,5).

After this introduction, there is a chain of *wayyiqtol* forms beginning with the he-goat's assault in 8,6. Expressing a longer series of past
events in strict chronological sequence[286] indicates that the he-goat really
is now in any case the main agent, once the background (the ram charging, then the he-goat appearing from a distance) has been depicted by
means of participles and nominal sentences in the preceding section. The
contrast between static background and dynamic action is reinforced
again in v. 6 itself by the juxtaposition of the *wayyiqtol* describing the he-
goat approaching the ram, now presented as determinate by a definite article (וַיָּבֹא עַד־הָאַיִל בַּעַל הַקְּרָנָיִם), and the participle depicting the ram still
standing in the background (אֲשֶׁר רָאִיתִי עֹמֵד לִפְנֵי הָאֻבָל, cf. v. 3).

The actual fight is thus expressed by one *wayyiqtol* following the
other, which illuminates primarily the swiftness of the he-goat's attack
(this was already indicated in v. 5). It runs towards the ram (וַיָּרָץ at the
end of v. 6; the rare and unexpected use of the preposition אֵצֶל after a
verb of movement, too, may highlight dramatically close proximity[287]),
strikes, breaks and conquers it (וַיַּשְׁלִיכֵהוּ – וַיִּשַׁבֵּר – וַיַּךְ – וַיִּתְמַרְמַר –
וַיִּרְמְסֵהוּ, all v. 7), without any further rhetorical elaboration. As a sign of
triumph, the he-goat finally tramples on its opponent, which may evoke
the utter havoc caused by the fourth beast in Dan 7,7. One gets the impression that each strike hits its mark, all in rapid succession, very much
like Caesar's *veni, vidi, vici*.[288] This impression is strengthened by the
unusually high percentage of *wayyiqtol* forms in comparison with the rest
of the text, since out of the 14 *wayyiqtol* forms in vv. 3-12, v. 7 contains
five, v. 6 two more, so half of all the *wayyiqtols* in this unit are to be
found in vv. 6 and 7.

---

[286] Waltke and O'Connor, *Syntax*, 1990, §33.2.1; Smith, *Origins and Development*,
1991, 27. The depiction of a chronological sequence of actions is more than just a
past-tense narration, cf. Comrie, *Tense*, 1985, 27-28.

[287] Behrmann, *Daniel*, 1894, 52; Bevan, *Daniel*, 1892, 131; Charles, *Daniel* 1929,
201. Normally, one would expect עד or אל, in later Hebrew ל, but cf. 8,17; 2 Chr
28,15.

[288] A rush of *wayyiqtol* forms automatically creates a fast-moving series of action
(Longacre, *Joseph*, 1989, 34-39), but (contrary to Longacre) it does not necessarily
mark the peak of a story, as pointed out by Heimerdinger, *Topic*, 1999, 73 (who refers
to 2 Sam 12,20).

The mention of an act of visual perception experienced by the visionary at the beginning of v. 7 (וּרְאִיתִיו),[289] just before the rapid chain of successive actions, gives a dramatic sense to the fight between the two animals. The beholder stands in the back, as becomes clear from the use of *qatal*. Yet he is still there – as if the fight took place in order to be witnessed. The *waw* here has a conjunctive sense ("weak *waw*", as opposed to "conversive[290] *waw*") expressing a *subsequent situation* which provides the background to the following narrative sequence.

This point deserves further comment. Since וּרְאִיתִיו is the first word in the sentence, it can hardly be a *wᵉqatal* form indicating a logical consequence. A *qatal* form with "weak *waw*" does indeed occur at times in later Hebrew, perhaps under Aramaic influence,[291] as a replacement for *wayyiqtol*.[292] But given the fact that the distinction between *wayyiqtol* and *qatal* is very sharp in the rest of this text and in the light of the similar beginning of v. 5 (where the *qatal* form describes a state of observation, *not* an event), it is sensible to postulate an essential difference between *wayyiqtol* and *waw* plus *qatal*. Such a difference may be, on the grammatical level, one of aspect and *Aktionsart* (durative *qatal* vs. punctual *wayyiqtol*), while it effectuates a distinction between background (*qatal*) and foreground (*wayyiqtol*) at the literary level.

Since plain *qatal* in the first position generally depicts the situational background, it appears thus more sensible to understand וּרְאִיתִיו as introducing a new, subsequent *situation* than as a subsequent *event*. While it would be theoretically possible that "weak *waw*" with *qatal* functions as a replacement for *wayyiqtol* here on grounds of historical

[289] The construction is parallel to v. 4: ראה in the *qatal* with direct object and an immediately following participle without וְהִנֵּה; cf. also the same formula in Dan 10,7; 12,5.

[290] The designation "conversive *waw*" is widespread and deeply rooted in traditional grammar, even though it is questionable whether this term really matches the linguistic facts. It is only used *in fugam vacui* here.

[291] A *qatal* form plus *waw* seems to function very often as a narrative tense (i.e., for depicting successive events) in Aramaic, even if it is not strictly analogous to *wayyiqtol*.

[292] As in Qoh 2,13; Ez 37,8; 41,8. See Driver, *Use of the Tenses*, 1892, §133 (esp. 162-163 with n. 3); Waltke and O'Connor, *Syntax*, 1990, §32.3. The interpretation as a "weak *waw*" is also accepted by Montgomery, *Daniel*, 1927, 332.

philology, the particular linguistic conventions of Daniel 8, which assign
a very distinct and restricted area of meanings to every verbal form, militate against such a view.

The insertion of וָרָאִיתִי at the beginning of a sentence is important for a wider interpretation of Dan 8,3-12. This particular insertion is,
together with the strong prominence of the verb "to see" in vv. 3.4.6,
another indication that the description is not intended as some kind of
encrypted historical allegory, but indeed as a *vision* actually witnessed by
the first-person narrator, a series of events evolving before his mental eye
as they are. It is a personal glance into the universal cosmic reality of the
supernatural realm, something which is for an instant *evident* to the observer.

e. The Horns of the He-Goat (vv. 8-12)

Having conquered and destroyed its antagonist, the he-goat disappears from the *wayyiqtol* level and thus from the mainline of the story.
The new unit, clearly separated by the appearance of new protagonists
(namely the horns), starts off with a fresh rendering of the background in
the light of what has happened before:

וּצְפִיר הָעִזִּים הִגְדִּיל עַד־מְאֹד
וּכְעָצְמוֹ נִשְׁבְּרָה הַקֶּרֶן הַגְּדוֹלָה
וַתַּעֲלֶנָה †אֲחֵרוֹת† [חָזוּת :MT] אַרְבַּע תַּחְתֶּיהָ
לְאַרְבַּע רוּחוֹת הַשָּׁמָיִם:
וּמִן־הָאַחַת מֵהֶם יָצָא קֶרֶן־אַחַת צְעִירָה [מִצְּעִירָה :MT]
וַתִּגְדַּל־יֶתֶר אֶל־הַנֶּגֶב וְאֶל־הַמִּזְרָח וְאֶל־הַצֶּבִי:
וַתִּגְדַּל עַד־צְבָא הַשָּׁמָיִם
וַתַּפֵּל אַרְצָה מִן־הַצָּבָא וּמִן־הַכּוֹכָבִים וַתִּרְמְסֵם:
וְעַד שַׂר־הַצָּבָא הִגְדִּיל
וּמִמֶּנּוּ הוּרַם [הֵרִים :K] הַתָּמִיד וְהֻשְׁלַךְ מְכוֹן מִקְדָּשׁוֹ:
וְצָבָא תִּנָּתֵן עַל־הַתָּמִיד בְּפָשַׁע
וְתַשְׁלֵךְ אֱמֶת אַרְצָה וְעָשְׂתָה וְהִצְלִיחָה:

Then the he-goat became very great indeed, but when it had

*reached the peak of its might, the great horn was broken, and in
its place four other ones²⁹³ came up, corresponding to the four
winds of heaven.*
*And out of one of Them had come one single, little horn and
grew exceedingly great toward the south, toward the east, and
toward the glorious (land).*
*It grew up to the host of heaven and cast down to the ground
some of the host and some of the stars and trampled upon them.*
*Even up to the prince of the host it grew, and from him the offer-
ing was taken away.²⁹⁴ Thus it overthrew the place of his sanctuary.*
*So a host had to be given over, in addition to the offering, in the
course of transgression. It threw truth down to the ground and
had success in what it was doing.*

The use of a *qatal* construction is appropriate for the introduc-
tion of a new *situation*: וּצְפִיר הָעִזִּים הִגְדִּיל עַד־מְאֹד. The Septuagint takes
this as ingressive by translating הִגְדִּיל with an aorist (καὶ ὁ τράγος τῶν
αἰγῶν κατίσχυσε). In the Greek, this verse thus constitutes a new, subsequent *event*. Such a translation corresponds to the tendency of the
Septuagint to avoid flashbacks and create one single series of successive
events (see above), but it does not match the Hebrew exactly.

The beginning of v. 8 follows the well-known pattern *waw* + X +
qatal, with "X" being the subject of the verb, that is, the pattern of the
"anterior construction".²⁹⁵ This construction is used for a past perfect²⁹⁶
and denotes something preceding. The *qatal* here has temporal value, but
it is not contemporaneous with the mainline story. From a literary point
of view, the anterior construction is often used for backgrounding.²⁹⁷
This usage is indeed much closer to the originally stative value of *qatal*
in narrative contexts than the ingressive rendering of the Septuagint.

---

²⁹³ MT: "a conspicuousness of four".

²⁹⁴ Or: "and he took the offering away" (following the Ketib).

²⁹⁵ Zevit, *Anterior Construction*, 1998, esp. 15-32 (with a slightly different terminology).

²⁹⁶ Cf. Gen 2,25-3,1; 6,7f; 7,18f; 13,12-14.

²⁹⁷ Zevit, *Anterior Construction*, 1998, 33-37.

Hence the first part of v. 8 most probably means: "And the he-goat *had grown* very great." This results from the defeat of its enemy, just like the growing of the ram at the end of v. 4 (depicted as a result by means of *wᵉqatal*), and furnishes the starting-point for what follows. The outcome of the he-goat's victory is almost identical to the initial situation where the ram could exercise its uninhibited superiority. This analogy is stressed by the use of the same lexeme and similar basic forms, namely of *qatal* and *wᵉqatal*.

The same is true for the next clause which again corresponds to the pattern *waw* + X + *qatal* (וּכְעָצְמוֹ נִשְׁבְּרָה הַקֶּרֶן הַגְּדוֹלָה), where "X" is an infinitive construct with temporal force. Although the subject of the *qatal* form follows the verb and so does not match the standard pattern, according to which the subject stands between the *waw* and the verb, this may again be a form of the anterior construction. It is just the case that the place of the subject has been taken by a specification of time through an infinitive with preposition: "and the great horn had (already) been broken". No reason is given as to why this happened, and yet the resulting situation serves as the background for a new chain of foreground events.

These events are brought about by new completely new agents. The importance of horns has only been alluded to so far, as they were given a rather prominent place in the description of both the ram and the he-goat. Now, however, they dominate the scene completely and become agents of finite verbs. First of all, the narrator mentions the sprouting of four horns in place of the old one, according to the four cardinal points:[298] וַתַּעֲלֶנָה חָזוּת אַרְבַּע תַּחְתֶּיהָ לְאַרְבַּע רוּחוֹת הַשָּׁמָיִם.[299] The new action brought about by the horns then starts immediately with a *wayyiqtol*[300] (וַתַּעֲלֶנָה). The reader thus finds himself back on the level of the mainline story.

---

[298] אַרְבַּע רוּחוֹת indicates a dynamic description of the directions proper rather than a static one of the cardinal points, cf. Main, "King Jonathan," in: *Biblical Perspectives*, eds. Stone and Chazon, 1998: 115-116.

[299] See the textual note above.

[300] The grammatical switch from *qatal* to *wayyiqtol* is analogous to the literary one from background to foreground, as *qatal* is generally used for backgrounding (Hatav, *Semantics*, 1997, 186-187), while *wayyiqtol* is a purely narrative form.

The same narrative and syntactical pattern occurs again in v. 9, where it is stated that out of one of the four new horns a little[301] one finally appears: וּמִן־הָאַחַת מֵהֶם יָצָא קֶרֶן־אַחַת מִצְּעִירָה. Again, the *qatal* form יָצָא denotes the background against which the rapidly proceeding mainline action takes place. The mainline action is rendered by means of an uninterrupted chain of several *wayyiqtol* forms in this and the subsequent verse (וַתִּגְדַּל – וַתִּגְדַּל – וַתַּפֵּל – וַתִּרְמְסֵם). Again, the relatively high percentage of *wayyiqtol* forms indicates rapidity, just as in vv. 6-7 (see above). Some commentators correct the 3rd masc. form יָצָא to a feminine יָצְאָה in order to establish full agreement with the feminine subject קֶרֶן. Consequently, the masculine form מֵהֶם, referring to the horns in the preceding verse, has been changed to the feminine מֵהֶן for the same reason by some manuscripts. But neither intervention is necessary.[302] Exceptions to normal agreement between subject and verb are most likely to occur when the subject follows the verb.[303] מֵהֶם may then reflect a further assimilation to the masculine form יָצָא,[304] although masculine suffixes tend to occur with female nouns, especially in the plural.[305]

In this context such a deviation from the general rule may not be totally unmotivated, for it is clear that horns have a particular significance in the whole of Dan 8,3-12. Their description is combined either with grammatical peculiarities, such as the rare byform קְרָנַיִם, otherwise unattested for this word (v. 3), or striking rhetorical devices, such as the *casus pendens* (at the end of v. 5). The grammatical anomaly (not: impossibility) here, stronger than the other highlighting features applied for horns elsewhere in this text, may again convey this sense of depicting something special and so attract attention. This is no wonder, since Dan 8,9f is near the climax of the whole unit, the attack on the astral host and the "abomination".

---

[301] Cf. the textual note above.

[302] For this phenomenon in general see Levi, *Inkongruenz*, 1987, *passim*.

[303] See GK §145.7; verb fronting causes only partial agreement (that is, gender agreement) with the subject in Classical Arabic as well.

[304] There is no evidence for a consistent use of ם- for the fem. plur. (Levi, *Inkongruenz*, 1987, 161).

[305] GK §135o, also with reference to Dan 8,9.

Once the horn has come up, it grows "toward the east, toward the south, and toward the glorious [land?][306]", which recalls the charging of the ram in all directions as described in v. 4. The overall impression recalls the fight between the ram and the he-goat, the victory and the triumph by asserting authority over the victim, but here everything is on a larger scale, besides the surreal imagery. A horn attacks the heavenly host, brings down some stars and tramples on them, that is, the "horizontal" aggression exerted so far is supplemented by a vertical one.

The final two verses of this unit, vv. 11-12, heavily focus on the consequences of the growing of the last horn. In total, they contain, despite their shortness, no less than seven verbal sentences and so apparently aim at an extremely graphic description of what is going on. This stylistic feature suggests to the reader that they depict the crucial point of the whole narrative. As if it were not enough that the horn had already attacked the heavenly host, it goes on to grow up to the prince of the host himself (וְעַד שַׂר־הַצָּבָא הִגְדִּיל). The fronting of the central idea for topicalization ("Yes, even to the prince of the host it grew!") illuminates the pivotal event and so interrupts the chain of *wayyiqtol* forms; the *qatal* form הִגְדִּיל[307] thus functions as a continuation of the preceding se-

---

[306] See the corresponding textual note above.

[307] Again there is a problem of agreement between the (now unmentioned) fem. subject and the masc. verb. Some (such as Marti, *Daniel*, 1901, 58) have proposed to correct the verbal form correspondingly (see the apparatus of the BHS). Bentzen, *Daniel*, 1952, 56, on the other hand, resolves this difficulty by assuming a direct reference to Antiochus Epiphanes beyond the metaphorical language. While it is true that in v. 11 the vision finally comes extremely close to leaving the purely supernatural world and being an encrypted reference to Antiochus' interference with the Temple cult, the generally fluctuating agreement in gender in vv. 8-12 between subject and verb with the horn as subject indicates that this assumption is not totally incomprehensible. But one would have to explain why in v. 12 the correct feminine gender is used again (correctly pointed out by Ginsberg, *Studies*, 1948, 50, in criticizing Bentzen), which makes an agreement with the "horn" unavoidable, although v. 12 syntactically, stylistically and semantically continues v. 11. So it may be more cautious to attribute these instances of incongruency to the fact that the horns in this part of the text are treated as if they were persons (cf. Levi, *Inkongruenz*, 1987, 161-184, with ample material). Kratz, "Visionen," in: *Schriftauslegung*, eds. Kratz, Krüger and Schmid, 2000: 227, however, sees the lack of agreement as evidence for a redactional addition, but in the light of the other instances of this grammatical phenomenon in the present text such a hypothesis is completely unfounded.

ries of events. The same construction is repeated in the next clause – again for the sake of topicalization of the main point introduced by *waw*, while the verb (*qatal*) is following afterwards (וּמִמֶּנּוּ [308] הוּרַם הַתָּמִיד). The last clause (וְהֻשְׁלַךְ מְכוֹן מִקְדָּשׁוֹ) then begins with a *wᵉqatal* and so, by analogy to the usage of this form in the whole of Dan 8,3-12, seems to depict the resulting situation, just as the two *wᵉqatal* forms at the end of v. 4: The daily offering has been taken away from the prince of the host, the dwelling of his sanctuary is now lying waste.

The particular significance of the offering is stressed by the uncommon expression הַתָּמִיד. The word תָּמִיד usually functions as an adverb ("continually"), at times used with nominal function as the second part of a construct. Its use as a definite noun on its own happens only in Daniel (8,11-13; 11,31; 12,11).[309] The interruption of the daily offering therefore automatically results in a situation in which the Temple is cast down, because the cult is abolished and the sanctuary has lost its function.

In the light of the interpretation given here, namely the specific character of the vision as a battle among supernatural forces and not as a symbolic representation of contemporary Jewish history, this unambiguous reference to the interference of Antiochus IV Epiphanes with the Jewish cult may at first seem awkward.[310] Is Dan 8,11 not a crystal clear

---

[308] Cf. the textual note above.

[309] The reason for this noteworthy uniqueness is unclear; the traditional explanation (cf. Montgomery, *Daniel*, 1927, 336; Brockelmann, *Syntax*, 1956, §127a) assumes that the word in this "technical" sense is an ellipsis of עולת התמיד (cf. Num 28,10ff; also in "Late Biblical Hebrew": Neh 10,34; so, too, the explanatory rendering of the Vulgate: *iuge sacrificium*), while Nuñez, "Usage and Meaning," in *To Understand*, ed. Merling, 1997: 95-102, argues that תמיד here is a proper noun meaning "continuance, continuity". His principal argument against the traditional interpretation, however, that תמיד as an ellipsis of עולת התמיד would be too ambiguous to mean "[daily] offering" (because תמיד also occurs with other nouns), is not fully convincing. For elliptic expressions *are* ambiguous and are only clarified by the context, which is the case in Daniel 8. But be that as it may, the wording is again striking.

[310] Its rather untypical character did not escape the acumen of Montgomery, *Daniel*, 1927, 325 (even though he did not elaborate on this point): "in this chap. the writer shows far more zeal for the concrete, as in vv. 10.11, where he abandons the proper elements of vision."

sign that the whole passage is an allegorical allusion to the *Religionsnot* in the 160s? However, a possible answer to this slippery question may derive from an adequate understanding of the subsequent verse.

Verse 12 concludes this last part of the whole unit. It begins, like the first two clauses of v. 11, with the apparently most significant element plus *waw* fronted and thus topicalized (וְצָבָא), followed by the verb (here a modal *yiqtol* – "it *had to be* given over" – instead of the usual *qatal*) and a double adverbial complement. Modal *yiqtol* forms are very rare in this unit, the only other instance being וְכָל־חַיּוֹת לֹא־יַעַמְדוּ in 8,4 (the other animals *could not* withstand the ram), where the construction is parallel: *waw* + subject + *yiqtol*. A possible reason for the employment of a modal nuance here could be the emotional tone at a moment of outmost abomination, just as it may express something like compassion in 8,4. It is in any case remarkable that the only two examples of modal *yiqtol* forms here are used with innocent subjects who have been defeated by a greater power, namely the "host" in this verse and the "living beings" who could not withstand the ram in v. 4, see below for some more "emotional" features in the style of Daniel 8. Additionally, וְהִנֵּה is missing in the entire section, so the impression of a visual experience is much less strong than in the preceding units.

The similarity in the syntactical pattern thus suggests that v. 12 is closely connected with v. 11, so it may be expected to continue the train of thought that starts there. This first clause of v. 12 is exceedingly difficult,[311] but an interpretation which leaves the text intact and understands the enigmatic צָבָא just as it is, as a "host", encounters far fewer problems than other proposals.[312] One may note that the "host" has already been mentioned in the two preceding verses; it is therefore familiar to the reader. The idea that the host of the "holy ones", here with two adverbial complements "in addition to the offering" (עַל־הַתָּמִיד)[313] and "in the course of transgression" (בְּפָשַׁע),[314] are handed over (תִּנָּתֵן)[315] to the "little

---

[311] The Greek versions exhibit an inflated text here in which several glosses and misreadings have become part of the text itself, cf. Jeansonne, *Old Greek*, 1988, 87.

[312] See the detailed discussion in Collins, *Daniel*, 1993, pp. 334-335.

[313] For עַל with the meaning "in addition to" cf. Gen 28,9; Num 31,8.

[314] The בְּ must be temporal, cf. Collins, *Daniel*, 1993, p. 335.

horn" is known from Dan 7,25 (וְיִתְיַהֲבוּן בִּידֵהּ), and this fits the context, an attack on the heavenly army, very well indeed. The vision would then end in the same realm in which it had begun and evolved for most of the time, namely in the supernatural sphere, while the only direct contact with concrete history would be reduced to the interruption of the daily offering alluded to in v. 11. What really matters is the heavenly battle between supernatural forces, with which the vision as a whole is mainly concerned.

Since the Temple is an immediate point of contact between the divine and the human sphere, between myth and history,[316] it establishes a vertical connection between both realms, into which human worshippers only enter.[317] According to a widespread Early Jewish belief, angels are the true agents of liturgy.[318] Hence the parallelism between the struggle of the cosmic forces and the attack on Jewish religion at a specific time

---

[315] The *yiqtol* can *perhaps* form a 3rd masc. sg. with a *t*-prefix (cf. Isa 53,10, which is more or less the paradigm case for such an assumption), so there may not be a problem of agreement with the masc. subject צָבָא. This hypothesis is not totally unproblematic, and the problem has been controversial for quite a few years. Moran, "*Taqtul," *Bib* 45 (1964): 80-82, rejects the existence of such a form in Amarna Canaanite), but cf. van Dijk, "*Taqtul," *VT* 19 (1969): 440-447, who affirms its existence, see esp. 442. The question has been examined afresh by Althann, *Studies*, 1997, 25-59, who concludes "that the alleged instances of this form [that is, *taqtul as a third masculine singular, H.G.] can be explained in other ways" (58). Among these alternative explanations, a deliberate change of person for rhetorical effect seems to resolve the difficulties of many passages discussed (such as Deut 32,14; Isa 38,13; 42,20; 53,10; Job 34,17; Lam 2,22 etc.). Something similar may be the case with Dan 8,12, especially since this is indeed a climactic moment in the course of the narrative, so a forceful rhetorical effect would not be out of place. However, there are still some difficult cases (e.g., Isa 57,3; Ezek 12,25; Job 20,9) which even Althann attributes to "a certain poetic licence" (59). In any case, the unusual form in Dan 8,12 would call for the reader's attention, but the textual basis is by far not sound enough to allow for a definite statement.

[316] This idea is already well attested in Mesopotamia, cf. Maul, "Fadenkreuz," *Heidelberger Jahrbücher* 42 (1998): 27-41, esp. 30ff.

[317] See Gzella, "Angelologie," *ETL* 79 (2002), 468-481, for instances of such a theology in Early Judaism.

[318] Cf. Mach, *Entwicklungsstadien*, 1992, 114-278.

becomes transparent for an instance. So even the clear historical allusion in v. 11 does not turn the whole scene into a symbolic representation of worldly history – the fights between the ram and the he-goat, the horn and the stars remain just what they are supposed to be, struggles in the supernatural world which parallel the conflict in the visible world. But as soon as the Temple is affected, the connection between both is apparent, because the sanctuary is part of both realms.

The rest of the verse follows a pattern already familiar from other sections of this unit. It proceeds in a straightforward way with a *wayy-iqtol* rendering a subsequent punctual event, "it cast down truth[319] to earth" (וַתַּשְׁלֵךְ אֱמֶת אַרְצָה).[320] The whole unit finishes off with two consecutive *wᵉqatal* forms (וְעָשְׂתָה וְהִצְלִיחָה), of which the second adverbially modifies the first, so the expression as a whole means "it was acting successfully".[321] They appear to have a function analogous to the *wᵉqatal* verbs in v. 4 (see above for a more detailed discussion), whose pattern they take up, namely a summary and a general consideration of the logical consequences of the foreground action. With v. 13 the visionary comes back to into the mainline story. This also indicates that the unit deliberately breaks off at this point. It will be recalled that from a narratological viewpoint the same visionary has disappeared from the mainline story after v. 7 and thus has ceased from intruding into the dramatic

---

[319] "Truth" here presumably means the Jewish law, as many important modern commentaries (Montgomery, *Daniel*, 1927, 338; Hartman and Di Lella, *Daniel*, 1978, 226; Collins, *Daniel*, 1993, 335) unanimously state.

[320] The vocalization of וְתַשְׁלֵךְ as a jussive form in the MT is anomalous. A jussive does not fit the context at all, because an indicative would be required. However, this is not the only case of a grammatical jussive with indicative meaning, see JM §114l. Even if one assumes that the pointing as a jussive was due to defective writing, it is often impossible to say how it came about, given the fact that a plain indicative would be the most natural way of pointing. The explanation given by GK §109k, namely rhythmic considerations, sounds very much like an argument *in fugam vacui*. Again, normal grammar is twisted, but not overstrained, and the reader is yet for another instant confronted with a form at which he has to stop for a moment and think. Two manuscripts of the Hebrew text have a Pual pointing with אֱמֶת as the subject ("truth was cast down", corresponding to the passive in the Greek versions), but this may well be a secondary correction of an original pointing as a jussive not understood anymore.

[321] Cf. Montgomery, *Daniel*, 1927, 340; Dan 11,32; 1 Kgs 8,32.

situation with his first person comments. This narrative technique shifts the reader's attention to the scene beheld by the visionary.

f. Subjectivity and Objectivity of Style and Their Effects

In order to assess the stylistic aspects in Dan 8,3-12, the analysis of the narrative will have to be supplemented by some observations about how the narrator manipulates the reader's emotions and leads them into a certain direction. In doing so he makes ample use of an overall climactic structure. Whereas the first section (vv. 3-4) is presented as the report of an eye-witness (ראה, וְהִנֵּה) who can rely on personal experience and so makes a certain claim to objectivity, the second section (vv. 5-7) begins with a comment on the narrator's reflection (בין in the Hiphil) and his attempt to make sense of what he sees, if indeed בין is used here as a technical term from wisdom literature and not as synonymous to ראה, as in Ps 94,7.[322] After v. 7, the self-references of the storyteller in the 1st pers. stop abruptly, in v. 8 the place normally taken by a 1st pers. *qatal* verb at the beginning of a new section is occupied by an infinitive absolute with a temporal meaning (וּכְעָצְמוֹ).

The effect of this dramatic development of the situation is immediate, to the effect that the distinction between narrator and narration carefully uphold by continuous self-references (8,3: וָאֶשָּׂא עֵינַי וָאֶרְאֶה *bis*; 8,4: רָאִיתִי; 8,5: וַאֲנִי הָיִיתִי מֵבִין; 8,6: רָאִיתִי; 8,7: וּרְאִיתִיו) is suspended. Likewise, with the omission of these remarks the narration becomes more subjective. On the one hand the 1st pers. references used in the preceding sections were applied as a means of objectivity and reliability, emphasizing that the narrator tells just what he has seen. This is in general their conventional literary function in a vision report, as has been pointed out above on the narrative frame in vv. 1-2 and 27. On the other hand, the third section is also marked by an agglomeration of explicitly pejorative terms, such as "abomination" and "casting down" sanctuary

---

[322] In the light of the association of ראה with the contents of sensual perception and the ample use of wisdom terminology in Daniel 8, it seems possible to assume such a semantic distinction, but it is not certain.

and truth,[323] while the use of markers of immediate sense perception, such as וְהִנֵּה, is much reduced.

But this impression of a development from an "objective" to an "emotional" literary presentation is, although basically true, too simple. Simultaneously with the "objective" nuance which the repeated stress on the fact that the visionary is an eye-witness creates, there is from the outset also a highly "subjective" or "personal" dimension accompanying the report. This latter dimension becomes the stronger the closer the narrative gets to its climax. At first, there only seems to be a subtle notion of arrogance in the intransitive Hiphil of the root גדל used for the ram in 8,4, for the he-goat in 8,8 and for the rising horn in 8,11. The $w^e qatal$ appears to indicate that this is the outcome of its domination over the other animate beings, see above.

Since the form derives from an intransitive verb, it has in principle the same force as the Qal used in vv. 9-10, but carries a sense of arrogance, just as in Ps 55,13 and in Jer 48,26,[324] unless God is the agent, as in 1 Sam 12,24 or Ps 126,2-3. From Dan 8,11f it becomes clear that וְעַד שַׂר־הַצָּבָא הִגְדִּיל refers to the peak of hybris, an attack against the heavenly powers and their prince, and the same is true for Ps 55,13 and Jer 48,26. Therefore there is some reason to see a similar, but more subtle and less explicit nuance of hybris also behind the same form in Dan 8,4.8.

The modal or "emotional" meaning of the Hiphil of גדל here becomes even more evident from the context. Note that this Hiphil is used with qatal forms that belong to the general background level of the narrative (vv. 8.11) or the evaluation of a situation (v. 4) in such a way that a durative or habitual Aktionsart appears. In the foreground action proper in vv. 9-10, signalled by wayyiqtol, the author uses the Qal. This is unlikely to be a coincidence. The same reason, namely the addition of an "emotional" nuance, may apply to the two modal yiqtol forms in 8,4 and 8,12, as they are both employed in a context of defeat and destruction of figures which have not been described as aggressors, namely the

[323] Correctly noted by Koch, "Visionsbericht," in: Apocalypticism, ed. Hellholm, 1989: 418.
[324] See Waltke and O'Connor, Syntax, 1990, §27.5 and 440, n. 17, on the modal sense of such a use of the Hiphil; cf. JM §54.e.

animals attacked by the ram and the heavenly host attacked by the little horn. So there is perhaps a notion of compassion present here.

A further important stylistic feature in this section is the use of keywords and the rather special way they are employed. In fact, this is a characteristic trait of the language of the Hebrew Daniel (see the introductory chapter on the language of the Book of Daniel). By means of repeating the same lexemes (i.e., the Hiphil of גדל) and also the same overall pattern (appearance, dominion, defeat / disappearance), the ram, the he-goat and the little horn are put on the same narrative axis. They all are somehow horned beings: they defeat their enemies, as the triumphant gesture of casting the enemy to the ground and trampling on him is largely parallel in vv. 8 and 10, exert unchallenged superiority, grow great and, at least in the case of the ram and the he-goat, are then suddenly replaced by something else which emerges from the background. The vision report breaks off before the reader learns how the final, little horn is going to end, but the general pattern of the two preceding sections may indicate that it, too, is doomed to failure at some stage.

The grammatical discussion of these keywords provides further support for the view that all three sections of Dan 8,3-12 form a unit, since several of the respective key-terms appear in an unusual fashion, even from a purely morphological and syntactical perpective, which emphasizes their importance.[325] The striking, emotional[326] use of גדל in the Hiphil has just been discussed, but in addition to that it is noteworthy how the word "horn" is treated in the text, see above in the respective sections of the narrative analysis for detailed information. The horns of the ram (v. 3) are introduced by a very rare and for this word unattested byform (קְרָנַיִם) of the regular dual, they are then described at great length, information on the horn of the he-goat is provided by means of a *casus pendens* construction at the end of a verse (v. 5), and the gender of

---

[325] It is true that the concept "emphasis" is often used as a universal solution for puzzling linguistic features (cf. Muraoka, *Emphasis*, 1985, xi: "The impression is thus created that 'emphasis' is a ready panacea for Hebraists' (and Semitists') headaches of all sorts." But in this case there seems to be enough cumulative evidence to determine a decisively "emphatic" character of the passage.

[326] Emphasis is indeed largely a question of emotion, since it belongs to the psychological rather than the logical sphere (cf. Muraoka, *Emphasis*, 1985, xiii-xiv).

the word "horn" fluctuates continuously between masc. and fem. in vv. 8-12. Lastly, the clear-cut distinction between the indeterminate ram and the determinate he-goat which bears the definite article, though not having been introduced before, is unusual. The combination of all these features creates surprise, and then also suspense and dramatic vividness. At the same time this particular linguistic garb highlights some essential points of the action which the reader must not miss, just like modern typographical means, such as italics, underlining etc. As the content of the vision is close to the limit of what can be understood, so its linguistic presentation approaches the limit even of the merely grammatical possibilities of language.[327]

g. Entering the Text: The Reader's Experience of Time

By developing such a climactic structure through which the reader is guided by means of recurring, easily recognizable keywords and through the repetition of situational background, action, final evaluation similarly structured sub-units, the narrator makes full use of the reader's *experience of time*. This is a category not commonly applied to the analysis of biblical narratives, but it contributes something to the understanding of Daniel 8. The actual vision is at first explicitly mediated by the narrator, who is still strongly present through the repeated use of the first person singular. Yet it uses from the outset images very familiar to the original addressees, such as horns as symbols of power or a ram and a he-goat, known as metaphors for rulers abusing their power from prophetic literature. There will be more to say on the connotations of the imagery. The description of these animals engaged in a fight is a well-liked *sujet* in Ancient Near Eastern pictorial representations and thus perhaps part of the reader's cultural knowledge.

Step by step the reader is being absorbed in the text. The he-goat, although not mentioned before, is presented with the definite article, just

---

[327] Such a play with the possibilities and limits of language for emphasis reappears in the Apocalypse, cf. the shift from accusative to nominative in 2,20, the masc. participle for a neuter subject (πνεύματα) in 5,6 or maybe also the genitive (γεμόντων) for an accusative object in 21,9 (here the manuscript **1006** has the expected form γεμούσας, but that is no strong external evidence).

as if it had been introduced before or indeed as if it were self-evident. Consequently the general character of indetermination prevailing in the preceding sub-unit is given up. In addition to that, the first-person narrator disappears to the background, the climactic triple repetition of struggle, victory and defeat creates a basic rhythm which becomes each time more familiar and at the same time more appealing, even though the imagery becomes increasingly eccentric. Through introducing new elements, the narrator keeps up the reader's attention, until the "little horn" at the end attacks the stars.[328]

At this point the reader should be ready to see things in a different way than before; he has become more familiar with the inner logic of the text as to be able to guess that this final, surreal attack is just going to end as the previous, more "realistic" ones did, even though the battle narrative breaks off here. Having been accustomed to this recurring pattern, it is clear to him that this is the way things work. The vision of the little horn, at the same time both familiar and unfamiliar, is thus not anymore incomprehensible, but has been connected to the preceding scenes more deeply rooted in the reader's imaginary world.

As time passes the reader will return again and again to the text to reflect upon it, he experiences a certain progress in understanding, until he is ready to grasp the meaning of the final event. Having understood the basic pattern, he is able to apply it to contemporary history as well; the theme of the latter part of Daniel 8 is already being prepared here. There is no precise instruction as to how the reader must deal with the text. He is nonetheless constantly invited strongly but subtly to share the narrator's mediation and this way he will in the end find himself in the situation of the visionary. It is the narrator, however, who, by means of linguistic devices, progressively leads his reader into the text.

h. Conclusion: Verbal Forms and Narrative Presentation

The syntactical and literary analysis has thus far attempted to shed some light on the three different levels in the visionary's account. Each of these three levels is closely associated with characteristic grammatical forms, namely the setting expressed by nominal sentences, parti-

---

[328] This is an instance of how the author twists a simile for hybris, see below.

ciples and *qatal*, the mainline action rendered by *wayyiqtol* and the evaluation of the resulting new situation individuated by the use of *wᵉqatal*. The description of the setting, or background, comes before the action (the ram in vv. 3f and the he-goat's arrival in v. 5 prior to the he-goat's attack in vv. 6f), while the evaluation of the situation through *wᵉqatal* can follow on the background description (v. 4) as well as on the foreground (v. 12). This background description and the concluding evaluation of the situation have a precise function as structural markers, signalling the beginning and the end of a subsection. Such an effective application of verbal forms proper to Hebrew, especially *wayyiqtol* and *wᵉqatal* as opposed to *waw* plus *qatal*, and the "backgrounding" use of the participle render it rather doubtful that Daniel 8 has been translated into Hebrew from an Aramaic original.[329]

Yet the division between these three levels of the narrative is not at all static. On the contrary, by using the same subject, such as the visionary or the he-goat, sometimes with a *qatal* form or a participle, sometimes with a *wayyiqtol*, the figures prominent in the overall narrative can move freely between background and foreground, they can be highlighted by being placed on the mainline action and then disappear again to the background. So the narrator is part of the foreground by being the subject of two *wayyiqtol* verbs in v. 3, then he disappears to the background, from which he nonetheless continues to observe the situation as it unfolds. He is the subject of ראה *qatal* forms in vv. 4, 5 and 7; the use of the same verb in vv. 4 and 7 as well gives an impression of continuity. He remains in the background until he appears with a different verb again on the *wayyiqtol* level in v. 13, as soon as a new situation comes about. In a similar fashion the he-goat in v. 5 stands initially in the background, while approaching from afar, and then it suddenly enters the center of the stage in vv. 6 and 7 for the fight with the ram. At this point the ram, having being defeated, recedes to the background again (*qatal* in anterior construction in v. 8) and its place on the *wayyiqtol* level is taken by a new entity, the horns.

Thus, the association of the three levels of narration with three different types of verbal forms allows not only for a further means of

---

[329] This is an old hypothesis cf. Ginsberg, *Studies*, 1948, 41-61. It has been accepted, among others, by Hartman and Di Lella, *Daniel*, 1978, 232.

structuring the text, but also for an effective technique to move the characters from one level to another. For an interpretation of the vision this is insofar significant as it stresses the mimetic nature of the narrative. At the same time the text keeps referring to the visionary himself, who moves back and forth from background to foreground, but is always present while the story is unfolding itself. A re-reading of the text in the light of the specific nuances it may convey within its particular cultural framework will function as a first step towards the metaphorical application of the vision.

3. A Metaphorical Reading

The literary analysis of the animal fight undertaken in the preceding section is an attempt to understand the function of the imagery within the narrative context itself. Here the imagery appears as if it were part of a worldly reality, namely a series of events that take place in chronological and logical sequence presented by the narrator within a specific setting. The action is called "mimetic" in the sense of a dramatic performance evolving before the eyes of a spectator. The next step is to determine how far this imagery alludes to experiences and concepts which have a particular significance in the cultural context of the speaker, above all in the area of royal typology.

This does not mean that the images could be treated as if they were heraldic symbols and that their decipherment would consist in identifying objects or realities they might represent. The figure depicted as acting in the supernatural realm should not be taken as mere metaphor for things that happen in the human realm. There is no one-to-one correspondence between the two. In the case of the ram and the he-goat, the identification of an *unambiguous referent* is impossible. It will be seen that the allegedly strongest arguments for such a view do not rest on firm ground. On the contrary, applying model categories known from its cultural heritage, especially the text of the Sacred Books, seems to be a way for ancient Israelite society to understand new experiences and take consciousness of them.[330] The transposition of the vision to contemporary history is therefore not a matter of decipherment, but of application.

a. Intertextual Possibilities: Daniel as Scribal Literature

As is normal in setting up a *Traditionsgeschichte* of a late biblical text, some valid connotations of the imagery in Daniel 8 can be sought within the biblical tradition itself. It is generally agreed that the final redaction of the Book of Daniel took place shortly before the death of Antiochus IV Epiphanes, that is, presumably between 168 and 164 BC. The authors and redactors could, in the long process of composition down to the final shape, make use of some established collection of normative writings, though still admitting of a certain liberty.

According to a number of recent – even though reasonably diverse – sociological studies on the Book of Daniel this composition is, at least in its final form, the work of a learned group with a clear "scribal" profile.[331] This group evidently maintained a certain interest in reinterpreting biblical prophecy.[332] Such an observation in turn provides a good reason for believing that the authors of Daniel had a considerable familiarity with the actual texts of the Scriptures and perhaps other, non-canonical material to which they had access. Moreover, they seem to

---

[330] Cf. Koch, "Visionsbericht," in: *Apocalypticism*, ed. Hellholm, 1989: 425: "Apokalyptisches Erleben hingegen resultiert aus exegetischer Meditation."; Collins, *Apocalyptic Imagination*, 1998, 17-19. Collins, however, stresses that the "symbolic character of apocalyptic literature is shown especially by its pervasive use of allusions to traditional imagery." But do allusions to literary tradition necessitate symbolism?

[331] See Davies, "Scribal School," in *Book of Daniel*, eds. Collins and Flint, 2001: 247-265, esp. 255ff: The Book of Daniel goes back to a scribal community and exhibits scribal values, namely a definition of what constitutes correct behaviour, based on observation of (or enlightment about) the way the world works. Also Albertz, "Social Setting," in *Book of Daniel*, eds. Collins and Flint, 2001: 171-204, sees the group behind the final redaction of the Book Daniel as "learned scribes, outstanding in their piety and widely acknowledged as the religious elite during that period" (201), which he tries to identify as the Hassidim. Less specific is Grabbe, "Dan(iel) for All Seasons," in *Book of Daniel*, eds. Collins and Flint, 2001: 229-246, who nonetheless characterizes the author of Daniel 7-12 as "an educated person" (243).

[332] The most obvious case is the explanation of the "seventy years" until the rebuilding of the Temple, originally found in Jer 25,12 and 29,10, in Dan 9,24ff.

consciously use these texts as a groundwork and foundation for their own theological outlook and other intellectual efforts.[333]

It is on the one hand apparent that Jewish literature between the Testaments is characterized by a "Renaissance of the Myth", to use a term coined by Aage Bentzen,[334] a certain revival of Ancient Near Eastern mythology. The celestial journeys in the Book of the Watchers (1 Enoch 17ff), for example, combine Babylonian and Greek conceptions of the netherworld,[335] while the Septuagint, however, either preserves or maybe even re-introduces old West Semitic mythological elements. A model case for this may be the rendering of the "Son of Man" in Dan 7,13 as coming *on* the clouds of heaven, ἐπὶ τῶν νεφελῶν τοῦ οὐρανοῦ ὡς υἱὸς ἀνθρώπου, thus reflecting the Canaanite idea of Baal as the rider on the clouds – *rkb 'rpt* –, while the Masoretic Text has "with", כְּבַר אֱנָשׁ עִם־עֲנָנֵי שְׁמַיָּא, which is rather faint.[336] Other parts of the Septuagint establish new allusions to Greek mythology[337] or indeed eliminate mythological expressions present in the Hebrew text. This latter approach in itself presupposes a certain knowledge of mythology; of all the Septuagint books, it is most commonly applied in the Psalter.[338]

---

[333] Beyerle, too, observes that the role and function of the highly educated intellectual elite, whom he considers responsible for the Book of Daniel in its present form, becomes apparent through the reception and re-interpretation of motifs and forms that originate mostly from earlier prophecy: Beyerle, "Social Setting," *Book of Daniel*, eds. Collins and Flint, 2001: 212. This "prophetic" profile is certainly not a social category, as there was a wide range of "prophetic" activity in the period between the Testaments, but it says something about the literary outlook of the author(s) of Daniel 7-12, cf. Davies, "Scribal School," in *Book of Daniel*, eds. Collins and Flint, 2001: 249.

[334] Bentzen, *King and Messiah*, 1970, 73-80.

[335] Wacker, *Weltordnung*, 1982, 144-175.

[336] It is of course impossible to decide whether the LXX only preserves an older expression (presumably reading עַל־עֲנָנֵי שְׁמַיָּא), corresponding more closely to the West Semitic ideas in the background, or whether the translators have independently adjusted the image according to their own knowledge of the ancient mythologumena. The latter hypothesis cannot be ruled out completely.

[337] Especially in the translation of the Book of Job and Isaiah: Gzella, *Lebenszeit*, 2002, 189.

[338] Gzella, *Lebenszeit*, 2002, 185-194. In the light of the striking amount of demythologizing renderings in the LXX Psalter, the attempt of Schaper, "Renaissance

But uncovering such isolated parallels in compositions of extremely diverse historical origins remains unsatisfactory and contributes little or nothing to the understanding of the history of literature or religion. Unless one can reconstruct precisely the *Vermittlungsweg*, namely the path by which an ancient mythological motif could have reappeared in a text that has been finished in the mid-2nd century BC, one cannot plausibly speak of a "background" or even an "influence", not to mention a precise "model". But such a reconstruction is often impossible. Instead, one must restrict oneself to a mere comparison, and this has often rather little intrinsic value.[339]

For determining the overall connotations of the imagery used in Daniel 8, material from preceding biblical texts may therefore be most relevant as a source of inspiration from which a later author could have drawn. Again, the attempt to determine allusions and overtones in the imagery must not be confused with a "symbolic" interpretation of the vision, since the difference between the "sense" of an image in its context and its "reference" to something else remains intact – the usage of culturally "laden" imagery is not an instance of deciphering information, but of applying categories from texts already known in order to make sense of something hitherto unknown, that is, the glance into a transcendent and supernatural reality.

The use of such categories, however, makes a specific application of the vision easier. Since rams and he-goats are at times applied as suggestive metaphors for kings in biblical texts, this provides a clue for the readers's understanding of the vision. He may therefore infer that the Persian Empire and the Greek conquest are a realization of the cosmic battle. However, such a knowledge does not necessitate the view that the protagonists of the vision narrative are *identical* with any historical entities. The "royal" connotations triggered by the imagery in Daniel 8 seem rather to evoke a *general idea* of kingship as the strongest expression of

---

der Mythologie," in *Der Septuaginta-Psalter*, ed. Zenger, 2001: 171-183, who tries to find examples of exactly a "Remythologisierung" in the Greek Psalter, appears untenable.

[339] Cf. for this problem Zeller, "Ägyptische Königsideologie," in *Religionsgeschichte*, eds. von Dobbeler, Erlemann and Heiligenthal, 2000: 541-552.

worldly power, whose conflict with divine power appears as one of the principal concerns of the whole Book of Daniel.

b. Astral Symbolism and Royal Imagery – A Reanalysis

The general obsession of a past generation of biblical scholars with astral symbolism[340] has gained a further stimulus due to the hypothesis that zodiacal allusions are lying at the heart of the ram and the he-goat as images for the kings of Persia and Greece in Daniel 8.[341]

The core of this argument is a fragmentary list attributed to Teucer of Babylon who is supposed to have lived in the first century AD[342] which contains an elenchus of signs of the zodiac and associates each sign with a specific country. The ram (κριός) represents Persia, the he-goat (αἰγόκερως) Syria. This explanation has found considerable approval in scholarship,[343] but there are two serious problems. First, the connection of signs of the zodiac with particular countries is, despite the great popularity of zodiacal depictions in late antique Jewish synagogues,[344] unattested so far in the second century BC.[345] This *argumentum e silentio* may perhaps only rest on a coincidence of transmission, but its force is increased considerably by the observation that, second, in

---

[340] See, e.g., Zimmern, "Jakobssegen," *ZA* 7 (1892): 161-172, who tries to detect associations of the various tribes in the Blessing of Jacob with symbols of the zodiac.

[341] As far as I see, this goes back to a private communication of F.C. Burkitt to F. Cumont, see Cumont, "Géographie astrologique," *Klio* 9 (1909): 263-273.

[342] Boll, *Sphaera*, 1903, 6-11.

[343] Caquot, "Quatre Bêtes," *Semitica* 5 (1955): 6-13, who developed Cumont's theory with regard to Daniel 7 and 8; Bentzen, *Daniel*, 1952, 69; Hengel, *Judentum*, 1988, 336-337; even Collins, *Daniel with an Introduction*, 1984, 87, asserts that it "is now generally acknowledged that the symbolism of the ram and the he-goat is astrological and refers to the constellations thought in the Hellenistic age to preside over Persia and Syria", although he is more cautious in his 1993 commentary and concludes, after having mentioned some counter-arguments: "The relevance of the astral geography, then, is questionable." (Collins, *Daniel*, 1993, 330)

[344] See Stemberger, "Bedeutung des Tierkreises," in his *Studien*, 1990, 177-228, who nonetheless accepts the alleged astral symbolism of Daniel 8 as a possible background (189).

[345] Lucas, "Daniel," *VT* 50 (2000): 71.

Teucer's list the he-goat corresponds to Syria and not, as in Dan 8,21, to Greece (יָוָן).[346] For these reasons, there is at least no unified astrological scheme behind the depiction in the Book of Daniel and the association of the ram with Persia in Teucer's list or indeed any other similar concept. So both testimonies could at least equally well be two reflections of the same tradition which are unconnected among themselves.

In addition to that, two other possible reasons why at least the ram might be associated especially with Persia,[347] are highly doubtful. First, Ammianus Marcellinus (19,1,2) mentions that king Shapur II (fourth century AD) at the head of his army wore the head of a ram. It is noteworthy that even Hengel[348] and Collins, in his commentary,[349] consider this remark of Ammianus Marcellinus pertinent enough to mention it when discussing Daniel 8 (mid-second century BC).

Although the general credibility of Ammianus' history has been the subject of some scholarly controversy,[350] there is no reason to doubt the authenticity of this comment. The historiographer's remark appears to be a detail illustrating vividly a certain importance of the ram in *Sasanian* royal typology. However, it does not really say anything about its value as a characteristic mark of the *Achaemenid* kings. Given the prominence of rams in Ancient Near Eastern figurative art and the at most very feeble ideological connections between the Achaemenids and

---

[346] Cf. Day, *Conflict*, 1985, 154, who shows that Caquot's elaborate symbolism draws on *different* astrological systems. Apparently, no one scheme can be found which exhibits the same connections between animals and countries as in Daniel 8 (or Daniel 7, for that matters). See also Lucas, "Source," *TynBul* 41 (1990): 161-185, esp. 165-171. The only possibility to save this analogy would be to postulate that Alexander and his successors were considered kings of Syria rather than of Greece (so Jeremias, *Das Alte Testament*, 1916, 631), even though one has to bear in mind that the Seleucids are generally referred to as "Greeks" in Syriac literature (in dating formulae, for example). But even if one accepts this reasoning, such a construction would not solve the problem of a *Vermittlungsweg* between a much later zodiacal symbolism and the Book of Daniel.

[347] For some more material on the ram in Persian iconography cf. Hävernick, *Daniel*, 1832, 258 with n. 1.

[348] Hengel, *Judentum*, 1988, 337, n. 494.

[349] Collins, *Daniel*, 1993, 330, n. 23.

[350] Rosen, *Studien*, 1970, esp. 18-19.

the Sasanians, it appears impossible to establish a direct line between the statement of Ammianus Marcellinus and the vision in Daniel 8.

This is also true for a passage in the Pahlavi *Records of Ardashir i Papakan* (the so-called *Karnamag*) which provides a theoretical parallel to the imagery under discussion.[351] This text is an unhistorical and rather novellistic account on the origins of the Sasanian dynasty in Iran.[352] It was presumably written towards the end of the Sasanian rule, that is, roughly at the end of the sixth and beginning of the seventh century AD. Most probably it uses older material.[353] When Ardashir, the founder of the Sasanian dynasty in Iran, fled from the court of Ardavan, he was followed by a big and fat ram (*warrar*),[354] which is then[355] explicitly interpreted as the majesty / glory of rulership (*xwarrah ī xwadāyīh*) following the one who is destined to reign the country. This concept presumably denotes something like the Greek idea of Tyche or the Roman one of Fortuna.[356] As soon as the ram is seen sitting on the horse with Ardashir, this means that the majesty of the kings "has reached him". This piece of evidence may perhaps be connected at the remotest with Ammianus Marcellinus' remark on Shapur II, especially since both refer to Sasanian Persia, but it is hardly feasible how it can be used to illuminate the vision in Daniel 8. Numerous Neo-Persian linguistic features in the text point to a long recensional history of the material, and without independent evidence it appears impossible to say whether the ram had any place in pre-Sasanian royal ideology.

The conclusion is that neither the use of the ram and the he-goat as zodiacal symbols nor the role of the ram in Sasanian royal typology, very distant from Achaemenid culture, can be unambiguously connected

---

[351] An annotated translation of the Pahlavi text directly from the manuscripts is provided by Nöldeke, "Artachšîr i Pâpakân," *Beiträge zur Kunde der Indogermanischen Sprachen* IV (1879): 22-69. For bibliographical notes cf. Cereti, *Letteratura Pahlavi*, 2001, 192 (with parts of the text in transcription and translation).

[352] For the political history cf. Frye, *Ancient Iran*, 1984, 291-296.

[353] Nöldeke, "Artachšîr i Pâpakân," *Beiträge zur Kunde der Indogermanischen Sprachen* IV (1879): 23ff.

[354] Ibid., 44.

[355] Ibid., 45.

[356] Cf. Wiesehöfer, *Ancient Persia*, 1996, 167.

with the animal fight in Daniel 8. In addition to the striking lack of any rudimentarily plausible *Vermittlungsweg*, such a symbolism would be contrary to the logic of the text, since there is no hint whatsoever at a possible symbolic understanding of Dan 8,3-12, such as, for example, an explicit marker of comparison: "Worldly empires are like a ram and a he-goat..." In fact, all this material has practically no clear bearing on the understanding of the symbolism. Rather than looking for a precise identification, one may get closer to the sense of the vision by examining the *connotations* which these figures evoke against their biblical background.

c. Biblical Connotations of Rams and He-Goats

The use of rams and he-goats as images in the prophetic tradition allows the reader to grasp something of their significance in Daniel 8. Both animals are traditionally associated with power and virility, and thus also with leadership and kingship, throughout the history of biblical texts, far into Early Judaism.[357] Hence the corresponding terms אַיִל and עַתּוּד were widespread metaphors for "ruler" and used so naturally that the literal meaning was perhaps not always fully realized anymore.[358]

Such a metaphorical usage is well attested in most Semitic languages.[359] In Hebrew, this metaphor is already present in very ancient

---

[357] Cf. the *Animal Apocalypse* (1 En 89,42-48; 90,13).

[358] HAL, for example, has a proper section on the metaphorical use of אַיִל.

[359] For West Semitic parallels cf. the Phoenician Maʿṣub inscription (KAI 19) from 222 BC (and therefore reasonably close to the final redaction of Daniel), which mentions in l. 2 a portico אש בן האלם, "which the mighty ones (lit.: 'the rams') have built". Since these people are then specified as "envoys of Milk-ʿAštart", there can be no doubt that אלם is used as a metaphor for influential persons here, and because it is unlikely that the Phoenicians called their magistrates "gods", אלם will mean "rams" here (cf. Meyer, "Untersuchungen," *ZAW* 49 [1931]: 3). See also Donner and Röllig in their commentary ad loc. (KAI II, 28), who also refer to Ex 15,15, likewise already Cooke, *Text-book*, 1903, 49 and Dahood, "Review of KAI," *Or. N. S.* 34 (1965): 86. Just about the same will be true for a Phoenician temple tariff inscription from Cyprus (presumably mid-5th century or early 4th), which appears to speak of "leaders of the new-moon festival" (אלן חדש, l. 3), see Gibson, *Phoenician Inscriptions*, 1982, no. 33B, and his note ad loc. (126) for doubts why officials receiving payments (and *not* offerings) are more likely to be called "rams", namely "chiefs", than "gods". Ugaritic parallels can be found in Miller, "Animal Names," *UF* 2 (1970): 177-186. From a

texts, such as the "rams of Moab" in Ex 15,15,[360] but it features predominantly in prophecy – see Ez 17,13; 31,11; 39,18[361] (אַיִל); Isa 14,9
(עַתּוּד). Other animal metaphors convey other connotations. Something
like nobility / pride / beauty instead of pure power may be implied by the
image of gazelles in 2 Sam 1,19. There הַצְּבִי יִשְׂרָאֵל may therefore mean
"the noble ones of Israel", cf. Isa 23,9.[362] The "fat cows" in Am 4,1, by
contrast, presumably evoke the connotation of a complacent, self-
sufficient and luxurious life. In addition to that, there are also several
ambiguous passages featuring a metaphorical use of אַיִל. In these cases it
is often not clear whether this or a similar-looking, but semantically different word is meant.[363]

    In the context of Daniel 8, the connotations of rams and he-goats
as metaphors for worldly powers entering into conflict with the divine
and hence meeting their own destruction are especially significant. Even
if, for the sake of the hypothesis, the animals in the vision in Daniel 8 are
hardly intended as metaphors, they still evoke the association of power-
ful and rebellious leaders who in the end will be defeated. Also the combination of he-goats and rams in several prophetic catalogues of animals

---

merely lexical point of view, one may refer to the analogous use of *kabš^un*, "ram,
bellwether, leader" in Arabic, cf. Wehr, *Arabisches Wörterbuch*, 1985, s.v. (1084).

[360] Cf. Cross and Freedman, *Ancient Yahwistic Poetry*, 1997, 44, n. 44.

[361] The metaphorical use of the animal list (אֵילִים כָּרִים וְעַתּוּדִים פָּרִים מְרִיאֵי בָשָׁן כֻּלָּם)
is evident because of the parallelism with "heroes" (גִּבּוֹרִים) and "princes of the earth"
(נְשִׂיאֵי הָאָרֶץ).

[362] The relevance of this passage for the present discussion has been pointed out by
Rosenthal, "Review of Ginsberg," *Or. N. S.* 16 (1947): 401-402. For the image of the
gazelle see Cant 4,5; 7,4.

[363] Such as Ps 58,2; Job 41,17 (here אֵלִים presumably means "gods"); the אֱלִילִים in
Ez 30,13 possibly reflects אֵילִים, cf. the parallelism with נָשִׂיא, "princes", in the next
stichos (this was apparently also the interpretation of the LXX translators, who render אֱלִילִים with μεγιστᾶνες), see Zimmerli, *Ezekiel*, 1969, 726. In 2 Kgs 24,15 at
least the Qere reads "rams", and in Jer 4,22 the LXX has ἡγούμενοι where the MT
has אֱוִיל ("foolish") and thus appears to have read אֵילִים (though it cannot be decided
with certainty whether the *Vorlage* of the LXX version actually had this reading or
whether the translators only have presupposed it). For the difficulties of Ps 29,1 cf.
Gzella, "Kalb und Einhorn," in *Der Septuaginta-Psalter*, ed. Zenger, 2001: 264-267.

to be slaughtered or judged, representing unjust rulers (Ez 39,18; Isa 34,6f),[364] is a noteworthy feature.

A reader of Daniel 8 who is familiar with prophetic metaphors will realize the intertextual references to the condemnation of the abuse of power in the background of this imagery. Taken together these references will lead the reader to understand the indirect characterization of the protagonists in Daniel by the narrator, even though no single reference will by itself enable the reader to grasp the charaterization.

In this context, a word has to be said about the unusual vocabulary for the "he-goat" in Dan 8,5. It is noteworthy that, instead of the more common term עַתּוּד (always in the plural), the text features the at first strikingly strange expression צְפִיר־הָעִזִּים ("the he-goat of goats"). One possible reason for this is that the author wants to distinguish sharply between the ram and the he-goat, because their antagonism is precisely the point of this text, whereas they are very often mentioned in strict parallelism elsewhere (see above), up to the point that עַתּוּד, as it seems, even can mean "ram", as in Gen 31,10.12.[365] The choice of words would thus prevent the distinction from becoming obscure.

But there might be another motive. The word צָפִיר is undoubtedly an Aramaic loan-word[366] which occurs only in later books of the Hebrew Bible (Ezr 8,35; 2 Chr 29,11). Although it is attested elsewhere in the Old Testament, it might still have been felt as unusual and therefore striking. Its use therefore points the reader to specific connotations, namely to the "demoniac" connotations goats could evoke in the world of the Bible:[367] Goat-demons, mostly labelled שְׂעִירִם, "hairy he-goats", but the

---

[364] Already noted by Miller, "Animal Names," *UF* 2 (1970): 177-186 (with n. 37), although he makes no reference at all to Daniel 8. F. L. Cross (personal communication, cited by Miller, "Animal Names," *UF* 2 [1970]: 186) suggests that Jdg 5,8, too, originally meant "they chose new leaders", reading אֵילִים = "rams" instead of אֱלֹהִים (which might be a theological clarification of an original אלם) and שְׂעִירִים = "he-goats" instead of שְׂעָרִים (which would both have been שערם in writing and hence not distinguishable).

[365] Cf. Holladay, *Jeremiah* 2, 1989, 416.

[366] Cf. Wagner, *Aramaismen*, 1966, 99 (no. 248).

[367] See the synopsis by Janowski, "Satyrs,", in *Dictionary of Deities and Demons*, eds. van der Toorn, Becking and van der Horst, 1999, 732-733.

other synonyms for "he-goat" are also used, are attested as the objects of
veneration. This is the case in Lev 17,7 and 2 Chr 11,15 – this latter passage suggests that Jeroboam I had established a special cult for them.
According to some texts, they were closely associated with demoniac
dances, see for example Isa 13,21: וּשְׂעִירִים יְרַקְּדוּ.[368] The apocalyptic
wasteland, which they were believed to inhabit after God's judgment on
the nations (Isa 34,14), may in the end resemble somehow the apparently
uninhabited, void landscape at the river Ulai which is the setting of
Daniel 8. The he-goat acquires, in a cultic perspective rather than a prophetic one, a demoniac connotation by its association with Azazel, the
lord of the goat-demons who inhabits the desert and is given the scape-
goat (Leviticus 16).[369]

The precise nature of these goat-demons is hard to determine,[370]
as there is no description of their physical appearance. But in the light of
the evidence outlined so far, it seems to be only of secondary importance
whether the שְׂעִירִם were originally demons appearing in the guise of he-
goats or whether they were, as Snaith maintains, simply animals – their
sinister connotation is unambiguous. Moreover, Snaith's division in the
usage of שְׂעִירִם between storm-demons and mere goats does not appear
to be valid for a writer at the time of the final redaction of the Book of
Daniel, since many later exegetical traditions, which will surely have their
roots in Early Judaism, do actually correlate the שְׂעִירִם in Lev 17,7 with
those in Isa 13,21 and explain them mutually (SifreLev 17,7). Furthermore, the Targumim to Lev 17,7 (Targum Neofiti, cf. Rashi's commentary to this verse);[371] Isa 13,21; 34,14;[372] 2 Chr 11,15 all translate שְׂעִירִם

---

[368] Dance, although often used in a profane or a metaphorical sense, can have a religious connotation which associates it with the Baal cult, cf. 1 Kgs 18,26 and see
Mulder, "רקד," in TWAT, eds. Botterweck et al., 1993, VII, 665-668, esp. 666(!), on
the Baal-Marqod.

[369] See in general Wohlstein, "Tier-Dämonologie," ZDMG 113 (1963), 483-492, esp.
487-489.

[370] Snaith, "Meaning of שְׂעִירִם," VT 25 (1975): 115-118, has tried to distinguish between storm-demons (Lev 17,7; 2 Chr 11,15) and normal desert animals without particular demoniac connotations (Isa 13,21; 34,14).

[371] The Targum Ps.-Jonathan translates שְׂעִירִם as "idols" but adds an explanatory
gloss: "who are comparable to demons". Cf. Böhl, "Metaphorisierung," Frankfurter
Judaistische Beiträge 15 (1987): 144.

with שׁידין, "demons",[373] which makes it clear that they understood the שְׂעִירִם in all of these passages as demoniac creatures.[374] This also applies to Rabbinic writings, such as GenR 65,10; LevR 22,5; bBer 62b; bBBatr 25a, which all testify to the tendency that שְׂעִירִם disappears and is being replaced by שֵׁדִים.[375]

Whether these "demoniac" features associated with the he-goat in the Israelite prophetic tradition are rooted in the wider realm of Ancient Near Eastern religion can hardly be said with certainty. Depictions of figures having normal human bodies but with a goat's head or horns are very common throughout the Ancient Near East from very early times onwards. The iconographic context often suggests that these beings had a religious significance, although it is not clear whether they were mere demons or proper gods, nor whether they were good or evil. All one seems to be able to say about them is that appear to have been somehow connected with fertility.[376] Therefore one cannot establish a straightforward connection with the he-goat in Daniel 8, even though it seems evident that the author of Daniel 8 draws on a common iconographic tradition. There is certainly no clear referenct, divine or demoniac, of which he could have been thinking.

There is nevertheless an Old Babylonian statue from about 1700 BC featuring a four-faced god treading on a goat, which has commonly been interpreted as Marduk treading victoriously on the chaos monster Tiamat, a motif well known from the creation epic *Enuma eliš*.[377] If this interpretation is correct, it might say something about the far-reaching demoniac connotations of goats in the Ancient Near East, especially

---

[372] Cf. the edition by Stenning, *Targum of Isaiah*, 1949, 47.113.

[373] The meaning is unambiguous, cf. Sokoloff, *Dictionary*, 1990, s.v. (538); Levy, *Wörterbuch*, 1924, s.v. (IV, 510).

[374] This identification is also made explicit by LevR 22,8 and Sifra Ahare Mot, Perek 9,8.

[375] Cf. Maier, "Geister, " in *RAC* 9 (1976): 680.

[376] Cf. von der Osten-Sacken, *Ziegen-'Dämon'*, 1992, 163ff. Herself, von der Osten-Sacken argues in favour of the view that these beings were gods, since many pictorial representations were found in the context of temples.

[377] Jacobsen, *Treasures of Darkness*, 1976, 166.

since the iconographic context appears to be one of triumph, just as in
Daniel 8. But it is not clear if one can indeed go that far in that direction.

d. The Apocalyptic Transformation of Battle Typology

Apart from the connotations of the ram and the he-goat themselves, which are closely associated with strength and leadership due to
the metaphorical use of the respective terms, there is also a certain connection with the idea of kingship through the usage of royal battle typology in the action described in Dan 8,3-12. Such a connection does not
necessitate the belief that they function as metaphors in Daniel 8. Central
motifs repeatedly applied to them in these verses, like strength (8,4.7)
and swiftness of movement (8,5), breaking the forces (= the horn;[378] 8,7-
8) of the enemy and affirming authority by trampling on him (8,7.10),
keep recurring in various Ancient Near Eastern royal inscriptions, from
Mesopotamia[379] over Egypt[380] up to the periphery of the cuneiform cultures in Western Syria.[381] Especially in Assyria, such descriptions of royal
battles were often interspersed with animal imagery,[382] while they art part
of the "epic poetry" register in the Hebrew Bible – "charging (נגח in the
Piel) with horns" up to the ends of the earth (Dan 8,4) also occurs in

---

[378] Horns were often associated with royal power in biblical imagery, cf. 1 Sam 2,10;
Ps 89,18; 132,17. Given this fact, it is unnecessary to assume a connection with depictions of horns on Seleucid coins, to which Morenz, "Tier mit den Hörnern," *ZAW*
63 (1951): 151-154, refers. For further bibliography cf. Staub, "Tier mit den
Hörnern," in *Hellenismus und Judentum*, eds. Keel and Staub, 2000, 37-85, esp. 54-
55.

[379] RIMA 2/II (ed. Grayson) A.0.102.28, ll. 7-10 (and ll. 43f for the idea of fast
movement); see also A.0.102.30, ll. 8-12; A.0.102.12, l. 36: "to subdue at my feet rulers who oppose me"; A.0.102.95, l. 7; for Shamshi-Adad V see A.0.103.1, col. i, l.
35: "trampler of the lands", for Adad-narari III: A.0.104.8, ll. 4f. The language of
these texts is of course highly formulaic.

[380] Cf. Osing, "'Poetische Stele'," in: *Literatur und Politik*, eds. Assmann and Blumenthal, 1998, 75-86.

[381] Cf. the Phoenician royal inscription from Karatepe (ca. 720 BC), KAI 26A; see
also KAI 222A, ll. 38f.

[382] Marcus, "Animal Similes," *Or. N. S.* 46 (1977): 86-106.

Deut 33,17, נגח (Piel) alone in Ps 44,6,[383] the idea of "breaking" in Num 24,8, the "treading" on enemies in Hab 3,19, both together in Ps 18,39 ‖ 2 Sam 22,39 (cf. Ps 47,4; 58,11; Mal 3,21). There is, as has been seen in the preceding sections, no encrypted reference to a particular ruler, but the generic pattern of a struggle in the supernatural world assumes central notions of kingship.

But again, these allusions to royal typology in Daniel 8 are complemented by a demoniac notion, namely the assault on the stars which the "little horn" endeavours. In fact, Daniel 8 presents an apocalyptic transformation of the royal battle commemorated by many a king's inscription. Here the message is that victory in battle very easily leads to hybris. Hybris, in turn, is a characteristic mark of the rebellious enemy of God.[384] It has already been alluded to in the court tales (cf. Dan 6,8)[385] and in the preceding description of the ram and the he-goat, marked by the repetitive use of the "emotional" Hiphil of גדל (see above). Therefore one may say that this kind of hybris has already been condemned by the narrator, albeit in a rather indirect fashion.

The motif of attacking the stars, however, is a topos for illustrating a maximum of arrogance. Even though it may have originated as a form of royal self-praise at some stage,[386] it carries extremely negative overtones in the imagery of the Bible. The Tower of Babel in Genesis is a well-known symbol for human ambition; apart from that, one may also recall the mockery of the king of Babylon in Isa 14,13 of whom it is said: וְאַתָּה אָמַרְתָּ בִלְבָבְךָ הַשָּׁמַיִם אֶעֱלֶה מִמַּעַל לְכוֹכְבֵי־אֵל אָרִים כִּסְאִי.[387]

---

[383] Behrmann, *Daniel*, 1894, 52, rightly remarks that נגח is said of the winner who pushes down his foes.

[384] Volz, *Eschatologie der jüdischen Gemeinde*, 1934, 89.

[385] The arrogance of a foreign ruler is one of the central themes of Daniel; cf. Kalms, *Sturz des Gottesfeindes*, 2001, 156.

[386] Cf. Sargon's claim to have touched with his hand the jambs of heaven in an Old Assyrian self-praise edited by Günbattı, "Kültepe'den bir tablet," *Archivum Anatolicum* 3 (1997), 131-155, l. 63.

[387] It is wholly unclear whether there is a particular myth in the background (*pace* Niditch, *Symbolic Vision*, 1983, 230); the identification of Hellel Ben Shachar with a specific enemy of God (namely the devil, cf. LXX and Vulgate to Isa 14,12) is in any case late. See Spronk, "Down with Hêlēl," in *"Und Mose schrieb dieses Lied auf"*, eds. Dietrich and Kottsieper, 1998, 717-726.

In Dan 8,11 the traditional topos of trying to reach the stars is combined with the battle motif, insofar as the rebel does not only attempt to grasp into the supernatural realm (תִּגְדַּל), but also brings to fall the heavenly bodies (וַתַּפֵּל אַרְצָה) and tramples on them (וַתִּרְמְסֵם). Particularly the latter two elements are, as has been seen, topoi from the language of battle descriptions. The novelty is that this act of hybris has some initial success, it is thus not a merely rhetorical hyperbole, as in Isa 14,13, where the king's project remains a pure ambition, but a real attack on cosmic powers. The literary adaptation of this topic in Daniel 8 employs the archaic mythical idea of the stars as heavenly warriors, the armed forces of Yahwe[388] who actively participate in battle. Compare Judg 5,20, an instance of Early Hebrew Poetry (cf. Isa 40,26):

מִן־שָׁמַיִם נִלְחָמוּ הַכּוֹכָבִים
מִמְּסִלּוֹתָם נִלְחָמוּ עִם־סִיסְרָא

The stars fought from heaven,
they fought against Sisera from their courses.

Such a belief constitutes the essence of the "military-celestial transaction", that is, the association of military leaders, ranks and stations with stars and positions of galaxies and *vice versa*.[389] In the context of Daniel 8, these topoi are evidently no metaphorical language. Since the battle described in Dan 8,3-12 takes place in the supernatural realm, an attack on the stars as the divine host is no longer an *adynaton*, a widely-used rhetorical figure emphasizing how utterly impossible something is, but a real possibility. Hence, the application of the "military-celestial transaction" in Daniel 8 is another instance of the so-called "Renaissance of the Myth" in Early Judaism,[390] contextually employed in

---

[388] Cf. Smith, *Origins of Biblical Monotheism*, 2001, 63.

[389] For further information see Levine, *Numbers 21-36*, 2000, 201: a hero can be called a "star" (cf. Num 24,17).

[390] Cf. Albani, "Sternbilder," in *Das biblische Weltbild*, eds. Janowski and Ego, 2001, 181-226, esp. 201-204, who thinks that there was a fundamentally new consideration of the religious significance of the stars in Israel due to contact with Mesopotamian religion. This is a theoretically possible *Vermittlungsweg*, but it has to be borne in

order to illuminate the cosmic dimensions an attack upon earthly cult and sanctuary has – it is no rebellion, but nothing less than an outright battle against the divine forces.

Against this background it is not too difficult to see that the innovative combination of the royal battle imagery, the hybris of the rebellious enemy of God and the mythic view of the stars as divine warriors, which are all fairly traditional motifs, serves a particular function within the theology of power developed in the Book of Daniel. It will be observed that whereas the king in royal battle accounts blatantly speak about his own piety, the battle of the "little horn" in Dan 8,10-12, while still making use of the traditional typology, has become the peak of abomination.

The whole scene in its apocalyptic transformation stresses the close connection between kingship and supernatural forces, but completely turns it upside-down. It is in fact a counter-history to royal ideology, as it presents the idea of kingship in its opposition to the forces of order. Yet on the basis of the literary tradition of the rebellious enemy of God it is also obvious that he will be utterly destroyed.[391] This is, however, not covered by the first part of the vision report anymore, which, as in a dramatic act, breaks off at the climax and leads to the first part of the application of the vision. Such an application is left to the reader's knowledge and imagination.

---

mind that the most striking instances of such a new orientation take place in Hellenistic times, when Israelite contact with Mesopotamian ideas was much more feeble. Furthermore, many of the later biblical compositions take up ancient Canaanite motives, rather than Babylonian ones.

[391] Kalms, *Sturz des Gottesfeindes*, 2001, *passim*.

5
The Commentary Section

The animal fight and its aftermath breaks off exactly at the very moment when the most abominable sacrilege, the attack upon the daily offering and the sanctuary, take place. The climactic structure of the narrative indicates that this is indeed the pivotal point at which the forces of evil attempt to destroy the contact between the human and the divine realm. Up to this point, as has been argued, the mimetic narrative consists in the description of a power struggle in the supernatural world. The second half of Daniel 8, however, tackles the corresponding historical reality of this power struggle, its manifestation in political history up to the time of the final redaction. It attempts a contextualizing interpretation and application of a cosmic universal pattern, much in the way exegetical commentary literature of that time (whose style the latter half of Daniel 8 parallels) tries to actualize biblical prophecies. This part of the vision thus also adds a wisdom dimension to the historical allusion, a phenomenon that recurs throughout the Book of Daniel.

1. The Angelic Conversation (8,13-14)

The conversation between two "holy ones", namely the angels,[392] serves as a transition from the pivotal point of the whole battle narrative to the interpretative section of the vision. It will be observed that the seer was reporting this event. With respect to its form and content, this dialogue thus provides a bridge between the above-mentioned major units. Its literary presentation also has a specific function for the outlook of the entire vision, since there is no clear distinction between vision and interpretation. Instead, the mimetic action described in vv. 3-12 continues as one single reality.

---

[392] Cf. Collins, *Daniel*, 1993, 335, who rightly emphasizes that the "holy ones" have a revelatory function here.

a. The Literary Presentation of the Dialogue

The battle narrative in the strict sense stops at 8,12. With 8,13 the focus shifts first to the narrator again and later to two previously unmentioned characters. This shift marks a strong caesura. Moreover, v. 13 introduces a new form of sensual perception by switching from vision to audition, which will remain dominant up to the end of the chapter and therefore ties vv. 13f to the second half of Daniel 8. However, there is also a strong link with what comes before, for the angelic dialogue is an immediate reaction to the abomination accomplished by the "little horn" in 8,12.

At this point the narrator reappears from the background, to which he had disappeared after v. 7, but the chronological sequence of events remains unbroken, as indicated by the series of *wayyiqtol*: וָאֶשְׁמְעָה in v. 13, then a change to the third person and shift of focus through the double וַיֹּאמֶר in vv. 13 and 14. Therefore v. 13 is an immediate consequence of the abomination of the sanctuary. The rapid series of subsequent events in 8,10-12 had already finished with a summary on the resulting situation. As argued earlier the two *wᵉqatal* forms function as a structural marker. Following on this summary, and hence as a reaction to the present state of affairs, the narrator overhears the conversation.

The introduction of this new section is extremely unusual. It combines visual and auditive perception in contrast to the traditional vision or dream reports which normally communicate only one of the two kinds of perception. In the context of Daniel 8 the application of this literary device is understandable, for what Daniel sees is not some fanciful imagination, but a glance behind the human realm, and this glance is rendered much more realistic by the combination of visual and auditive perception. This idea is also strengthened by the continuation of the mainline story. The new series of *wayyiqtol* forms starting at v. 13, while the background scenario is still the content of vv. 3-12 (for the content of vv. 13-14 describes a reaction to this), thus emphasizes that the visionary has not yet finished looking into the supernatural realm, he just continues.

Moreover, the presence of the angels forcefully argues against an allegorical interpretation, since these transcendent beings, whose "reality" can hardly have been doubted by the narrator, are said to share what they themselves have witnessed. Up to this point, together with Daniel, they have been assuming the role of independent spectators of the "mimetic" battle narrative, commenting upon it without referring to the visionary at all. Everything which happens thus appears to be presented with a great "objectivity", guaranteed by some further reliable witnesses. This seems to be the way angels perceives the world.

b. The Dialogue Itself

The content of the reported dialogue, in turn, supplies further information that is implied by the battle narrative, but has not been stated in a more explicit way. It rather outlines how the situation described at 8,12 will keep going on. Formally, the question of the first "holy one"[393] to someone else (פלמוני, an otherwise unattested syncope of פלני and אלמוני)[394] is a lament:

עַד־מָתַי הֶחָזוֹן הַתָּמִיד וְהַפֶּשַׁע שֹׁמֵם †תֵּת וְקֹדֶשׁ† וְצָבָא מִרְמָס

"For how long is the vision, the regular offering, the transgression that makes desolate and his making sanctuary and host a trampling?"

The text is somewhat corrupt. The least problematic emendation apparently consists in reading חתו קדש, "his making sanctuary and host a trampling".[395] Whatever the original text might have been, it must refer directly to the action described in vv. 10-12 (use of the words צָבָא, רמס,

---

[393] According to the rabbinic tradition, the first "holy one" is the angel Michael, cf. Braverman, *Jerome's Commentary*, 1978, 95.

[394] Cf. Ruth 4,1; 1 Sam 21,3; 2 Kgs 6,8. Both, the Old Greek and Theodotion translate the expression as if it were a proper name (τῷ φελμουνι), and in subsequent interpretative tradition it was indeed at times thought to be the name of an angel (among other explanations), cf. Köbert, "Alte Erklärung," *Bib* 35 (1954): 270-272. The Vulgate, on the other hand, has the correct translation *alteri nescio cui*.

[395] See Montgomery, *Daniel*, 1927, 341; accepted by Collins, *Daniel*, 1993, 336. The translation of the Greek versions seems to be a tentative suggestion to make sense of an already corrupt text. For a further discussion cf. the textual commentary above.

קֶדֶשׁ, פֶּשַׁע, נתן, all present in these verses).[396] This part also seems to begin with the outcry of despair – עַד־מָתַי, "How long?", known from Psalms of lamentation to contain the feelings of someone oppressed without any prospect of help.[397] From the use in other texts it is clear that this expression is addressed to God and hence by its mere uttering also pronounces faith in the one who has already determined the end of every suffering.

This nuance of faith and hope is immediately affirmed by the reply of the other angel in v. 14:

$$\text{וַיֹּאמֶר אֵלָיו [}^{398}\text{אֵלַי :MT]}$$
$$\text{עַד עֶרֶב בֹּקֶר אַלְפַּיִם וּשְׁלֹשׁ מֵאוֹת וְנִצְדַּק קֹדֶשׁ}$$

And he answered him: "For two thousand three hundred evenings and mornings. Then it will be the case that the sanctuary will be set right."

The answer to the other angel's question provides a clear statement to the effect that the end of the abomination after 2300 evenings and mornings (does that peculiar wording mean that *every* suspended sacrifice is counted?)[399] has already been determined and the violence against the sacred has already been condemned. The judgment will be effectuated some time in the very near future, more precisely, in a period

---

[396] Rightly noted by Marti, *Daniel*, 1901, 59, and Montgomery, *Daniel*, 1927, 342, although the latter supposes that the terms after "iniquity" are a series of glosses.

[397] Ps 6,4; 79,5; 80,5; 90,13; cf. Isa 6,11; Jer 12,4; Zech 1,12. For its forerunner *adi mati* in Babylonian penitential psalms see Montgomery, *Daniel*, 1927, 341. The reference to Zech 1,12, where the situation is very similar, is perhaps most revealing for the author's attempt to copy his predecessor (so Niditch, *Symbolic Vision*, 1983, 232, without stating a reason why he should do so). A possible motif would be a general orientation towards prophetic language, as has already been observed in the application of the ram and the he-goat as protagonists in Dan 8,3-12.

[398] See the textual commentary above.

[399] On the other hand, one may also think that the morning and evening offering was seen as one unit rather than two events which could be counted separately, cf. for this view Schwantes, "'*Erebbōqer*," *AUSS* 16 (1978): 375-385. As the insertion ἡμέραι in the Old Greek and Theodotion indicates, this interpretation was already known in antiquity.

of time close to the two and a half years mentioned in Dan 7,25 and 12,7. It is now apparent that the "little horn" in the vision will finish just like the ram and the he-goat. Afterwards the sanctuary will function normally again. Moreover, the reference to a specific time introduces the historical dimension into the vision, which is elaborated in the historical application of the cosmic scene. The counting of the time of the sacrifice here provides a normative chronological measure which ties together cosmic and human time.

2. The Application of the Vision (8,15-26)

While the angelic discourse in vv. 13f seems to have obvious connections with the mainline story of the animal fight in vv. 3-12, the interpretation of the vision needs a rather long and complicated epiphany of the *angelus interpres* which serves to link it to the mainline story. This literary device sets vv. 15-26 apart from the first half of Daniel 8, although the setting remains clearly the same. This way the vision of the animal fight is put in the same transcendent realm as the subsequent angelic interpretation. The adaption of the *pešer* style and the addition of elements not belonging to the proper vision report indicate that the explanation suggested by Gabriel is in fact an actualizing application, not a decipherment of the vision as such.

a. The Epiphany of the Interpreter (8,15-18)

After the introductory angelic discourse in vv. 13f the application proper of the vision in vv. 19ff is prepared by the epiphany of Gabriel. The corresponding description follows a fairly conventional pattern. It depicts the visual and auditive elements which accompany the appearance of a divine being, the resulting panic of the beholder,[400] and a subsequent form of encouragement. Between v. 14 and v. 15 there is an explicit caesura. The phrase וַיְהִי בִּרְאֹתִי here introduces a new section, ex-

---

[400] Cf. Dan 10,9; Ez 1,28; 3,23; Apc 1,17 (here, too, the revivification of the visionary is effectuated by the touch of the angel); 1 En 14,14.24; 4 Ezra 10,29f; Niditch, *Symbolic Vision*, 1983, 223.

actly like וַיְהִי בִּרְאֹתִי in v. 2 that functions to mark a shift in the geographical setting. Then וַיְהִי marks a break between the preceding verses and the following narrative sequence. Despite the fact that it is a *wayyiqtol* form, it does not denote an event, but, together with בִּרְאֹתִי,[401] the situation in the background of the new mainline story. So it is the only *wayyiqtol* form which can initiate a narrative sequence.[402] The two unnamed "holy ones" have disappeared to the background again, while the narrator emerges from it; his conscious presence is markedly illuminated by the self-reference אֲנִי דָנִיֵּאל, already known from the frame. It is as if he had come to himself again and now, as a chronologically subsequent step (*wayyiqtol*), seeks understanding (וָאֲבַקְשָׁה בִינָה). For a moment, the level of communication between the narrator and the reader is reestablished when the first person singular appears again.

The presentative marker וְהִנֵּה here signals the shift of attention to something else. In this new situation someone "like a human being" (גבר is perhaps already an allusion to the name Gabriel) is standing before the visionary: וְהִנֵּה עֹמֵד לְנֶגְדִּי כְּמַרְאֵה־גָבֶר. This phrase constitutes a parallel to the introduction of the ram in v. 2 (וְהִנֵּה אַיִל אֶחָד עֹמֵד), which introduces the scene of the animal fight there; the parallelism is reinforced by another, at a first glance superfluous mention of the river Ulai in v. 16.[403] The reader therefore realizes that the setting beheld in the first part of the textual unit remains the same, but also that a new background has been built up, against which a new mainline story will unfold. Thematically, a new unit begins, but it is still set in the environment where the animal fight had taken place before. The narrator is conscious of this fact. Such a continuity of setting, in turn, makes it plausible that it was the author's intention to render the content of vv. 3-12 as a part of the same transcendent reality as the divine revelation. He tries to achieve this by putting the animal fight at the same narrative level as the appearance of the angels.

---

[401] On its own, וַיְהִי is semantically void, cf. Bartelmus, *HYH*, 1982, 114.

[402] Schüle, "Bedeutung", in *Studien*, ed. Wagner, 1997: 118.

[403] בֵּין אוּלָי does not necessarily have to be an Akkadian calque ("riverine peninsula"; so, with reference to J. J. Finkelstein, Lucas, "Daniel," *VT* 50 [2000]: 72-73); for the rather unusual construction (that is, בֵּין with only one noun) cf. Num 17,2 ("amidst").

The interpretation of the vision directly follows a fairly complex introductory section in which the *angelus interpres* approaches the visionary step after step. The whole narrative is mimetic, as the sequence of *wayyiqtol* forms indicates. At first, the attention is again on the sensual perception of the narrator at the beginning of v. 16. The categories applied in this part of the text, including the geographical setting, are all human (וָאֶשְׁמַע קוֹל־אָדָם בֵּין אוּלָי), but mysteriously unspecific.[404] This description of the visionary's auditive experience is followed (still v. 16) in strict chronological sequence (וַיִּקְרָא וַיֹּאמַר) by a reported command in the injunction to the angel (הָבֵן לְהַלָּז אֶת־הַמַּרְאֶה), while the divine instruction directly refers to the narrator (לְהַלָּז):[405] this application of the vision[406] apparently takes place according to the narrator's purposes.

Subsequently the angel approaches the visionary from a distance until he stands close to him, much in the same way the he-goat had approached the ram. Note the series of *wayyiqtol* וַיָּבֹא אֵצֶל עָמְדִי, v. 17; cf. the phrase וַיָּבֹא עַד־הָאַיִל in v. 6. The narrator seems to be absorbed by the cosmic environment, as the figures which populate the divine realm now appear to reach out for him. Just upon the angel's arrival, the seer is struck with terror (וּבְבֹאוֹ נִבְעַתִּי, with fronting of the temporal specification וּבְבֹאוֹ and correspondingly a following *qatal* form), falls down and is addressed directly by the spiritual being (all these events are depicted by means of *wayyiqtol* forms); the reported address itself (which forecasts an eschatological interpretation of the vision taken up in v. 19) contains an imperative, whose consequence is expressed in v. 18 in the same form as the result of the angel's approach in v. 17: fronting of the temporal specification with a following *qatal* form, then the next event(s) by means of *wayyiqtol* forms. The visionary falls in a kind of trance:

---

[404] The "voice of a man" has been variously identified; according to Jerome's commentary, it is the voice of the angel Michael, while the rabbinic tradition understands it as the voice of God speaking in human language (Braverman, *Jerome's Commentary*, 1978, 95).

[405] Cf. GK §§34f for הַלָּז; the phrase is presumably an echo of Zech 2,8.

[406] מַרְאָה is here certainly synonymous for חָזוֹן (again used in v. 17), cf. Bentzen, *Daniel*, 1952, 58 (against Ginsberg, *Studies*, 1948, who thinks this points to a misunderstood Aramaic word).

וּבְדַבְּרוֹ עִמִּי נִרְדַּמְתִּי עַל־פָּנַי אָרְצָה
וַיִּגַּע־בִּי וַיַּעֲמִידֵנִי עַל־עָמְדִי

*And while he was speaking with me, I was in a trance, face to the
ground. Then he touched me and made me stand on the place
where I stood.* [407]

b. Vision and History (8,19-25)

The interaction between Daniel and Gabriel increases the distance
between the vision itself and its application, which is apparently meant by
the narrator. But at the same time it also gives some authoritative look to
the application. One may recall that for the people behind the Book of
Daniel, wisdom comes from God and divine revelation.[408]

Although the mainline story, sustained by means of the series of
wayyiqtol, and its transcendent setting remain basically the same, the interpretation given by the angel is nonetheless presented as an independent textual unit. Its utmost importance is marked by a solemn and
lengthy introduction of the mediator figure. Formally, the caesura in v.
19 is expressed by the use of the presentative marker הִנְנִי and the annun-
ciation of a different literary genre, an instruction (מוֹדִיעֲךָ, from the root
ידע, itself being of course a wisdom term).

This is followed by an overall characterization of the vision as a
future event which will take place long after the time of the fictional
Daniel of the Book: אֲשֶׁר־יִהְיֶה בְּאַחֲרִית הַזַּעַם כִּי לְמוֹעֵד קֵץ, "what will be
at the end of the wrath, since it is for the appointed time of the end", cf.

---

[407] For נִרְדַּמְתִּי as referring to the trance of a seer cf. Gen 15,12; Job 4,12-16; the Septuagint of Gen 2,21 is clearly a witness to this nuance and has ἔκστασις (a term that
belongs to the language of mysticism) for תַּרְדֵּמָה. The same semantic ambiguity between "deep sleep" and "trance" can be found in the Greek word κῶμα. See also Goldingay, *Daniel*, 1989, 214-215.

[408] Grabbe, "Dan(iel) for All Seasons," in *Book of Daniel*, eds. Collins and Flint,
2001: 230; cf. Davies, "Scribal School," in *Book of Daniel*, eds. Collins and Flint,
2001: 252.

Hab 2,3 for the wording.[409] Such a remark pointing to the distant future has already been made in v. 17: כִּי לְעֶת־קֵץ הֶחָזוֹן, "it is the end of time to which the vision refers". The repetition therefore reinforces the importance of the fact that the following explanation is in fact a prophecy for a future time.

The actual interpretation can be sorted out into a series of different identifications of the protagonists in the animal fight according to the specific historical allusions (vv. 20-22). This "catalogue" of identifications concludes with a dramatic presentation of what will happen. Such a division is confirmed by the distinct use of verbal forms in both parts. For vv. 20-22 present a number of nominal sentences which asyndetically explain the figures featuring in vv. 3-12, following the sequence in which they appear: the ram – the kings[410] of Media and Persia (v. 20); the he-goat – the king of Greece; the big horn – the first king (v. 21; presumably Alexander the Great);[411] that being broken (Alexander's death in 323 BC) and four rose up (participle as background and *wayyiqtol* for the subsequent action)[412] in its place – four kingdoms (the division of Alexander's reign after the battle of Ipsos 301 BC) will stand up (*yiqtol*[413]

---

[409] In the later Books of the Bible, there is an increasing association of קֵץ, "end", with nuances of time, cf. Brin, *Concept of Time*, 2001, 264.

[410] The plural מַלְכֵי indicates that the speaker means entire dynasties. But to conclude from this evidence that אַיִל must be collective (so Hasslberger, *Hoffnung*, 1977, 74) is absurd and shows how the assumption of a strict parallelism between vision and application distorts the meaning of the text.

[411] It is obvious that the reference to the description of Alexander the Great as "the one of the two horns" in the Qur'an (Sura 18,82), to which some commentators refer, is a coincidence (correctly stated by Behrmann, *Daniel*, 1894, 51; Marti, *Daniel*, 1901, 57) and has nothing to do with Dan 8,3-12, not only because the animals are no metaphors for worldly kings, but also because the analogy would not stand the fact that the he-goat has only *one* horn (8,5).

[412] The finite form complements the participle, cf. Waltke and O'Connor, *Syntax*, 1990, §33.3.5. The participle here functions as a mere keyword in order to recall the content of the vision as briefly as possible, cf. GK §116w. Consequently, the style is very dense.

[413] Again a grammatical peculiarity – a *y*-prefixed form יַעֲמֹדְנָה instead of the expected תַּעֲמֹדְנָה (as in the first part of v. 22) for the fem. pl. subject מַלְכָיּוֹת. The reading תַּעֲמֹדְנָה of two Hebrew manuscripts, accepted by some commentators (Marti, *Daniel*, 1901, 61-62; Bentzen, *Daniel*, 1952, 58), is the *lectio facilior* and may be a

with future time reference). The change of linguistic coding appears to be responsible for the future tense reference of the *yiqtol* forms in this section, while the *yiqtol* forms in vv. 4 and 12 of the narrative section had a modal meaning. The influence of the syntax beyond sentence-level and the literary genre on the use of specific verbal forms is absolutely transparent here.

The identification of persons, following the same order as the text, strongly reminds of the style of the "continuous" *pešer*[414] (as opposed to the "thematic" one).[415] Many scholars nowadays tend to agree that *pešer* can also be taken as a method of interpretation or as a sub-genre of commentary literature.[416] One may therefore compare the identifying equations in Dan 8,20-22 (mostly asyndetical, but in the form Y הוּא X in v. 21b) with the "Y הוּא X" pattern in the Habakkuk *pešer* from Qumran (1QpHab col. xii, ll. 3ff: the Lebanon "is" the Council of the Community etc.; cf. vii,5.8.14; see also 4QpIsa[b] ii,11) or the backwards reference אֲשֶׁר־רָאִיתָ ("which you have seen") in 8,20 with the אֲשֶׁר אָמַר formula of the commentary style.[417] The mention of a proper name of contemporary history, too, is also a recurrent feature in the *pešer* style (cf. King Demetrius in 4QpNahum 3-4.1.2).[418]

This technique is also applied elsewhere in the Book of Daniel, for example in 2,37f; 4,17.19; 5,26;[419] the use of the analogous formula τοῦτ' ἔστιν in New Testament Greek[420] points to a widespread use of the respective method in Early Judaism. In the context of Daniel 8, this may

---

secondary correction; explaining this phenomenon as an Aramaism (Bevan, *Daniel*, 1929, 138) seems strained. Similar constructions recur in Gen 30,38 and 1 Sam 6,12. (For masc. plur. for fem. plur. cf. Levi, *Inkongruenz*, 1987, 154-160.)

[414] Rightly observed already by Brownlee, *Midrash Pesher*, 1979, 23.

[415] The distinction between *pesher continue* and *pesher thématique* was originally established by Carmignac, "Document sur Melkisédeq," *RevQ* 7 (1969-1971): 342-378.

[416] Brooke, "Qumran Pesher," *RevQ* 10 (1979): 483-503.

[417] Cf. Elliger, *Studien*, 1953, 124-125.

[418] Correctly pointed out by Collins, *Daniel*, 1993, 339.

[419] Elliger, *Studien*, 1953, 156-157, comments explicitly on the convergence of method in 1QpHab and the Book of Daniel.

[420] Lim, "Qumran Scrolls," in Religion, eds. Collins and Kugler, 2000: 60-62.

be additional evidence for the view that the identifications in 8,20-22 are not meant as a decipherment of the vision, but as a contextualizing application of the cosmic pattern to political history at the time of the final redaction of the Book of Daniel.

With v. 23 the style changes markedly.[421] Here instead of the basic identifications in the form of nominal sentences, which evidently furnish some clues for the interpretation about what will happen, there is a dramatic rendering of the character in nominal and verbal sentences (note the use of *yiqtol* with future time reference, just as in the prose section vv. 20-22). The person and the deeds of Antiochus IV Epiphanes are described along this perspective. This "prophetic narrative" continues until v. 25. The description of his deeds presumably refers to the abolition of the perpetual sacrifice and the installation of a foreign cult in the Temple (1 Macc 1,59).[422] These incidents would have been known to the readers of the Book, and they may additionally have been imagined as so abominable as not to be mentioned, so the encrypted references could well be a kind of euphemism. The layout of the BHS makes this stylistic distinction even clearer by printing these verses in poetic lines.

The literary genre also moves from actualizing commentary to prophecy. Moreover, it has been suggested by some scholars that the expression יַעֲמֹד מֶלֶךְ ("a king will rise up") is a characteristic formula in Neo-Babylonian dynastic prophecies,[423] while the meaning "to arise" (referring to the appearance of a king) is unusual for עמד in Hebrew and occurs only[424] here as well as in the dynastic account in Dan 11,2.3.

It is noteworthy that this "dramatic" account, depicting the character of the future king, does not pretend to be an elaboration of the pre-

---

[421] Koch, "Visionsbericht," in: *Apocalypticism*, ed. Hellholm, 1989: 419.

[422] For the historical background cf. Lust, "Cult and Sacrifice," in *Book of Daniel*, eds. Collins and Flint, 2001: 671-688 (with bibliography).

[423] Grayson, *Historical-Literary Texts*, 1975, 17-34, esp. 21. It has to be borne in mind, however, that the Mesopotamian understanding of history was fundamentally different from the apocalyptic one, cf. Grayson's remark on page 4.

[424] In 2 Kgs 10,4; 23,3 the meaning is different ("to withstand" and "to stand" respectively).

ceding vision. On the contrary, it is strikingly independent from it,[425] since nowhere in Dan 8,10-12 it is said that the "little horn" is cunning and crafty, nor are the sufferings of the Jewish people mentioned there (8,24-25a).[426] This leads to a twofold conclusion: first, the deeds of Antiochus receive special emphasis, since they are so outrageous that the linguistic and literary code changes completely (within the same genre, namely prophecy) when it comes to their description; second, Dan 8,23-25 is not meant to be exactly parallel to Dan 8,10-12, although the general theme is taken up. In fact, the latter section is an elaboration of the vision in the light of wisdom terminology (עַז־פָּנִים[427] and מֵבִין in v. 23, שִׂכְלוֹ in v. 25[428]) and concepts (cunning as improper use of wisdom). Particularly the second conclusion fits the overall impression of the vision in Dan 8,3-12 as *non*-allegorical very well. The "little horn" is not a symbol whose referent is Antiochus IV Epiphanes, as is often assumed,[429] but an evil force in the supernatural world which manifests itself in the human

---

[425] Kratz, "Visionen," in *Schriftauslegung*, eds. Kratz, Krüger and Schmid, 2000: 227 ("Allerdings stimmen Bild und Deutung in 8,9-10.23-25 [...] nicht wirklich überein."), is one of the very few scholars who have drawn attention to this fact. But he is surely mistaken in concluding that it must be explained in the light of redactional activity, since the text does not even claim to make vision and interpretation strictly parallel.

[426] In Dan 8,10-12 the object of the horn's aggression, on the other hand, is the heavenly host, see above.

[427] The notable expression עַז־פָּנִים is presumably an intertextual reference to Prov 7,13 (the impudence of the harlot bringing destruction upon her victim), as has been pointed out by Lebram, "König Antiochus," *VT* 25 (1975): 741-742. "Strong of face" in this context means "to be devoid of proper human sensibilities", cf. Fox, *Proverbs*, 2000, 245.

[428] If the MT (defended by Montgomery and others) is to be trusted. For emendations cf. Collins, *Daniel*, 1993, 340-341.

[429] Interestingly, this *communis opinio* has been questioned by Gulley, "Danielic Little Horn," in *To Understand*, ed. Merling, 1997: 191-197, who argues that because of the apocalyptic time-frame the prophetic view of the vision must be far broader and cannot end in the 160s BC. A distinction between the mythical and supernatural combat on the one hand and its particular and historical application on the other hand, however, would solve this problem without playing down the importance of the *Religionsnot* caused by Antiochus for the final redaction of the Book of Daniel, to which Gulley has to resort, because he does not make such a distinction.

realm in the guise of the Hellenistic ruler. Finally, there is another affir-
mation that this ultimate aggressor will be destroyed (lit.: "broken", taking up the language of the vision; so both, the supernatural evil force and
its historical manifestation are meant) without the intervention of a human hand, that is, by divine power: וּבְאֶפֶס יָד יִשָּׁבֵר ("but without anybody's hand he will be broken", v. 25b; see the introductory chapter on
language for the importance of the keyword "hand" in Daniel 1).

c. Apocalypticism and Scribal Culture (8,26)

The dramatic description of the events under Antiochus IV is
brought to a conclusion in v. 26 by a reinforced backward reference to
the vision the seer has just beheld. This conclusion affirms the truth of
what the visionary has seen, but also its temporal distance from the present of the narrative.

The fronting of וּמַרְאֵה ... אֱמֶת הוּא with resumptive pronoun for
topicalization emphasizes that the predication "true, reliable" is applied
to the vision (here מַרְאֶה, instead of חָזוֹן, which is consistently used elsewhere) itself. The second clause of the verse, in turn, is an adversative
address to the visionary ("but as for you..."), giving the order to keep silent about ("seal it up") what he has seen. The reason for this is that the
events beheld will only be fulfilled in a distant future:

$$\text{וְאַתָּה סְתֹם הֶחָזוֹן כִּי לְיָמִים רַבִּים}$$

> *"As for you, however, seal up the vision, for it refers to many
> days."*

The clear verbal allusion to v. 14 in the description of the vision
as מַרְאֵה הָעֶרֶב וְהַבֹּקֶר (this is used almost as a summary title: "The Vision
of the Evening and the Morning")[430] and the reference to its explanation
(אֲשֶׁר נֶאֱמַר, "which you have seen") however, seem to suggest that it is
the *historical realization* of the vision which is for לְיָמִים רַבִּים, not the
universal pattern: The temporal specification הָעֶרֶב וְהַבֹּקֶר is evidently not

---

[430] Correctly seen by Montgomery, *Daniel*, 1927, 352.

part of the animal fight, but of the angelic conversation, which initiates the interpretative application.

Thus, the wording of this text, too, appears to make a distinction between the mimetic description of a cosmic battle, that is, the content of vv. 3-12 in the strict sense, and its visible side in particular history. It has been seen that such a distinction is being uphold throughout Daniel 8. The pattern itself is therefore not bound to a particular time in history. It is rather the actualization and manifestation of powers working in history which takes place in temporal and spatial categories.

The order to "seal up" the vision is at face-value apparently an attempt to make it look more real, because it explains why, though supposedly written down in the reign of Belshazzar, it had remained hidden until Antiochus.[431] This also the case with the analogous (and, for the first part, similarly phrased) statement in Dan 12,4:

וְאַתָּה דָנִיֵּאל סְתֹם הַדְּבָרִים וַחֲתֹם הַסֵּפֶר עַד־עֵת קֵץ

"As for you, Daniel, seal up the words and keep the book secret until the time of the end."

At the same time, the reported command to hide knowledge gained by means of a divine revelation makes this knowledge more "esoteric". This is not an exclusive feature of prophecy and apocalypticism, but it is also a topos regularly associated with scribal culture and tradition. The cultural superiority resulting from the mastery of writing was cemented through hiding the knowledge written down. One may thus compare this to the command to hide the contents of the tablet from the ignorant people, and to make it known only to those who possess the necessary understanding found in several Mesopotamian colophones.[432] The angel's advice so reinforces the wisdom dimension of the Book of Daniel by establishing a link to scribal typology.

---

[431] Montgomery, *Daniel*, 1927, 352, with reference to older commentators and to 1 En 1,2.

[432] See Hunger, *Kolophone*, 1968 (still indispensable), and cf. the wording in nos. 40; 98; 110; 151; 206; 303; 533; 562.

6
Conclusion

The general conclusion from the analysis of Daniel 8 undertaken so far is that the vision is not a "historical allegory" which presents political history in the form of a symbolic animal fight, but that it is a momentary, God-given glance into the supernatural realm. Such a view rests on the highly developed mimetic narrative, during which the narrator constantly emphasizes that the events have taken place before his eyes just as he describes them and that he has been an attentive and conscious observer.

Moreover, this interpretation is corroborated by the absence of any obvious symbolism and the integration of angelic figures, which then function as interpreters, into the same mainline story. What is revealed to the seer is the cosmic universal pattern of a power-struggle in the transcendent realm in the way the angels see it.

The interpretation of the vision, in contrast, is a contextualizing and actualizing application, resembling very much *pešer* style commentaries. It tries to show that the eternal struggle between supernatural forces becomes manifest in the political history within the human realm. However, at the same time it points out by means of various linguistic and stylistic devices that the two realms are not at all identical, as becomes clear from the fact that typical words and ideas used in the description of Antiochus IV Epiphanes do not occur in the vision narrative.

Daniel 8, while elaborating on the contacts between two distinct realms, the supernatural and the human, inserts itself into a central concern of the whole book, namely how one should understand conflict between wordly and divine power. The powers of evil may express themselves in misguided worldly kingship and consequently dare to defile the sacred and try to destroy the contact with the divine via the sanctuary, but they are already doomed to failure. Their end is determined, and hence the enemy of the forces of order will be annihilated, as will be enacted in the course of events in contemporary history.

This is the effort of the Book of Daniel: to propose a theodicy to which the persecutions under Antiochus IV Epiphanes had given rise. It is the path taken by a pacifistic, intellectual opposition of Jewish scholars in order to reconcile the experience of oppression with the faith in the sacred nature of humanity within God's design and under his protection. These scholars express their central concerns by taking up theological ideas and literary traditions already rooted in their culture when they compose this complex work, laden with meaning, that becomes a source of consolation for those who are able to make sense of it.

The message of the Book of Daniel is also couched in subtle linguistic garb. For this reason, a multi-dimensional approach combining textual criticism, linguistic analysis, and literary appreciation proves useful. The bewildering strangeness of apocalyptic theology which has greatly advanced the rise of mathematics, astronomy and the natural sciences during the Middle Ages[433] can still contribute greatly to a scholarly study of language.

It should in any case be clear by now that the Hebrew of the Book of Daniel is a very carefully crafted composition. Daniel 8 reveals this. Its authors apply a maximum of syntactical possibilities, a rich, peculiar and complex lexicon and various literary genres (narrative, dialogue, commentary, prophecy) within one single chapter. Since the linguistic code thus switches several times, it becomes possible to observe within a handful of verses the impact of the literary context with its respective conventions on the meaning of individual verbal forms. On this note, one can reasonably make further reflections on the grammatical "anomalies" and "exceptions" in vocabulary and spelling practice. By considering seriously such "anomalies", one will for sure gain a deeper understanding of the various linguistic devices employed in the text that will otherwise remain unexplored.

Lastly, the discussion of individual problems has shown how an in-depth contextual analysis can contribute significantly to clarify certain textual critical matters and translation technique in antiquity. Since many aspects of the text of Daniel still await further scrutiny, more systematic philological explorations along these lines will likely bring new insights into of this remarkable and often enigmatic composition.

---

[433] See Fried, *Aufstieg*, 2001, for a synopsis.

Bibliography

Abegg, M. G., Jr.
   1998   "The Hebrew of the Dead Sea Scrolls." In *The Dead Sea Scrolls after Fifty Years: A Comprehensive Assessment*, Vol. 1, eds. P. W. Flint and J. C. VanderKam, 325-358. Leiden: Brill.

Albani, M.
   2001   "'Kannst du die Sternbilder hervortreten lassen zur rechten Zeit ...?' (Hi 38,32). Gott und Gestirne im Alten Testament und im Alten Orient." In *Das biblische Weltbild und seine altorientalischen Kontexte*, FAT 32, eds. B. Janowski and B. Ego (eds.), 181-226. Tübingen: Mohr-Siebeck.

Albertz, R.
   1992   *Religionsgeschichte Israels in alttestamentlicher Zeit*. Grundrisse zum Alten Testament 8. Göttingen: Vandenhoeck.
   2001   "The Social Setting of the Aramaic and Hebrew Book of Daniel." In *The Book of Daniel: Composition and Reception*, VT.S 83, eds. J. J. Collins and P. W. Flint, 171-204. Leiden: Brill.

Althann, R.
   1997   *Studies in Northwest Semitic*. biblica et orientalia 45. Rome: Pontifical Biblical Institute.

Assmann, J.
   1977   "Die Verborgenheit des Mythos in Ägypten." *Göttinger Miszellen* 25: 7-43.

Auerbach, E.
   1946   *Mimesis. Dargestellte Wirklichkeit in der abendländischen Literatur*. Bern: Francke.

Baldwin, D. D.
   1997   "Free Will and Conditionality in Daniel." In *To Understand the Scriptures. Essays in Honor of William H. Shea*,

ed. D. Merling, 163-172. Berrien Springs, Michigan: Institute of Archaeology.

Baltzer, K.
2001   *Deutero-Isaiah. A Commentary on Isaiah 40-55.* Transl.
        M. Kohl, ed. P. Machinist. Hermeneia. Minneapolis: For-
        tress.

Barr, J.
1987   "Translators' Handling of Verb Tense in Semantically Am-
        biguous Contexts." In *VI Congress of the International
        Organization for Septuagint and Cognate Studies Jerusa-
        lem 1986*, SCSt 23, ed. C. E. Cox, 381-403. Atlanta:
        Scholars Press.

Bartelmus, R.
1982   *HYH. Bedeutung und Funktion eines hebräischen "Al-
        lerweltswortes". Zugleich ein Beitrag zur Frage des he-
        bräischen Tempussystems.* Arbeiten zu Text und Sprache
        im Alten Testament. St. Ottilien: EOS.

Bauer, W.
1988   *Wörterbuch zum Neuen Testament*, 6th ed. Berlin and New
        York: De Gruyter.

Behrens, A.
2002   *Prophetische Visionsschilderungen im Alten Testament.
        Sprachliche Eigenarten, Funktion und Geschichte einer
        Gattung.* AOAT 292. Münster: Ugarit-Verlag.

Behrmann, G.
1894   *Das Buch Daniel.* HAT 3.3,2. Göttingen: Vandenhoeck.

Bentzen, A.
1952   *Daniel.* HAT 1,19. 2nd ed. Tübingen: Mohr-Siebeck.
1970   *King and Messiah*, ed. G. W. Anderson. Oxford: Basil
        Blackwell.

Bevan, A. A.
1892   *A Short Commentary on the Book of Daniel.* Cambridge:
        Cambridge University Press.

Beyer, K.
1989   "Woran erkennt man, daß ein griechischer Text aus dem
        Hebräischen oder Aramäischen übersetzt ist?" In *Studia
        Semitica necnon Iranica. Festschrift Rudolf Macuch*, eds.

M. Macuch, C. Müller-Kessler and B. G. Fragner, 21-31. Wiesbaden: Harrassowitz.

Beyerle, S.
2001   "The Book of Daniel and its Social Setting." In *The Book of Daniel: Composition and Reception*, VT.S 83, eds. J. J. Collins and P. W. Flint, 205-228. Leiden: Brill.

Blass, F. and A. Debrunner
1990   *Grammatik des neutestamentlichen Griechisch*, 17th ed., ed. F. Rehkopf. Göttingen: Vandenhoeck.

Böhl, F.
1987   "Die Metaphorisierung (Metila) in den Targumim zum Pentateuch." *Frankfurter Judaistische Beiträge* 15: 111-149.

Boll, F.
1903   *Sphaera. Neue griechische Texte und Untersuchungen zur Geschichte der Sternbilder*. Leipzig: Teubner.

Bombeck, S.
2001   "Das althebräische w-Perf. für Gegenwart und Vergangenheit in den hinteren Propheten und den Psalmen." In *Sachverhalt und Zeitbezug. Festschrift Adolf Denz*, Jenaer Beiträger zum Vorderen Orient 4, eds. R. Bartelmus and N. Nebes, 21-34. Wiesbaden: Harrassowitz.

Braverman, J.
1978   *Jerome's Commentary on Daniel. A Study of Comparative Jewish and Christian Interpretations of the Hebrew Bible*. CBQ Monographs 7. Washington, D. C.: The Catholic Biblical Association of America.

Brin, G.
2001   *The Concept of Time in the Bible and the Dead Sea Scrolls*. STDJ 39. Leiden: Brill.

Brinkman, J. A.
1968   *A Political History of Post-Kassite Babylonia 1158-722 B.C.* Analecta Orientalia 43. Rome: Pontifical Biblical Institute.

Brockelmann, C.
1956   *Hebräische Syntax*. Neukirchen: Verlag der Buchhand-

lung des Erziehungsvereins.

Brooke, G. J.
1979 "Qumran Pesher: Towards a Redifinition of a Genre."
RevQ 10: 483-503.

Brownlee, W. H.
1979 *The Midrash Pesher of Habakkuk*. SBL Monographs 24.
Missoula: Scholars Press.

Burridge, R. A.
1992 *What are the Gospels? A Comparison with Graeco-
Roman Biography*. Cambridge: Cambridge University
Press.

Butler, S. A. L.
1998 *Mesopotamian Conceptions of Dreams and Dream Ritu-
als*. AOAT 258. Münster: Ugarit-Verlag.

Caquot, A.
1955 "Sur les quatre Bêtes de Daniel VII." *Semitica* 5: 6 13.

Carmignac, J.
1969-71 "Le document de Qumrân sur Melkisédeq." *RevQ* 7: 342-
378.
1972-75 "L'emploi de la négation אין dans la Bible et à Qumrân."
RevQ 8: 401-411.

Cereti, C. G.
2001 *La letteratura Pahlavi. Introduzione ai testi con riferi-
menti alla storia degli studi e alla tradizione mano-
scritta*. Milano: Associazione Culturale Mimesis.

Charles, R. H.
1929 *A Critical and Exegetical Commentary on the Book of
Daniel*. Oxford: Oxford University Press.

Collins, J. J., ed.
1979 *Apocalypse: The Morphology of a Genre*. Semeia 14.
Missoula: Scholars Press.

Collins, J. J.
1984 *Daniel. With an Introduction to Apocalyptic Literature*.
The Forms of the Old Testament Literature 20. Grand
Rapids: Eerdmans.
1993 *Daniel. A Commentary on the Book of Daniel*. Hermeneia. Minneapolis: Fortress.

1998   *The Apocalyptic Imagination. An Introduction to Jewish Apocalyptic Literature.* 2nd ed. Grand Rapids: Eerdmans.

Comrie, B.
1976   *Aspect.* Cambridge Textbooks in Linguistics. Cambridge: Cambridge University Press.

1985   *Tense.* Cambridge Textbooks in Linguistics. Cambridge: Cambridge University Press.

Cooke, G. A.
1903   *A Text-book of North-Semitic Inscriptions.* Oxford: Oxford University Press.

Cross, F. M. and D. N. Freedman
1997   *Studies in Ancient Yahwistic Poetry.* Grand Rapids: Eerdmans.

Crowe, S. P.
1992   *The Armenian Version of Daniel.* Atlanta: Scholars Press.

Cumont, F.
1909   "La plus ancienne géographie astrologique." *Klio* 9: 263-273.

Dahood, M.
1965   "Review of: KAI." *Or. N. S.* 34: 84-87.

Dandamaev, M.
1984   "The Diaspora. A: Babylonia in the Persian Age." In *The Cambridge History of Judaism*, Vol. 1, eds. W. D. Davies and L. Finkelstein, 326-342. Cambridge: Cambridge University Press.

Davies, P. R.
1980   "Eschatology in the Book of Daniel." *JSOT 17*: 33-53.

2001   "The Scribal School of Daniel." In *The Book of Daniel: Composition and Reception*, VT.S 83, eds. J. J. Collins and P. W. Flint, 247-265. Leiden: Brill.

Day, J.
1985   *God's conflict with the dragon and the sea.* Cambridge: Cambridge University Press.

Dietrich, M., O. Loretz and J. Sanmartín
1995   *The Cuneiform Alphabetic Texts from Ugarit, Ras Ibn Hani and Other Places.* KTU Edition No. 2. Abhandlungen zur Literatur Alt-Syrien-Palästinas und Mesopo-

tamiens 8. Münster: Ugarit-Verlag.

Dirksen, P. B.

1988   "The Old Testament Peshitta." In *Mikra: Text, Translation, Reading and Interpretation of the Hebrew Bible in Ancient Judaism and Early Christianity*, eds. M. J. Mulder and H. Sysling, 255-297. Assen: Van Gorcum.

Donner, H. and W. Röllig

1962-64   *Kanaanäische und Aramäische Inschriften*. 3 Vols. 5th revised ed. of Vol. 1 2002. Wiesbaden: Harrassowitz.

Driver, S. R.

1998   *A Treatise on the Use of the Tenses in Hebrew and Some Other Syntactical Questions*. 4th ed. Grand Rapids: Eerdmans.

Ebner, M., H. Gzella, H.-G. Nesselrath and E. Ribbat

2001   *Lukian. Die Lügenfreunde*. Sapere 3. Darmstadt: Wissenschaftliche Buchgesellschaft (2nd, unaltered ed. ibid. 2002).

Eggler, J.

2000   *Influences and Traditions Underlying the Vision of Daniel 7:2-14. The Research History from the End of the 19th Century to the Present*. OBO 177. Göttingen: Vandenhoeck.

Ehrlich, A. B.

1908-14   *Randglossen zur Hebräischen Bibel. Textkritisches, Sprachliches und Sachliches*. Leipzig: Hinrichs.

Eldar, I.

1988   "An Ancient Genizah Treatise on Interchangeable Letters in Hebrew." *Tarbiz 57*: 483-510.

Elliger, K.

1953   *Studien zum Habakuk-Kommentar vom Toten Meer*. Beiträge zur historischen Theologie 15. Tübingen: Mohr-Siebeck.

Eskhult, M.

1990   *Studies in Verbal Aspect and Narrative Technique in Biblical Hebrew Prose*. Acta Universitatis Upsaliensis, Studia Semitica Upsaliensia 12. Stockholm: Almqvist & Wiksell.

Ewald, H.
  1870   *Ausführliches Lehrbuch der hebräischen Sprache des Alten Bundes.* 8th ed. Göttingen: Verlag der Dieterichschen Buchhandlung.

Fitzmyer, J. A.
  1971   *The Genesis Apocryphon of Qumran Cave 1. A Commentary.* biblica et orientalia 18A. 2nd ed. Rome: Pontifical Biblical Institute.

Fleischman, S.
  1990   *Tense and Narrativity. From Medieval Performance to Modern Fiction.* Austin: University of Texas Press.

Fox, M. V.
  2000   *Proverbs 1-9.* AB 18A. New York: Doubleday.

Fredericks, D. C.
  1988   *Qoheleth's Language: Re-Evaluating Its Nature and Date.* Ancient Near Eastern Texts and Studies 3. Lewiston: Mellen Biblical Press.

Fried, J.
  2001   *Aufstieg aus dem Untergang. Apokalyptisches Denken und die Entstehung der modernen Naturwissenschaft in Mittelalter.* München: Beck.

Frye, R. N.
  1984   *The History of Ancient Iran.* Handbuch der Altertumswissenschaft III/7. München: Beck.

Gane, R.
  1997   "Genre Awareness and Interpretation of the Book of Daniel." In *To Understand the Scriptures. Essays in Honor of William H. Shea*, ed. D. Merling, 137-148. Berrien Springs, Michigan: Institute of Archaeology.

Gardner, A. E.
  2001   "Daniel 7,2-14: Another Look at its Mythic Pattern." *Bib* 82: 244-252.

Geertz, C.
  1973   *The Interpretation of Cultures. Selected Essays.* New York: Basic Books.

Gehman, H. S.
  1925   "The 'Polyglot' Arabic Text of Daniel and Its Affinities."

JBL 44: 327-352.

1927 "The Sahidic and Bohairic Versions of the Book of Daniel." *JBL* 46: 279-330.

Gelston, A.

1997 "Was the Peshitta of Isaiah of Christian Origin?" In *Writing and Reading the Scroll of Isaiah. Studies of an Interpretative Tradition*, Vol. 2, VT.S 70,2 eds. C. G. Broyles and C. A. Evans, 563-582. Leiden: Brill.

Gesenius, W. and E. Kautzsch

1909 *Hebräische Grammatik*. 28th ed. Leipzig: Vogel.

Gianto, A.

1996 "Variations in Biblical Hebrew." *Bib* 77: 493-508.

1998 "Moods and Modality in Classical Hebrew." *IOS* 18: 183-198.

Gibson, J. C. L.

1973 *Textbook of Syrian Semitic Inscriptions. Volume III. Phoenician Inscriptions*. Oxford: Oxford University Press.

Ginsberg, H. L.

1948 *Studies in Daniel*. New York: The Jewish Theological Seminary of America.

Gnuse, R. K.

1997 *Dreams and Dream Reports in the Writings of Josephus. A Traditio-Historical Analysis*. AGAJU 36. Leiden: Brill.

Goldfajn, T.

1998 *Word Order and Time in Biblical Hebrew Narrative*. Oxford Theological Monographs. Oxford: Oxford University Press.

Goldingay, J. E.

1989 *Daniel*. WBC 30. Dallas: Word Books.

Gordon, A.

1982 "The Development of the Participle in Biblical, Mishnaic, and Modern Hebrew." *Afroasiatic Linguistics* 8: 121-179.

Grabbe, L. L.

2001 "A Dan(iel) for All Seasons: For Whom was Daniel Important?" In *The Book of Daniel: Composition and Reception*, VT.S 83, eds. J. J. Collins and P. W. Flint, 229-

246. Leiden: Brill.

Grayson, A. K.

1975 *Babylonian Historical-Literary Texts.* Toronto Semitic Texts and Studies 3. Toronto: University of Toronto Press.

1991 Assyrian Rulers of the Early First Millennium BC. Royal Inscriptions of Mesopotamia. Assyrian Periods 2. Toronto: University of Toronto Press.

Greenberg, M.

1983 *Ezekiel 1-20.* AB 22. New York: Doubleday.

Gross, W.

1987 *Die Pendenskonstruktion im Biblischen Hebräisch. Studien zum althebräischen Satz I.* Arbeiten zu Text und Sprache im Alten Testament. St. Ottilien: EOS.

Gulley, N.

1997 "Why the Danielic Little Horn is not Antiochus IV Epiphanes." In *To Understand the Scriptures. Essays in Honor of William H. Shea,* ed. D. Merling, 191-197. Berrien Springs, Michigan: Institute of Archaeology.

Günbattı, C.

1997 "Kültepe'den akadlı Sargon'a âit bir tablet." *Archivum Anatolicum* 3: 131-155.

Gunkel, H.

1895 *Schöpfung und Chaos in Urzeit und Endseit. Eine religionsgeschichtliche Untersuchung über Gen 1 und Ap Joh 12,* Göttingen: Vandenhoeck.

Gzella, H.

2001a "Das Kalb und das Einhorn. Endzeittheophanie und Messianismus in der Septuaginta-Fassung von Ps 29 (28)." In *Der Septuaginta-Psalter. Sprachliche und theologische Aspekte,* HBS 32, ed. E. Zenger, 257-290. Freiburg: Herder.

2001b see Ebner, M.

2002a *Lebenszeit und Ewigkeit. Studien zur Eschatologie und Anthropologie des Septuaginta-Psalters.* BBB 134. Berlin: Philo.

2002b "Beobachtungen zur Angelologie der Sabbatopferlieder

im Spiegel ihrer theologiegeschichtlichen Voraussetzungen." *ETL* 79: 468-481.

2003   "Hebräische Verbformen mit modaler Bedeutung im Spiegel der alten Bibelübersetzungen." Forthcoming in *Kleine Untersuchungen zur Sprache des Alten Testaments und seiner Umwelt (KUSATU). Beiträge des 6. Mainzer Hebraistischen Kolloquiums am 9. November 2002*, ed. R. G. Lehmann, Waltrop: Spenger.

Hagan, H. (= W.)

1986   *The Battle Narrative of David and Saul. A Literary Study of 1 Sam 13 - 2 Sam 8 and Its Genre in the Ancient Near East.* Unpublished Dissertation. Rome: Pontifical Biblical Institute.

Harrington, D. J.

1999   "The Ideology of Rule in Daniel 7-12." *SBL Seminar Papers*: 540-551.

Hartman, L. F. and A. Di Lella

1978   *The Book of Daniel.* AB 23. New York: Doubleday.

Hasslberger, B.

1977   *Hoffnung in der Bedrängnis. Eine formkritische Untersuchung zu Dan 8 und 10-12.* Arbeiten zu Text und Sprache im Alten Testament. St. Ottilien: EOS.

Hatav, G.

1997   *The semantics of aspect and modality. Evidence from English and biblical Hebrew.* Studies in Language Companion Series 34. Amsterdam: John Benjamins.

Hävernick, H. A. C.

1832   *Commentar über das Buch Daniel.* Hamburg: Friedrich Perthes.

Heimerdinger, J.-M.

1999   *Topic, Focus and Foreground in Ancient Hebrew Narratives.* JSOTSS 295. Sheffield: Sheffield Academic Press.

Heininger, B.

1995   *Paulus als Visionär. Eine religionsgeschichtliche Studie.* HBS 9. Freiburg: Herder.

Hengel, M.

1988   *Judentum und Hellenismus: Studien zu ihrer Begegnung unter besonderer Berücksichtigung Palästinas bis zur Mitte des 2. Jh.s v. Chr.* 3rd ed. Tübingen: Mohr-Siebeck.

Henze, M.
  1999   "The Ideology of Rule in the Narrative Frame of Daniel (Daniel 1-6)." *SBL Seminar Papers*: 527-539.

Hirsch, E. D., Jr.
  1967   *Validity in Interpretation.* New Haven: Yale University Press.

Holladay, W. L.
  1989   *Jeremiah 2.* Hermeneia. Minneapolis: Fortress.

Huehnergard, J.
  1997   *A Grammar of Akkadian.* HSS 45. Atlanta: Scholars Press.

Humphreys, W. L.
  1973   "A Life-Style for Diaspora: A Study of the Tales of Esther and Daniel." *JBL* 92: 211-223.

Hunger, H.
  1968   *Babylonische und assyrische Kolophone.* AOAT 2. Neukirchen-Vluyn: Butzon & Bercker.

Husser, J.-M.
  1999   *Dreams and Dream Narratives in the Biblical World.* The Biblical Seminar 63. Sheffield: Sheffield Academic Press.

Jacobsen, T.
  1976   *The Treasures of Darkness. A History of Mesopotamian Religion.* New Haven: Yale University Press.

Janowski, B.
  1999   "Satyrs." *Dictionary of Deities and Demons in the Bible*, 2nd ed., eds. K. van der Toorn, B. Becking and P.W. van der Horst, 732-733. Leiden: Brill.

Japhet, S.
  1968   "The supposed common authorship of Chronicles and Ezra-Nehemiah investigated anew." *VT* 18: 330-371.

Jason, H.
  1977a   *Ethnopoetry. Form, Content, Function.* Forum Theologiae Linguisticae 11. Bonn: Linguistica Biblica.
  1977b   "Precursors of Propp: Formalist Theories in Early Russian Ethnopoetics." *Journal of Poetics and Theory of Litera-*

ture 3: 471-516.

Jeansonne, S. P.
1988   *The Old Greek Translation of Daniel 7-12*. CBQ Mono-
         graphs 19. Washington, D. C.: The Catholic Biblical As-
         sociation of America.

Jeffers, A.
1996   *Magic and Divination in Ancient Palestine and Syria*.
         Studies in the History and Culture of the Ancient Near
         East 8. Leiden: Brill.

Jeremias, A.
1916   *Das Alte Testament im Lichte des Alten Orients*. 3rd ed.
         Leipzig: Hinrichs.

Joosten, J.
1999   "Pseudo-Classicisms in Late Biblical Hebrew, in Ben Sira,
         and in Qumran Hebrew." In *Sirach, Scrolls, and Sages:
         Proceedings of a Second International Symposium on the
         Hebrew of the Dead Sea Scrolls, Ben Sira, and the Mish-
         nah, Held at Leiden University, 15-17 December 1997*,
         STDJ 33, eds. T. Muraoka and J. F. Elwolde, 149-159.
         Leiden: Brill.

Joüon, P.
1986   *Ruth. Commentaire philologique et exégétique*. subsidia
         biblica 9. Rome: Pontifical Biblical Institute.

Joüon, P. and T. Muraoka
1993   *A Grammar of Biblical Hebrew. Part Three: Syntax*. sub-
         sidia biblica 14/II. Rome: Pontifical Biblical Institute.

Justus, C. F.
1981   "Visible Sentences in Cuneiform Hittite." *Visible Lan-
         guage* XV,4: 373-408.

Kalms, J. U.
2001   *Der Sturz des Gottesfeindes. Traditionsgeschichtliche
         Studien zu Apokalypse 12*. WMANT 93. Neukirchen-
         Vluyn: Neukirchener.

Keel, O.
1992   *Das Recht der Bilder gesehen zu werden. Drei
         Fallstudien zur Methode der Interpretation altorienta-
         lischer Bilder*. OBO 122. Göttingen: Vandenhoeck.

Kamesar, A.
1993   *Jerome, Greek Scholarship, and the Hebrew Bible. A Study of the "Quaestiones Hebraicae in Genesim"*. Oxford: Oxford University Press.

Kermode, F.
1980   *The Genesis of Secrecy*. Cambridge / Mass.: Harvard University Press.

Khan, G.
1988   *Studies in Semitic Syntax*. London Oriental Series 38. Oxford: Oxford University Press.

King, L. W.
1912   *Babylonian Boundary-Stones and Memorial-Tablets in the British Museum*. London: Longman.

Köbert, R.
1954   "Eine alte Erklärung von '*palmoni*' (Dan. 8, 13)." *Bib* 35: 270-272.

Koch, K.
1989   "Vom profetischen zum apokalyptischen Visionsbericht." In *Apocalypticism in the Mediterranean World and the Near East. Proceedings of the International Colloquium on Apocalypticism Uppsala, August 12-17, 1979*, 2nd ed., ed. D. Hellholm, 413-441. Tübingen: Mohr-Siebeck.

König, F. E.
1897   *Historisch-comparative Syntax der Hebräischen Sprache*. Leipzig: Hinrichs.

Koschmieder, E.
1952   *Die noetischen Grundlagen der Syntax*. Sitzungsberichte der Bayerischen Akademie der Wissenschaften, Philosophisch-historisch Klasse, 1951, Heft 4. München. Reprinted in: id., *Beiträge zur allgemeinen Syntax*, Heidelberg 1965: Winter.

Kratz, R. G.
2000   "Die Visionen des Daniel." In *Schriftauslegung in der Schrift. Festschrift Odil H. Steck*, BZAW 300, eds. R. G. Kratz, Th. Krüger and K. Schmid, 219-236. Berlin and New York: De Gruyter.

Kropat, A.
1909   *Die Syntax des Autors der Chronik verglichen mit der seiner Quellen. Ein Beitrag zur historischen Syntax des Hebräischen.* BZAW 16. Gießen: Töpelmann.

Kühner, R. and B. Gerth
1898   *Ausführliche Grammatik der griechischen Sprache*, Vol. II. 3rd ed. Hannover and Leipzig: Hahnsche Buchhandlung.

Kuhrt, A.
1995   *The Ancient Near East*, Vol. II. London: Routledge.

Kutscher, E. Y.
1974   *The language and linguistic background of the Isaiah Scroll (1QIsa^a).* STDJ 6. Leiden: Brill.
1982   *A History of the Hebrew Language.* Ed. R. Kutscher. Jerusalem: Magnes; Leiden: Brill.

Kvanvig, H. S.
1988   *Roots of Apocalyptic: The Mesopotamian Background of the Enoch Figure and of the Son of Man.* WMANT 61. Neukirchen-Vluyn: Neukirchener.

Larsen, M. T.
1996   *The Conquest of Assyria. Excavations in an Antique Land 1840-1860.* London: Routledge.

Lebram, J. C. H.
1975   "König Antiochus im Buch Daniel." *VT* 25: 737-772.

Leichty, E.
1970   *The Omen Series Šumma izbu.* Locust Valley: Augustin.

Levi, J.
1987   *Die Inkongruenz im biblischen Hebräisch.* Wiesbaden: Harrassowitz.

Levine, B. A.
2000   *Numbers 21-36.* AB 4A. New York: Doubleday.

Levy, J.
1924   *Wörterbuch über die Talmudim und Midraschim.* 2nd ed. With additions and corrections by L. Goldschmidt. Berlin and Wien: Benjamin Harz.

Lim, T. H.
2000   "The Qumran Scrolls, Multilingualism, and Biblical Inter-

pretation." In *Religion in the Dead Sea Scrolls*, eds. J. J. Collins and R. A. Kugler, 57-73. Grand Rapids: Eerdmans.

Lipiński, E.

2001   *Semitic Languages. Outline of a Comparative Grammar.* Orientalia Lovaniensia Analecta 80. 2nd ed. Leuven: Peeters.

Löfgren, O.

1927   *Die äthiopische Übersetzung des Propheten Daniel.* Paris: Geuthner.

1936   *Studien zu den arabischen Daniel-Übersetzungen. Mit besonderer Berücksichtigung der christlichen Texte.* Uppsala Universitets Ärsskrift 4. Uppsala: Lundequistska bokhandeln.

Longacre, R. E.

1989   *Joseph: A Story of Divine Providence. A Text Theoretical and Text Linguistic Analysis of Genesis 37 and 39-48.* Winona Lake: Eisenbrauns.

1994   "Weqatal Forms in Biblical Hebrew Prose. A Discourse-modular Approach." In *Biblical Hebrew and Discourse Linguistics*, ed. R. D. Bergen, 50-98. Dallas: Summer Institute of Linguistics.

Lucas, E. C.

1990   "The Source of Daniel's Animal Imagery." *TynBul* 41: 161-185.

2000   "Daniel: Resolving the Enigma." *VT* 50: 66-80.

Lust, J.

1987   "Exegesis and Theology in the LXX of Ezekiel. The Longer 'Pluses' and Ezek 43:1-9." In *VI Congress of the International Organization for Septuagint and Cognate Studies Jerusalem 1986* (SCSt 23), ed. C. E. Cox, 201-232. Atlanta: Scholars Press.

2001   "Cult and Sacrifice in Daniel. The Tamid and the Abomination of Desolation." In *The Book of Daniel: Composition and Reception*, VT.S 83, eds. J. J. Collins and P. W. Flint, 671-688. Leiden: Brill.

Mach, M.
1992   *Entwicklungsstadien des jüdischen Engelglaubens in vor-rabbinischer Zeit*. TSAJ 34. Tübingen: Mohr-Siebeck.

Maier, J.
1976   "Geister (Dämonen): B.III. d. Talmudisches Judentum." *RAC*, 9:668-688. Münster, Westf.: Aschendorff.

Main, E.
1998   "For King Jonathan or Against? The Use of the Bible in 4Q448." In *Biblical Perspectives. Early Use and Interpretation of the Bible in the Light of the Dead Sea Scrolls*, STDJ 28, eds. M. E. Stone and E. G. Chazon, 113-135. Leiden: Brill.

Marcus, D.
1977   "Animal Similes in Assyrian Royal Inscriptions." *Or N.S.* 46: 86-106.

Margoliouth, D. S.
1889   *A Commentary on the Book of Daniel by Jephet Ibn Ali the Karaite*. Anecdota Oxoniensia. Semitic Series 1.3. Oxford: Oxford University Press.

Marti, K.
1901   *Das Buch Daniel*. Kurzer Hand-Commentar zum Alten Testament 18. Tübingen and Leipzig: Mohr-Siebeck.

Maul, S. M.
1998   "Im Fadenkreuz von Raum und Zeit. Zum Verhältnis von Weltbild und Herrschaftskonzeption im Alten Orient (Festvortrag anläßlich des 70. Geburtstages von Prof. Dr. Karlheinz Deller am 21.2.1997)." *Heidelberger Jahrbücher* 42: 27-41.

McCarthy, D.
1980   "The uses of *wehinnēh* in Biblical Hebrew." *Bib* 61: 330-342.

McFall, L.
1982   *The Enigma of the Hebrew Verbal System: Solutions from Ewald to the Present*. Historical Texts and Interpreters in Biblical Scholarship 2. Sheffield: Almond Press.

McKnight, E. V.
1988   *Post-Modern Use of the Bible. The Emergence of*

Reader-Oriented Criticism. Nashville: Abingdon.

McLay, T.
1996   *The OG and Th Versions of Daniel*. SBLSCS 43. Atlanta: Scholars Press.

Meyer, E.
1931   "Untersuchungen zur phönikischen Religion." *ZAW* 49: 1-15.

Meyer, R.
1992   *Hebräische Grammatik*. Reprint of the 3rd ed. 1966-1972. Berlin: De Gruyter.

Miller, P. D.
1970   "Animal Names as Designations in Ugaritic and Hebrew." *UF* 2: 177-186

Montgomery, J. A.
1927   *The Book of Daniel*. ICC. New York: Charles Scribner's Sons.

Morag, S.
1973   *The Book of Daniel. A Babylonian-Yemenite Manuscript*. Jerusalem: Kiryat Sepher.

Moran, W. L.
1964   "**Taqtul* – Third Masculine Singular?" *Bib* 45: 80-82.

Morenz, S.
1951   "Das Tier mit den Hörnern." *ZAW* 63: 151-154.

Morrison, C. E.
2001   *The Character of the Syriac Version of the First Book of Samuel*. MPIL 11. Leiden: Brill.

Moulton, J. H.
1911   *Einleitung in die Sprache des Neuen Testaments*. Heidelberg: Winter.

Mulder, M.
1993   "רקד." *TWAT*, eds. G. Botterweck, H.-J. Fabry and H. Ringgren, VII:665-668. Stuttgart: Kohlhammer.

Munnich, O. (see also under J. Ziegler)
1999   *Susanna, Daniel, Bel et Draco. Editio secunda*. Septuaginta. Vetus Testamentum Graecum XVI/2. Göttingen: Vandenhoeck.

Muraoka, T.

1973   "Literary Device in the Septuagint." *Textus* 8: 20-30.

1985   *Emphatic words and structures in Biblical Hebrew.* Jerusalem: Magnes Press.

Niccacci, A.

1986   *Sintassi del verbo ebraico nella prosa biblica classica.* Studium Biblicum Franciscanum Analecta 23. Jerusalem: Franciscan Printing Press.

Niditch, S.

1983   *The Symbolic Vision in Biblical Tradition.* HSM 30. Chico: Scholars Press.

Nöldeke, Th.

1879   "Geschichte des Artachšîr i Pâpakân." *Beiträge zur Kunde der Indogermanischen Sprachen* IV: 22-69.

Nuñez, S.

1982   *The vision of Daniel 8. Interpretations from 1700 to 1800.* Berrien Springs, Michigan: Andrews University Press.

1997   "The Usage and Meaning of the Hebrew Word תמיד in the Old Testament." In *To Understand the Scriptures. Essays in Honor of William H. Shea*, ed. D. Merling, 95-102. Berrien Springs, Michigan: Institute of Archaeology.

Oppenheim, A. L.

1956   *The Interpretation of Dreams in the Ancient Near East.* TAPS 3. Philadelphia: The American Philosophical Society.

Osing, J.

1998   "Zur 'Poetischen Stele' Thutmosis' III." In *Literatur und Politik im pharaonischen und ptolemäischen Ägypten, Gedenkschrift Georges Posener*, IFAO 127, eds. J. Assmann and E. Blumenthal, 75-86. Cairo: Institut Français d'Archéologie Orientale.

Osten-Sacken, E. von der

1992   *Der Ziegen-'Dämon'. 'Obed- und Urukzeitliche Götterdarstellungen.* AOAT 230. Kevelaer: Butzon & Bercker.

Panofsky, E.
1932   "Zum Problem der Beschreibung und Inhaltsdeutung von Werken der bildenden Kunst." *Logos* 21: 103-119.

Parker, S. B.
1997   *Stories in Scripture and Inscriptions. Comparative Studies on Narratives in Northwest Semitic Inscriptions and the Hebrew Bible.* New York: Oxford University Press.

Parpola, S.
1993   *Letters from Assyrian and Babylonian scholars.* State Archives of Assyria 10. Helsinki: University Press.

Peshitta-Institute.
1980   *The Old Testament in Syriac According to the Peshitta Version*, Vol. III/4, Leiden: Brill.

Petit, T.
1990   *Satrapes et satrapies dans l'empire achéménide de Cyrus le Grand à Xerxès Ier.* Bibliothèque de la Faculté de Philosophie et Lettres de l'Université de Liège, fasc. 254. Paris: Les Belles Lettres.

Pfeiffer, R. H.
1952   *Introduction to the Old Testament.* London: Adam & Charles Black.

Pollak, W.
1988   *Studien zum Verbalaspekt. Mit besonderer Berücksichtigung des Französischen.* Bern: Lang.

Polzin, R. M.
1976   *Late Biblical Hebrew: Toward An Historical Typology of Biblical Hebrew Prose.* HSM 12. Missoula: Scholars Press.

Porter, P. A.
1985   *Metaphors and Monsters. A Literary-Critical Study of Daniel 7 and 8.* Coniectanea Biblica, Old Testament Series 20. Toronto: s.n.

Porteous, N. W.
1978   *Das Buch Daniel.* ATD 23. Transl. W. Beyerlin, O. Kaiser and R. Walz. 3rd ed. Göttingen: Vandenhoeck.

Qimron, E.
1986   *The Hebrew of the Dead Sea Scrolls.* HSS. Atlanta:

Scholars Press.

Rabin, Ch.
1973   *A Short History of the Hebrew Language.* Jerusalem:
            Publishing Department of the Jewish Agency.

Rahmer, M.
1861   *Die hebräischen Traditionen in den Werken des Hierony-
            mus.* Breslau: Verlag der Schletter'schen Buchhandlung.

Rainey, A. F.
2001   "Mesha' and Syntax." In *The Land that I Will Show You.*
            Festschrift J. M. Miller, JSOTSS 295, eds. J. A. Dearman
            and M. P. Graham, 287-307. Sheffield: Sheffield Aca-
            demic Press.

Rendsburg, G.
1990   *Linguistic Evidence for the Northern Origin of Selected
            Psalms.* SBL Monographs 43. Atlanta: Scholars Press.

Richter, W.
1963   "Traum und Traumdeutung im AT. Ihre Form und Ver-
            wendung." *BZ* 7: 202-220.

Roca-Puig, R.
1976   "Daniele: Due semifogli del codice 967: P. Barc. inv. nn.
            42 e 43." *Aegyptus* 56: 3-18.

Rooker, M. F.
1990   *Biblical Hebrew in Transition: The Language of the Book
            Ezekiel.* JSOTSS 90. Sheffield: Sheffield Academic Press.

Rosen, K.
1970   *Studien zur Darstellungskunst und Glaubwürdigkeit des
            Ammianus Marcellinus.* Bonn: Habelts Dissertations-
            drucke.

Rosenthal, F.
1946   "Review of: H. L. Ginsberg, *The Legend of King Keret.*
            BASOR Suppl. 2-3, New Haven 1946." *Or. N. S.* 16:
            399-402.

1995   *A Grammar of Biblical Aramaic.* Wiesbaden: Harras-
            sowitz.

Schaper, J.
2001   "Die Renaissance der Mythologie im hellenistischen
            Judentum und der Septuaginta-Psalter." In *Der Septua-*

ginta-Psalter. Sprachliche und theologische Aspekte, HBS 32, ed. E. Zenger, 171-183. Freiburg: Herder.

Schniedewind, W. M.
1999 "Qumran Hebrew as Antilanguage." *JBL* 118: 235-252.

Scholes, R. and R. Kellogg
1966 *The Nature of Narrative*, Oxford: Oxford University Press.

Schüle, A.
1997 "Zur Bedeutung der Formel *wajjehi* im Übergang zum mittelhebräischen Tempussystem." In *Studien zur hebräischen Grammatik*, OBO 156, ed. A. Wagner, 115-125. Göttingen: Vandenhoeck.

Schwantes, S. J.
1978 "'*Erebbōqer* of Dan 8:14 Re-examined." *AUSS* 16: 375-385.

Seeligmann, I. L.
1948 *The Septuagint Translation of Isaiah*. Leiden: Brill.

Segal, M. H.
1958 *A Grammar of Mishnaic Hebrew*. Oxford: Oxford University Press.

Ska, J. L.
1990 *"Our Fathers Have Told Us". Introduction to the Analysis of Hebrew Narratives*. subsidia biblica 13. Rome: Pontifical Biblical Institute.

Smith, M. S.
1991 *The Origins and Development of the waw-Consecutive*. HSS 39. Atlanta: Scholars Press.

2001 *The Origins of Biblical Monotheism. Israel's Polytheistic Background and the Ugaritic Texts*. New York: Oxford University Press.

Snaith, N. H.
1975 "The Meaning of שְׁעִירִם." *VT* 25: 115-118.

Soisalon-Soininen, I.
1965 *Die Infinitive in der Septuaginta*. Annales Academiae Scientiarum Fennicae, Ser. B, Tom. 132, 1. Helsinki: Suomalainen Tiedeakatemia.

Sokoloff, M.

1990   *A Dictionary of Jewish Palestinian Aramaic of the Byzantine Period*. Bar Ilan: Bar Ilan University Press.

Speyer, W.

1971   *Die literarische Fälschung im Altertum. Ein Versuch ihrer Deutung*. Handbuch der Altertumswissenschaft I/2. München: Beck.

Spronk, K.

1998   "Down with Hêlēl! The Assumed Mythological Background of Isa 14,12." In *"Und Mose schrieb dieses Lied auf". Studien zum Alten Testament und zum Alten Orient, Festschrift O. Loretz*, AOAT 250, eds. M. Dietrich and I. Kottsieper, 717-726. Münster: Ugarit-Verlag.

Staub, U.

2000   "Das Tier mit den Hörnern. Ein Beitrag zu Dan 7,7f." In *Hellenismus und Judentum. Vier Studien zu Daniel 7 und zur Religionsnot unter Antiochus IV*, ODO 178, eds. O. Keel and U. Staub, 37-85. Göttingen: Vandenhoeck.

Stemberger, G.

1990   "Die Bedeutung des Tierkreises auf Mosaikfußböden spätantiker Synagogen." In his *Studien zum rabbinischen Judentum*, 177-228. Stuttgart: Katholisches Bibelwerk.

Stenning, J. F.

1949   *The Targum of Isaiah*. Oxford: Oxford University Press.

Talshir, D.

1988   "A Reinvestigation of the Linguistic Relationship between Chronicles and Ezra-Nehemiah." *VT* 38: 165-193.

Taylor, R. A.

1994a   *The Peshitta of Daniel*. MPIL 7. Leiden: Brill.

1994b   "The Peshitta of Daniel: Questions of Origin and Date." In *VI Symposium Syriacum 1992. University of Cambridge, Faculty of Divinity 30 August - 2 September 1992*, OCA 247, ed. R. Lavenant, 31-42. Rome: Pontifical Oriental Institute.

Ulrich, E.

1987   "Daniel Manuscripts from Qumran. Part 1: A Preliminary Edition of 4QDan[a]." *BASOR* 268: 17-37.

1989 "Daniel Manuscripts from Qumran. Part 2: A Preliminary Edition of 4QDan^b and 4QDan^c." *BASOR* 274: 3-26.

1990 "Orthography and Text in Dana and Danb and in the Related Masoretic Text." In *Of Scribes and Scrolls. Festschrift John Strugnell*, eds. H. Attridge et al., 29-42. Lanham: University Press of America.

Unger, E.

1931 *Babylon. Die heilige Stadt nach der Beschreibung der Babylonier.* Berlin: De Gruyter.

Van der Kooij, A.

1981 *Die alten Textzeugen des Jesajabuchs. Ein Beitrag zur Textgeschichte des Alten Testaments.* OBO 35. Göttingen: Vandenhoeck.

Van der Peursen, W. Th.

1999 "Negation in the Hebrew of Ben Sira." In *Sirach, Scrolls, and Sages: Proceedings of a Second International Symposium on the Hebrew of the Dead Sea Scrolls, Ben Sira, and the Mishnah, Held at Leiden University, 15-17 December 1997*, STDJ 33, eds. T. Muraoka and J. F. Elwolde, 223-243. Leiden: Brill.

Van Dijk, H. J.

1969 "Does Third Masculine Singular *Taqtul* Exist in Hebrew?" *VT 19*: 440-447.

Vogt, E.

1994 *Lexicon linguae aramaicae Veteris Testamenti.* 2nd ed. Rome: Pontifical Biblical Institute.

Volz, P.

1966 *Die Eschatologie der jüdischen Gemeinde im neutestamentlichen Zeitalter. Nach den Quellen der rabbinischen, apokalyptischen und apokryphen Literatur.* Hildesheim: Olms (reprint of the Tübingen 1934 edition).

Wacker, M-Th.

1982 *Weltordnung und Gericht. Studien zu 1 Henoch 22.* FzB 45. Würzburg: Echter.

Wagner, M.

1966 *Die lexikalischen und grammatikalischen Aramaismen im alttestamentlichen Hebräisch.* BZAW 96. Berlin: De

Gruyter.

Waltke, B. K. and M. O'Connor
    1990   *An Introduction to Biblical Hebrew Syntax.* Winona Lake:
            Eisenbrauns.

Wehr, H.
    1985   *Arabisches Wörterbuch für die Schriftsprache der Ge-*
            genwart. 5th ed. Wiesbaden: Harrassowitz.

Weinrich, H.
    2001   *Tempus. Besprochene und erzählte Welt.* 6th ed. München:
            Beck.

Weitzman, M. P.
    1995   "Lexical Clues to the Composition of the Old Testament
            Peshitta." In *Studia Aramaica: New Sources and New Ap-*
            proaches, JSSSup 4, eds. M. J. Geller et al., 217-262. Ox-
            ford: Oxford University Press.

Weninger, S.
    2001   *Das Verbalsystem des Altäthiopischen. Eine Unter-*
            suchung seiner Verwendung und Funktion unter Berück-
            sichtigung des Interferenzproblems. Veröffentlichungen
            der Orientalischen Kommission der Akademie Mainz 47.
            Wiesbaden: Harrassowitz.

West, M. L.
    1973   *Textual Criticism and Editorial Technique.* Stuttgart:
            Teubner.
    1997   *The East Face of Helicon. West Asiatic Elements in*
            Greek Poetry and Myth. Oxford: Oxford University Press.

Wiesehöfer, J.
    1996   *Ancient Persia from 550 BC to 650 AD.* Transl. A. Azodi.
            London: Tauris.

Wohlstein, H.
    1963   "Zur Tier-Dämonologie der Bibel." *ZDMG* 113: 483-492.

Zeller, D.
    2000   "Ägyptische Königsideologie im Neuen Testament? Fug
            und Unfug religionswissenschaftlichen Vergleichens." In
            Religionsgeschichte des Neuen Testaments, Festschrift
            Klaus Berger, eds. A. von Dobbeler, K. Erlemann and R.
            Heiligenthal, 541-552. Tübingen and Basel: Francke.

Zevit, Z.
  1978   "The Exegetical Implications of Daniel VIII 1, IX 21." *VT* 28: 488-492.
  1998   *The Anterior Construction in Classical Hebrew.* SBL Monographs 50. Atlanta: Scholars Press.
Ziegler, J. (see also under O. Munnich)
  1954   *Susanna, Daniel, Bel et Draco.* Septuaginta. Vetus Testamentum Graecum XVI/2. Göttingen: Vandenhoeck.
Zimmerli, W.
  1969   *Ezekiel.* Biblischer Kommentar XIII/2. Neukirchen-Vluyn: Neukirchener.
Zimmern, H.
  1892   "Der Jakobssegen und der Tierkreis." *ZA* 7: 161-172.

Index of Authors

Finito di stampare
nel mese di Maggio 2003

presso la tipografia
"Giovanni Olivieri" di E. Montefoschi
00187 Roma • Via dell'Archetto, 10, 11, 12
Tel. 06 6792327 • E-mail: tip.olivieri@libero.it